Beyond

the
HORIZON

Into the Light, Returned from 'Death'

JOHN EDMONDS

BALBOA.
PRESS

A DIVISION OF HAY HOUSE

Balboa Press books may be ordered through booksellers or by contacting:

Balboa Press
A Division of Hay House
1663 Liberty Drive
Bloomington, IN 47403
www.balboapress.com.au
1-(877) 407-4847

ISBN: 978-1-4525-0900-6 (sc)
ISBN: 978-1-4525-0901-3 (e)

Printed in the United States of America

Balboa Press rev. date: 02/07/2013

I was given something very few were given, the day I died. The choice of either returning from 'death,' or remaining on another new continuant journey through heaven, and God willing, procuring a new journey.

Many lifetimes ago, to discover who I had been over 33 distant lifetimes before. An Inuit kinsman, father; a doctor; a seafarer, an ancient Pagan chieftain, a monk; and among them a lifetime with my dearest soul brother in a town called Bethany. The nights we shared in His love and proclamation, His wisdom, and His soul. Amidst the blazing winter fires, days and nights, we partook in the divine, His longing for the world and its troubles, which were to be sorrowfully forsaken for centuries to come. My sisters and I clothed Him, bathed Him, anointing His feet; and in return He saved my life not once but twice, yet our hearts pained to hear of His suffering. He was the One, the Messiah, Christ Jesus, my brother, flesh and blood, and I gave to Him my home as refuge. These are my words, His, and the word of God and my estoterical guide, JahAnanda, the same in which you too possess.

For John, Beyond the Horizon' ~ Into the Light, Return from 'Death' is his story, struggle, incredible and remarkable recollection outlining an epic journey, his present day, his calling, and revelations. One of the longest in the world dead, a journey far beyond the realm of the living on the earth where an awakened revealed purpose was laid to a set of agreements, to the choice that he was given in exchange for his life and direction, and that of the world. The fascinating and compelling non-physical experience and instruction he received during his time on the 'other side.' is the chronological account of an astonishing tale of survival, courage, revelation, and inconceivable willpower.

John rediscovered his truth and purpose after what was deemed virtually impossible; surviving twenty five minutes without a heartbeat. He now teaches meditation groups, spiritual awakening and connection through Satsang. Where egoism is cast aside upon where mankind should and could become further as pure spiritual and loving beings.

Testimonials

*'Immensely profound and deeply
touching, transformational, of
Truth and purity.
Each one of us can be awakened
into the expansiveness of heart
and soul essence and humility
through the message of this One
on the earth who so obviously is
of the Holy and Divine Consciousness'*
~ Victoria of Light, Author ~ Sacred Scriptures of Love

*'This chronicle is a compelling
Testament of the future of
the Earth. It reveals dimensions
Of spirit that need to be proclaimed
And understood better by a unified
And forgiving nation'*
JD ~ Channel of Egyptian Goddess of Justice, Maat

ABOUT THE AUTHOR

This is a three part trilogy; the first book of the series is a true story about kiwi Aotearoa, New Zealander, John Edmonds. His life was like any normal Kiwi, businessman, a self confessed father, son and, an unconscious and suffering soul.

On one hot November afternoon in 2008, his life was about to change forever. John had without warning, an NDE or Near Death Experience by a cardiac arrest. For twenty five minutes without a heartbeat, his body endured 8 defibrillation shocks to his chest, a multitude of drugs, four adrenaline shots to his heart, multiple broken ribs and sternum rupturing and consequently, severe brain damage. What has made this case so extraordinary was that his survival is noted as being one of the longest cases recorded in the world without a heart-beat. To survive such an extraordinary length of time dead he had only an estimated one in five billion chances of surviving such a gruelling period of time without oxygen.

After his resuscitation his body was put into a coma and then into an ice (hypo-thermal) bed for 18 hours in an attempt to prevent his brain from swelling and dying. In an extraordinary and medically unexplainable event, he almost inexplicitly lost it again the following day due to brain oxygen depletion complications.

For twelve months he underwent intensive rehabilitative therapy to help him walk, comprehend, remember, and integrating himself back into physical reality again. He was aware that he was not the same person he was in his past life albeit they were scattered fragments of another life, a distant time, an uncommon realm. The recollection of his journey due to the publicity and dizzying media attention his survival had attracted, he chose to remain private with his family and children until such time that he would feel comfortable sharing his experience.

'Beyond the Horizon' ~ Into the Light, Return from 'Death' is his story, struggle, incredible and remarkable recollection outlining an epic journey, his present day, his calling, and revelations. A journey far beyond the realm of the living on the earth and an awakened revealed purpose was laid to a set of agreements to the choice that he was given in exchange for his life and direction, and that of the world. The fascinating and compelling non-physical experience and instruction he received during his time on the 'other side.' is the chronological account of an astonishing tale of survival, courage, revelation, and inconceivable willpower.

For Tour Dates, Satsang Gatherings, Teaching's calendar, update's and more information about the author, you may visit www.jahananda.com.

Photo by: Catherine Heath Photography
Auckland, NZ

CONTENTS

Toku pepeha
Ko Whakapunake raua ko Panekiri nga maunga
Ko Te Wairoa-hopupu-honengenenge-matarangi-rau raua ko
Waikaretaheke nga awa
Ko Takitimu raua ko Mataatua nga waka
Ko Ngati Kahungunu-ki-te-Wairoa raua ko Ngai Tuhoe nga iwi
Ko Tanemitirangi raua ko Te Whanaupani nga hapu
Ko Huramua raua ko Waimako nga marae
Ko Hone toku ingoa
Tihei Mauriora!

ACKNOWLEDGEMENTS

The writing of this book would have not been possible without the undying love and support of the following people and some who were at my side when I wasn't, and during the following years of rehabilitative periods of adjustment.

To my mother Amiria, I love you mama. Raising your children on your own in giving them the best was not the easiest of duties. You dedicate yourself with everything you do with sincerest love, with passion, with precision, and grace. You are a teacher, a matriarch, a wife, a mother, a grandmother, a great grandmother and, an angel.

Forever indebted to Delwyn Pringle, my guardian angel, both you and Selina who were there, one can imagine being thrown into a situation that saving a life depended on your unbelievable efforts. The professional way you calmly conducted yourselves in calling 111 and the task of performing CPR before paramedics crew arrived, I will never forget what you both went through.

To the paramedic and fire crew Jason, Tommo and Andy. The instinctive actions, professionalism and persistence to work beyond any normal situation to push on in such hot, testing and what must have seemed hopeless conditions. It was through your diligence, perseverance, and determination which made the difference. I offer this tribute and testimony in recognition to all paramedics and fire crews who work with indomitable tenacity and dedication in what must seem sometimes a thankless and hopeless occupation.

To Dr Neils Duggan, a passionate, impressive, giving soul, husband and father. Neils came from Chicago to Aotearoa New Zealand for a new journey and new life, who had observed but had never conducted a hypo-thermic ice emersion procedure before but chanced it anyway. How can I ever repay you other than to offer my utmost gratitude and blessings to you and your family and forever I will be eternally indebted and grateful, thank you.

To all my whanau, kia ora ra. Ka nui te mihi aroha kia koutou katoa. To my brother Denis and his wife Celia, you have always been a leader from our childhood, in your work, and in our family. Your aroha and ability to lead any situation, working with doctors and hospital staff and visitors, and having to drop everything to move from Raglan to be there for me and the children I will never forget and love you always. To my brother Marty, sisters Ren and Pania, and their partners Jason, and Kabir, Brett and Sylvia, to travel from Perth and Melbourne during my time in the coma and being the most gracious siblings anyone could ever have. I love you all and am so grateful and indebted for your love, humour, and compassion. To Dr Stephanie Smith, Dr Rob Maunsell, Cardiologist Dr Scott Harding, nursing staff at Masterton and Wellington Hospitals, Linda Calkin, Derek and Chris Daniel, Sri Yanchiji-Guruji, Linda Spence, Sue Nicholson, Victoria of Light, Karl Baker, Mithun Prasannan, Emily McDowell, Jay Lane, Doug and Pravinia Bluck, Judy and Colin Lawrence, John and Judy Bunny, Paul Bates, Rawiri Hindle, David and Sandra Paku, Veronika Cox, Huia and Brian Cox, Evan and Julie Wilson for your love, wisdom, support and friendship.

My dearest friends, Philip and Dianne, you both are like a brother and sister. The special bond we have had for so many years only gets stronger through the struggles and happy times personal to us and the special quality of the love and connection we share now and forever. I look forward to our many years together. To Daryl, my buddy, my mate, you have always had a compassionate and selfless side to you that always meant dropping whatever you were doing to be at my side. What you did to be there for mama, those long nights sharing shifts, talking, crying, sharing, laughing and telling stories, I love you Dazz. To all the caregivers, nurses, rehabilitation staff, counsellors, friends, family, and the hundreds of messages of goodwill, love, and support I received from Aotearoa, New Zealand and the world. I thank you from the bottom of my heart. It was through the struggles, learning to walk again, think, and comprehend the reality of adjusting again back into this life again. Through your words of love and encouragement, this journey to repatriation would have made the road that much more difficult and challenging without your love and assistance. And, last but not least, I give my deepest love and undying reverence, offering, and devotion eternally to my papa Turi, and to God. Without all things, this existence and journey, this story would not be possible. Namaste, Arohanui kia koutou katoa.

DEDICATION

To my mother Amiria, stepfather Gerry, and my
children, I dedicate this book to you.

FOREWORD / PREFACE

Complain not about life, but focus on your blessings, even if they are shrouded in heartache. There is a silver lining in all things, all contrasts, if one looks close enough. There are many more people in the world who know what struggling and suffering really means in their day to day life more than me. I cannot speak more irreverently, from my heart to those who suffered and fought through the ravages of war, too numerous to mention, and those who gave their lives for their countries and for the world. Christ Jesus, Gautama Buddha, Muhammad, Martin Luther King, Mahatma Gandhi, Vivienne Bullwinkel, Dr Viktor Frankl, and Kate Sheppard to name but a few. All the men and women who gave for their countries come to mind though there are many more like these selfless and committed visionaries. Their wish was to see love, acceptance, compassion, and equality given to all people. To those who suffered the scourge of war and torture, or by ravaging disease, disaster, poverty and starvation, the families who had to go on with their lives again after, this story is in recognition to them.

Fear not pain or fear itself, for temperance is its ally, impermanence its friend. The silence of the breath, the mildness of the mind, the explicit beauty of the soul seeks and knows only love ~ JahAnanda

There is an indiscreet understanding of how important perspective is, in acknowledging the simple beauty of life even in trying times, and living with utmost gratitude even when things appear to be against us. Challenging times are to be cherished, it is only temporary, moments always come to pass, even in death, and the choice to be grateful and happy is simply a decision, that's all it takes no matter what. It is a choice. That is the power of intimate knowing. Ask someone who has just been told they won't ever see, walk, or hear again, or someone who has lost a limb, or a loved one. Or a child who has just lost their whole family to tragedy or war; to see the look on someone's face who has just been told that they have a terminal illness. Perspective is humbling. Serving others and living with gratitude no matter what, for that is the answer to happiness, love and tolerance. Life is short, and that too in itself is a gift, a gift that is taken by many for granted. Behold what you have, even if you have nothing left to hold or you think sometimes that life is boring, for there is always someone in the world suffering more than those who would dearly love to trade places. Be thankful. Make something of it, not tomorrow, but right now, in this moment.

'Death' brings an important realisation that children brought into the world which adults forgot. That the smallest simplest things in life are actually the most joyous and important, and the 'big' things in life are a complete wasteful illusional distraction.

Learn to laugh together, but not ridicule. Learn to forgive quickly than shame or judge another. Life is too short, more precious and wonderful than wasting it on examining another's faults for they are not their faults, be it a reflection of the lost soul, the enquirer, the judge, the examiner, the condemner, the observer. Learn to laugh more, lighten up more, to share a drink, a prayer, or a hug with someone. Hold out your hand to someone whose hands are wracked with pain and sorrow. Give someone a smile and you will surely get one back and make a friend.

'Learn from, Offer your hand, Value all experiences and living things, this Earth, Encourage one another. L-O-V-E.'

This story is dedicated to those who have suffered, are suffering, or searching. And those who have asked the question, what is my purpose in this life and, what really is 'Death' and how and should we prepare for it?

Heaven, Nirvana, Janna, Shangri-Lah, Dharma, call it what you may, for it is the most serene, exquisitely beautiful and awed sanctuary of light and absolute, unwavering, and eternal love.

The term 'unconditional love' may be a cliché, yet it is the universal answer towards mankind's destiny and understanding of reverent world peace. It is the source and pathway of wisdom, truth, awareness and compassion. It is a God given entity, the gift of all gifts. And you held it all this time. It is the greatest mission to spiritual destiny, earthly destiny, and cohabitant relationship desire with all in embracing Oneness. Issues which have caused pain, death, and suffering for thousands of years have only escalated and exacerbated, even today by holding it away from ones heart, to living with absolute love and acceptance.

Never be afraid. For now, you have a life. Take it in both hands and follow your heart. Always be free, remain free, and stay true, to be a source of love, forgiving, and honest to your word. Let no-one tell you who you are, what you should do, or why you should do what they say if your heart tells you to go your own path. What is a worse fate than that and if there is another, then is it really true? It takes courage to be free, to be oneself, to live pure, even if it meant living not like a sheep, by following the crowd, not to believe what others say, but what comes from the heart. That, I do know.

This story is about the beginning of an existence of a pure soul and of a suffering soul returning, one born into this world to the day of reckoning and awakening. These passages are of heart, observation, and forever a determinant duty. To serve, not of judgement but with will and unconditional love, and the joy in which we all seek eternally.

I am asked, 'Why did you return?', and, 'What is 'death?'. 'What did you experience in 25 minutes without a heartbeat, on the 'other side', if there really is an 'other side?' And, did you see anything at all, and if you did, what was it like? How do we prepare for 'death', and should we?

'Who is God?', and what relationship does spirituality have with religion? And lastly, 'What are we really here for?'

The answers to these questions are my own and no-one else's. They are my truth after this journey, and through the many years of unconscious conditioning and ritualising. There are two ways to know your truth, either to have an NDE and utilize what you are given, or to become truly awakened through choice, will and courage.

The first is a chosen path that is given to very few. The second is easier. It is having the fortitude, the daring, and the knowledge that the power and authority to do so lies already contained within. The reason why sadly much of the world achieves neither, it is hoped to explain within these pages. What can be said is that life can indeed be more fulfilling, more peaceful, more joyous, less stressful, and less indoctrinated by outside influences, opinions, control, and the dimensions of the ravaged unconscious physical mind.

Once one can master the valour to become who they truly are, it will be known. That until one becomes awakened and enlightened is realized and determined by mastering the art of will, courage, gratitude, persistency, and faith.

What is known is that time on the other side is timeless. That time doesn't really exist, only that of timelessness. I hope to explain this more clearly. There are no seconds, minutes, or hours. There are no watches, no clocks, no measurement or relevance to time at all as there is on this earth. It is what it is. It is its own truth and in time you too will know why.

I have lived in the past, the present, and the future, simultaneously in space and timelessness, and to some degree so too have you. This life is an indebted exchange and acceptance to agreements and to the great work here on earth, even though I am no longer part of it anymore.

This calling is to live outside the square, and more so realising the illusion of thinking that life is lived within a square. There is none and never was. Living life completely free with love in your heart in all things that you do, and knowing and trusting that Gods power and existence is real, and begins with awakened souls, with you, beside you, within you, and its grace is influential and commanding when you know, believe, and trust in this power.

Know too that your ascended passed loved ones are always with you. When one instils this simple philosophy to their lives, it has a quantum effect of truth to living and learning within karmic harmony, of acceptance and Oneness.

This destiny has been understood and acknowledged. The terms of these contrasts, signs, and awakenings, are gifts and blessings. To help others know, believe, and trust. To share, experience, instil, to inspire, and to teach, and under the auspice of Satsang, and to fulfil now this promise to this work, to lend a commanding hand to new aligning souls, understanding that they too have the same choice. This is my story.

CHAPTER I

Journey to 'Death' and Back

You couldn't ask for a more beautiful day, the day I died. It creeps up like a stealthy lion, a panther, or a snake; or by the simple hand of God tapping you on the shoulder holding a small ball with a number on it with your name etched and skilfully written in scrolled print below. You could be so blissfully unaware that today is the day, unlike a wedding day or the day you get a brand new red bike for your fifth birthday, or to see the Northern Lights, or to stand atop Gaurisankar for the very first time. The day of one's own death, sudden or not, is quite a different story especially one that you believe you don't really get to tell after the fact.

I am sure that if I knew I was going to die that I would have hastily tossed out the television, the house would mean nothing, the mortgage would mean even less, and most certainly the teeth whitening appointment at the dentist next week would be worthless, or my protruding nose hairs come to think of it. There'd be no use having perfect teeth in a mouth that has no life in it and the top ten of the top one hundred on ones delusional life's happiness list didn't make their new top one hundred on their newly hurriedly written bucket list. I didn't have that privilege to plan my last days, I didn't even have the privilege to saying goodbye and Ill love you always to my children and loved ones, but death is a funny thing, how it waves its deathly black cape over ones colourful life at the most inopportune moment. It's more amusing still how people live wastefully with two lists where the least most important is their holy grail and well, you know what I mean. It puts us Geminis in a more than demeaning light really. I thought that we were the only split personality souls, and if so, what then are the other eleven earthly star family souls living two or three lives when they have their own horoscope traits that describe who they really are, and more so, their own truth?

Maybe, I'm to find out the real answer. That perhaps I and the rest of the world are blindly and completely full of shit.

The Other Life

In the clinic, peering over Judy's shoulder, my eyes ran out the window and beyond, I couldn't see a cloud in the sky, just a sea of radiant blue. Down on the street below, people were going about their business, mothers shopping or talking to friends, children off to school, men waiting at the barbershop and reading the newspaper just to pass the time of day. Just seven more clients and I'll be out there too in the glorious sunshine.

For now, I am here, on this earth, the 21st century. A poignant saviour for many out there, a father, a friend, a brother, a son. An unconscious soul, an unconscious soul with a lifetime of flickering questions unanswered, whilst cradling ignorant, ravaged and gripped in blind confusion trying to survive and get ahead. An indelible child in an adult's body, a provider, a servant, and a saint it seemed. But above all, the day of reckoning had come, unbeknown to the one, who more than most, would come face to face to the reality of a dream disguised as a nightmare. The nightmare of all nightmares, a saviour to no-one but them-self, and this perfect death, was about to be real.

Life of the Unconscious Soul

I get an incredible thrill when I see the body of someone who has transformed their tired temple of television, potato chips, and beer, into this bounding gazelle, potential All Black, or new bride to be, well in my case, in training. It might take months of determined sweat and strain, ignoring questions of doubt to push on and upwards with their mindset picture always out in front of them unfolding, the imaginary crowd spurring them on like they were in Yankee Stadium, Lansdowne Road, or Eden Park, their eyes pinned on the goal cheering and urging them on.

That was my life, the representation of an encouraging passionate mentoring soul helping expose the real person under the layers of excuses and kilograms. I always had a passion and fascination for biology and how the mind works in conjunction with achieving and maintaining a high level of health and fitness. A 'fitnessy' kind of geek perhaps, but nevertheless, how a once previously sedentary, unhealthy and often obese person can refocus their mental attitude of committing to changing their less than ideal lifestyle habits into a new regime of lean endowed vitality and keeping them for the rest of their life. I was inspired to guiding them. Helping them escape the shell of unwanted, unnecessary kilos of over-riding excess of fat, excuses, self persecution, and guilt, I had heard them all, from being too busy, too sick, too tired, and big boned. I never understood that one. How can someone have bones bigger than another? Did that actually cause them to be twenty or thirty kilograms heavier? Can someone really carry twenty or thirty kilos of extra bones in their butt? Well, to them that's what it is, and me, I let pass sullenly over my head the 'Oh, I've heard them all before' thoughts float and dissipate out the window to evaporate into mist whilst they hold it as true as if it were a bible in their top pocket like precious demeaning truth, or lies. Yet if they have a desire to have a new body, a new way of life, a new attitude, even smaller bones, then I'm going to be their guide, their light and motivation. Day by day, week by week, we're going to work together, as a team. A partnership that will not suggest burgers and fries, but vitality and life!

But for this day, this moment, I will be free. For this life unbeknownst, unconscious or not, is about to bid a fond farewell. For now, only forty minutes to go, to tear off this shirt and barefoot, cut out into the fresh air and enjoy every glorious minute of it, even if just for two hours in the basking sun.

The lawns were yearning to be mowed. How lazy could one be? Not to have biked or even walked to work this morning, but nay, I never did like walking that much, not like cycling or riding a horse. Nevertheless, it's too late, I have the car, and by car, homeward I go.

Mairangi owned the barber shop below my work. She'd always be there sharing 'matters' with her clients, which she insisted wasn't gossip at all. She always had a smile, a hello, and a wave for everyone who walked or drove by, and a bowl of lollies in front of the mirror next to the combs, cutters, and hair tonic.

You can do a lot of thinking whilst mowing the lawns, or doing almost anything for that matter. Perhaps it's the feeling of the softness of the lawn at my feet and the smell of fresh cut grass. Other than the noise of the lawnmower and the spurting smoke fumes, it's kind of bliss really. And the sun feels so delicious to the skin.

In the distance, I spy Andre Dillons' topdressing plane go by over head heading towards the airport not far down the road from my house. How many times have I envied his job? Maths was my biggest struggle at school and if only I could divide, and calculate algebra, and decipher something by Pythagoras's Theorem, I never understood, I'd too be up there amongst the clouds, away from the hustle and bustle, being free. I spent much of my childhood growing up on the farm at Huramua gazing at planes going by and I didn't care or even wonder why no-one else on the farm had the same allure to flight. But for a few seconds I'd imagine me up there, free.

Mr Maddiley my high school maths teacher ensured me that any chance of flying was to be just a pipe dream. I remember like yesterday how unwavering he was, his expressionless face with a slight turned down mouth as if someone had farted in the classroom. He never looked at the class directly, but as though he was gazing into a big crystal ball which rolled around on the floor or out the windows as if he were somewhere else. I really think he was.

He always wore a leather glove when writing maths problems on the blackboard because his skin was allergic to chalk. He had a tweaked moustache and rain or shine, he wore khaki long shorts with an army jacket with either sandals or tramping boots depending on the weather, as if he was still reliving his past or an imaginary life still in the British army. He spoke in parables and words from a dictionary no-one else had ever read, and yet like most mathematicians, he was a prude particular gentleman who demanded order and kept order, and like his papers and pens, rulers and his bicycle, most everything else in his life, had its precise place.

'People who were constant nuisances at school were like a dump in the loo that needed two flushes'

I was a tidy student, a little confused, in his class mostly, and yet somehow to be a pilot according to Mr Maddiley, for me, aiming that high with my unfortunate lacking of mathematics acumen, was preposterously impossible. But for that moment now, with my hand on the lawn mower, I still had the whimsical grace and guild to nevertheless share my love of flying, and reverence to Andre up there for living his dream.

When I was forced to let go any suggestion of that dream ever becoming a reality. The passion returned again to give it another try many years later when Linda bought me a trial flight gift voucher from Masterton's local flying school. I relived my vision of flying jets and leading bombing raids in the night, or perhaps captaining a Jumbo jet across the crystal clear oceans, mountains and skies, entertaining the passengers with my Lou Rawls voice wasn't to be, that was, until Riki came along.

Here was my flesh and blood, like an antelope innocently and nonchalantly grazing on the safari plains, the eyes of the lion was ready to pounce, and play with his prey, manipulate, and drive this helpless poor creature insane for fifteen years or more to live my life through him. 'He's my pilot!' I espoused to myself. Linda and I could plainly see that he had the Gerdvilis/Kavalunis maths brain from his mother, and his grandmother, Meile. This young starling was to be seconded, tormented, and bored utterly for the remainder of his new life by a father who after many years of delinquent serenading, by transplanting another's dream upon a poor innocent soul like him. Like gravity pressed to the heart of the desired, the great blind sculptor of the universe appearing, but nonetheless, too far and unconsciously removed for one upon another naive and blameless, venturing poor wee human being.

Nevertheless, it was a welcomed and much appreciated timely awakening, and an embarrassment for his dad, but it was taken on the chin and ticked off as a lesson well learnt. He certainly paid his dad back duly with sweet revenge the day he karate kicked his dads life sized cardboard cut out Philip had given me from the video shop, of 'Miss Congeniality' which stood like a sexy Aquarian goddess idol in the corner window of the bedroom, as if she'd awaken and answer those warped dreams by coming to life, hopefully minus the pistol strapped to her leg.

Dads a dick, a child, a random geek who needs to act his age and grow up and I am not HIS pilot son, I am ME, nor is some pathetic piece of cardboard. Hiyah, Chop, Done! After that she never quite looked the same and the silly repugnant attempt to sticky tape her back to straighten the large karate kicked horizontal crease that bisected her cardboard body near her belly button just made her look more like she was Miss Congenital Scoliosis. Ironically, it was Rata who revealed more promise not that I added two and two together, being so enamoured with his older brother being 'Top Gun'. Rata didn't have a fear of heights and he really enjoyed flying but I never pushed the subject anymore. I decided to let them be, and free, and for me, just butt out and concentrate on being a normal father, whatever that meant.

Its nurturing father whispered, 'You're going to soar and become something great.' 'I am who I am now!' pondered the baby eagle, ~ JahAnanda

CHAPTER 2

Land of Milk and Honey

I was born into a small yet beautiful riverside town of Wairoa along with my brothers Denis and Marty on the North Island's east coast of Aotearoa, New Zealand.

Huramua was our family farm my grandparents Turi and Parehuia owned which was then passed on to mums elder sister Mako and her husband, Uncle Reay, and their seven children, my cousins.

The farm oozed with an extremely fascinating history from what I knew. My Papa Turi had an illustrious life in politics, sports, the First World War, farming, tribal affairs, and a host of community, high school, and local body politics. He was knighted by the Queen and thereafter he became more in demand and busier even in the latter periods of his life, however as kids on our own missions what Papa did was his joy and for us catching eels, fishing, climbing trees, milking cows and riding horses was ours.

Huramua, particularly in its earlier days to me, seemed like an incredible self sufficient oasis and a university of teaching a vast array of skills for the land, machinery, animals, and a most valued work ethic. The Wairoa River ran alongside Huramua and was changeable depending on the weather, the wind, or the rain in the upper reaches of Te Urewera and Te Reinga regions which would flood the lowland and turn the serene willow lined peacefulness into a swollen torrent of thunderous caramel with fallen trees which were washed down and out to the sea at Whakamahi. This paradise land was to be, unknowingly for me, the canvas upon which the journey and lessons of an innocent soul would be coloured red like blood and seething like the deep violet moon rising through the dark clouds of reason and purpose through experiencing and learning of one's destiny already planned a very long time ago.

Farmboy

Huramua had winding creeks, dairy and woolsheds, an assortment of orchard trees, citrus trees, and a large vegetable garden, with cows, sheep, horses, and pigs. Honey was made from the hives spread around the farm and as children growing up on the farm we always felt very blessed to have everything compared to the children who lived in the towns and cities. I remember feeling grateful that we had a blessed life and always thinking and feeling sad for the children in Africa and Bangladesh that we saw on television, who were living in poverty and starving.

It was during a period of revolutionary change which was during the 1960's and 70's. The Second World War or what I now know was really the Hundredth World War, had ended some years earlier of which many of my family were involved in, and the world was in the throes of another. Vietnam.

There was a strong sense of national comradery and allegiance with other countries and men who were thirsty to display their courage and national pride by enlisting themselves on an adventure of some kind, so they

were told, protecting who knows what against pretty much the same. Constrastingly, there was also another movement which as a normal rural kid would, became inquisitive and drawn to another worldwide phenomenon. Woodstock. I didn't know at the time what drugs were yet all the same the faces of the people seemed happier, the music definitely was evoking and the captivating lyrics of these songs continued to play on my mind day after day, and for many years to come.

As time passed I could see a paradox. On one hand there were a faction of countries including our own, and people wanting to kill, shoot, and blow up anybody by any means with anything and everything without considering the ramifications and personal pain and suffering that it would cause to perceived 'perpetrators' they called enemy and more importantly, innocent people. And, on the other, there were these happy joyous people who I became infatuated and drawn to, who promoted these then unfamiliar ideals called peace and love.

Not for one minute more did I think these countries were fit, responsible, or coherent enough to realise the incredible damage and injustice that was caused in the two previous world wars to millions of innocent people. Yet, like an overdosed bull high on testosterone, the bull upon Vietnam nevertheless and unrelentingly charged, minus its brain.

The Inquisitive Eyes of a Child

I had a wonder about flight as a child. If I was on the farm driving the tractor or moving stock; if a plane or topdressing plane or if a hawk flew by, always being told off for daydreaming or not concentrating and crash into a strainer post or make crocked the hedgerow. Imagining life on Huramua, just picture New Orleans and the Waltons, or picture Professor Longhair singing Tipitina, or Robert Johnson's rendition of Red Hot. It was that kind of life, laid back and innocent mojo rising fun. It was as though a black man from Mississippi had passed through Wairoa and sprinkled some blues into an amalgam with his soul and the soul of Maori music influenced heavily into its own style uncorrupted by the synthesised electronic subversion we hear today. If you could picture John-boy, Sue Ellen, Jim Bob, Ma and pa, Grandma Walton, and the whole gambit of bright eyed, muddy skinned brood on the farm with a shady creek and a bucket of herrings, craziness, and a field of corn, that was Huramua.

The House of God

In those days church and Sunday school was conducted by Mr Gordon and later by Canon Wi Huata. Wearing his Anglican ministers robe it was Wi Huata's beautiful dark skin and bulging twinkling eyes, his big smile, and above all, his passion and warmth, it was though his incredible voice which filled any church service with shivers and goose bumps. He was like our whanau's own Louis Armstrong as he wiped his sweaty brow with his white folded handkerchief and everyone couldn't help but join in song giving praise at the top of their voices. Well the adults did anyway. We kids were too busy poking tongues and swapping lollies with the other kids and then getting caught by mama or an aunt for not listening and paying attention, our punishment was a pulled ear or being bonked on the head with a bible. We would then sit up straight and quiet with the lolly hidden under our tongue which made poking it at each other again behind the aunties backs real hard so we did a pukana face and giggle instead.

I always found church to be different, confusing and strange. It didn't seem very Maori at all, kind of imported from somewhere far away, and yet we all dressed up and went along knowing that there was something important in this precious looking book called the bible. Because the bible had too many words in a language I couldn't understand I found the colouring books depicting biblical stories to be much more fun.

Mr Gordon and Canon Huata always tried their best to make learning about Jesus fun at church and at religious studies at school. We'd sing songs and listen to their stories even though I had questions which conjured in my mind even more questions about God, Jesus, and religion.

Recalling and thinking how amazing Jesus must have been, turning water into wine and parting the sea and bringing the sick to life and healing lepers, and if there wasn't anyone else performing such miracles like Jesus performed, that he really must have been a very special and unique person.

Whenever there was a tangi or funeral at the marae, the minister would talk about how the beloved person was resting in Gods arms and if it was someone close whom I loved, thinking, how come God had the pleasure of enjoying them in his arms whilst we who loved them more missed out. Or when a disaster happened, it was called an 'Act of God'. That's a bit unfair, why would God do such a thing? I began to believe that God must be a cruel selfish man and I chose to not believe much in God anymore. I remember when our son Tane passed away decades later, feeling less closer to God for taking him from us yet I felt uplifted strangely by spirit and if so then how could I feel spirit if it came from religion and I didn't really care to believe in it anymore.

Even though church was a time to dress up and meet friends and family I became more confused and disillusioned as to what was being taught at church, to be kind, loving, and how we should follow the 10 Commandments and for the next 6 days afterwards many of the churchgoers would be doing exactly the opposite. It was like they heard what was being preached went in one ear and came out the other, or either they disagreed with the sermon or chose more pertinently to follow their sinful ways. For a child going to Sunday school and church I began to realise that rather than the church being a waste of time, it was parishioners who were wasting the churches time. Making a mockery of the church, and of themselves and I learnt more about life, church, and people who lived their lives truthfully, and by those who sinned according to the church. For a child, life became a paradox wonder, and coincidently, became more confusing, more sad, and to realise the tarnish of sinful ways was a choice, yet why, and believing that I too was liable to the same and how weak and unscrupulously shameful it felt to follow the other sheep.

Recalling how the churches modus operandi' was to our own, what seemed to be much deeper Maori spiritual protocol and belief. Tangi or Maori funerals were quite different to western or Europeans funeral services. The European style, although sad, appeared removed of voluptuous outcry of emotional expression and longing-ness like we grew up with. I remember the feeling of immense love and connection, grief and spiritual presence around me at tangi but at traditional pakeha services, even if I knew them, it seemed so comparatively different and painfully restrained. Being understandably perplexed as to how or why a loved bereaved person or family member is put into a morgue until the day of the funeral yet we keep our loved ones, at home or on the family marae always puzzled and sometimes saddened me. Whatever the difference, it was realising and understanding, and accepting that, 'it is what it is' and there is no right or wrong, service, justice or injustice, other than accepting other cultures ways and differences. Experiencing wairua, the spirit, the power and connection made to the higher source is certainly felt in song, the wailing of the women and kuia, in the haka, the whaikorero or speeches of kaumatua or elders talking and sharing their experience of their lives with the deceased in song or waiata.

If a recognised person, chief, leader, or matriarch passed away the heavens and tupuna would share in their own grief seen in the opening up of the heavens with rain.

Papa's tangi was such an event. I was only thirteen at the time and his death came as sudden shock to me as I really didn't know that much about his failing health at the time and it hit me so hard to know that I wasn't going to see him again. For 8 days, cars, and bus load after bus load of mourners from all over Aotearoa would come onto the marae to pay their respects in the wero, waiata, whaikorero, and bringing together of iwi and hapu with kai which played a role in helping to break tapu which allowed people to come together and share grief in a more relaxed and convivial setting whilst still holding close, solidarity and respect.

For the Maori elders who sat on the Pae-pae, whose role it was to welcome and host visitors was, for them tiring especially if the tangi went for several days or more. But in Maoridom it was common and familiar, as protocol permitted, that it be done this way, as they had for thousands of years. This encouraged and fostered bringing together all people, tribes, hapu, and tauiwi, an opportunity to share in arohatanga and whakawhanaungatanga, the bringing and sharing together respect, love, peace, and reverence.

On the morning of papas' burial it was a beautiful bright blue sky sunny day. His coffin which had laid on Taihoa marae for the entirety of the tangi was now going to lie for a short time on another esteemed tribal marae, Takitimu. Named after one of the seven waka who travelled the vast Polynesian ocean in the Pacific, Takitimu was a sacred waka, a waka which carried chiefs, priests, noble prophets, and tohunga. This was the connection that papa had to both these marae and the spirit of great past leaders which represented them were paying their offering also to a mighty Totara fallen and acknowledging too the fine work that he had done. From there, papa and the entourage of mourners would then travel to Huramua, then to our Urupa on the farm at Matiti. Part way through the service at Takitimu was to be my first notable experience of spirit presence gathering together in mourning. The haunting yet uplifting haka by the tribal men symbolising warriors and wailing by the women dressed in black, their heads covered in black lace or cloth with fern fronds in their hair, and in their hands, filled my sombreness with some rectitude belonging. A resonant belonging uniquely exemplifying the mauri, or spiritual force, and the grief and love of our people, the tangata whenua, and our tipuna, those who had passed on, to us their presence was felt so strongly.

After several waiata Wi Huata lead a beautiful yet sullenly haunting Maori hymn, Piko Nei Te Matenga. From all directions it seemed, dark clouds rolled in from all directions followed by enormous gusts of wind and torrential rain. I remember the mourners who were sitting in front of the marae running to find shelter whilst still singing over the howling wind and rain and witnessing all the plastic and wood chairs being hurled across the lawn to the other side. The rain never let off and even at the Urupa the intense power of the heavens pouring their hearts and tears during Papas burial was something that had become engraved in my memory. Something I had not seen, felt, or heard before. To me, it was like an indelible foundation of a new belief. Attempting to understand to something much higher I couldn't at the time quite explain. Of connecting with our already connected loved ones was by and through an esteemed and long passed down protocol. To be Maori is something I've always treasured and proud to be Maori and when one feels the wairua, mana, and ahuatanga of the people and tipuna, such occaisions give an enamoured sense of peace, healing, and humility mixed with feeling of being blessed for my whanau, and to be Maori.

Hill-Billy Maori Kids

On the farm, mixing mash for the hens, ducks and Muscovy's was as much fun as it was, the sweet aroma of milk powder we mixed into milk for the calves each day. It was a lot of fun, knowing that in exchange for fresh eggs each day we were giving back to them warmth and shelter, and straw in which they could build their nests. And the aroma of stale bread, mash, broken up egg shells mixed with warm water and handfuls of dried corn kernels was a welcome nourishing daily meal for them. The sad bit for little kids was seeing the chooks at Christmas time running around with their heads chopped off with the axe, blood pouring out of their necks always made me want to throw up in disgust. But that was farm life, a life of incredible beauty, fun, freedom, and occasional sadness, particularly when orphaned lambs or calves died, or when any of the cows had eaten too much clover and succumbed to bloat. That was especially heartbreaking watching them gasping for their last breath, life seemingly and demeaning end and new life revolving, evolving, and so too the cycle of life and death for humanistic survival and prosperity, a puritan means to living from the land.

Dad

Our father left mum when I was five or so. I remember his last words, proudly saying, 'don't forget to learn Maori boy' That was too deep and confusing for a kid to understand I thought, thinking more like 'where are you going?,' and 'why?,' yet deep down, somehow I knew. After that our dad was nothing more than a picture in mums' storage chest.

Many years later, it was at my father's dad's funeral, someone who knew my grandad said how sad it was but what a wonderfully kind and caring man he was. He had been through an extreme period of suffering himself during his time in the British Army during the Second World War. Suffering what only could be described as post-war traumatic stress he may have unknowingly returned quite shocked and bewildered I imagine and because of his foreign nature had put enormous pressure on my grandmother, Irene. So devastating it must have been that when he finally left my grandmother, that he walked to the front door of their home and removed all his clothes. He politely folded them neatly and left them on top of the letter box and walked off down the street with nothing on and nothing taken from her but her own heartache and despondency. Joseph, my grand-dad spent the remainder of his especially private life with his sister Olive and alone, dedicating himself to finding himself and helping others, and painted as an artist until he passed away during the early 1990s.

It wasn't until that period that I found the courage to forgiving my father for what had occurred during his break-up with my mother. That, as a little boy himself, he had obviously been absent of love and affectionate guidance by his dad as a result of his own suffering and through that far reaching disintegration of such nurturing, no-one could have been to bear the blame for his contribution as a father. Through the years prior, we were told how he wasn't a man to be respected and in so doing, I harboured an incredible amount of shame and disrespect for what I had heard of him, something which I learned later would be the fault of listening to the opinions of others and believing it all as being true. That in itself was the most valuable lesson anyone can treasure, not believing anything until one knows all the facts. How suffering can be alleviated in this world until every amount of evidence is gathered until admissible truth is delivered. Until then, remain open minded, diligently calm, and loyal to the cause of democratic and totally respectful objectivity, as amusingly colourful and somewhat sad my grand-dad and my father's story may have seemed.

'Stifling within the unconnected unconscious body is a belief structure reflecting the next path of action. That thought has little significance to how the world and the soul wish to be since love is the foundation to all things. Greater than one believes the body will thus align to that of the world and of their soul' - JahAnanda

Timeless childhood memories

Times were very tough and mum worked from sunrise to sunset to pay the bills and put food on the table. We had no car, not that we cared, and seeing her off to work each morning, we had our own chores to do before she got home.

Mum had neat friends. Some worked with her at the local telephone exchange and maybe some she grew up with, but nevertheless they had wonderful times together. Working at the telephone exchange, and if someone knew about something going on, or if someone needed help then mum would be in charge. She has an amazing memory and can remember telephone numbers off the top of her head and rarely relied on a telephone book unless it was an out of town number. I think it was that she was always doing crosswords, and things like weaving, and art, the kind of stuff that needed a hell of a lot of patience. We obviously didn't as kids as we'd be either at school, at rugby practise, down the river either swimming or rowing, or up town hanging out, or at the farm, or stealing oranges and mandarins from West's Orchard.

What we as kids couldn't understand for years was when we would ask if she was going out somewhere, 'where you going mum?' shed always say, 'I'm going to see a man about a dog', strange though, after all these years, we never did get a dog. We never asked after that. I remember being told by aunts and uncles that she'd made a record and sang in a band and travelled with some Maori guy called Howard somebody, yet as kids we had our life and she had hers and life was good nonetheless.

Sing, sing, sing from the Soul!

Being raised amongst a herd of mostly older cousins on the farm, music became a real influence but none more so than mama. Every part of

Maori life involved singing and kai. Whether it was church, a tangi, hui, or just gathering around for a game of cards, someone would pull out their guitar and off we'd go. Talent quests would always be popular too and there'd be more entrants than places in competitions and you'd hear someone come up on stage saying that her friends and her thought that she looked and sounded just like Aretha Franklin or Tina Turner but I'd think to myself, didn't Aretha Franklin and Tina Turner have teeth? Nevertheless, it was all humorous fun and our pukus sure got a workout from laughing or crying too for that matter.

Being woken gently by the radio down the hall coming from the kitchen and then a particular song piquing her inspiration off she'd let loose from Kiri Te Kanawa, Gladys Knight, Aretha, Diana Ross, Petula Clark, Dusty Springfield, the list went on and on but it was the best alarm clock and if that didn't work we certainly knew about it.

Itch

On the farm, cousin Reaymond, or Itch as he is affectionately known with the bros, was perhaps one of my greatest influence's growing up on the farm. Maybe it was his passion for farming and music and something much higher that I didn't exactly know what it was, nevertheless we connected. What I came to understand about him was that he was a deep thinker, a peaceful soul, an inherent old soul with wisdom beyond his years. Itch knew that whatever happened outside of his own peacefulness, had no bearing to how he wanted to be and feel, and that is how he chose to live life first and foremost as an awakened soul, as a loyal son, a prodigious father, and as a husband to his wife Joylene.

Itch lived intuitively. His vehement yet quiet resolve and connectedness to the land unbounded by ritual and divergence of being lured by the world but through his own virulent and calm 'knowing' Itch consciously chose to maintain his innate and solemn inner peace and sanctity as something he considered sacrosanct. Whether he knew it or not, he is a deeply connected spiritual being. His connection to the earth, those around him, and those whom he loved who had passed on is an aspect of his acceptance and irreverent love for all things.

His extraordinary range of music genres was appealing and I was intrigued by the styles of music he enjoyed that I too became influenced, at that time which we were inspired at such a young age.

Woodstock was certainly a big part growing up and listening to Jimi Hendrix, Crosby, Stills, Nash and Young, Joni Mitchell, Joe Cocker, Janis Joplin, Richie Havens, Santana, Matthew Southern Comfort. The list was endless. The Rolling Stones, Jethro Tull, Uriah Heap, and thanks to my brother Marty, Black Sabbath. But nothing could have had such a bigger influence on Wairoa and Huramua was when Reggae music came to town. It was Wairoa to the 'T' so to speak, like a baby was to its mother's milk.

Lead by Bob Marley, the emergence of colossal lyrical reggae revolution reigned supreme. I remember even the Wairoa Carpenters Union in town used '*Redemption Song*' to open their monthly meeting one time which made me lament and chuckle a little, imagining these old white Anglo-Saxon men singing a reggae song and thinking too how much Bob Marley's lyrics had made an impact on peoples beliefs, worth, and sufferings. This guy Jah certainly had me thinking who exactly he was but I never did know exactly. I thought he was a big island guy that lived in Jamaica who had lots of love to spread, feeling free and Irie, and that he was pretty cool all the same.

'One good thing about music, when it hits you
You feel no pain.' Bob Marley

Music was influential and the family loved dressing up like John Lennon or Donna Summer. It was all pretty cool, expressive, and ways to dress in stuff that didn't always look like dungarees, gumboots, and a straw hat and in the back of my mind thinking about the children in the world who had their freedom taken away and how blessed we were.

Much of my musical influences came from Itch. There really wasn't anyone who knew music like he did and it was one of many past-times we shared fondly together but it was what was going on out there in the world, outside of the tiny bubble of this small town that really began to intrigue me about the suffering and hatred the world always seemed to be enduring.

The Mask of the Stranger

After seeing the disparity of how the world appeared from a child's eyes, was a time when I came across a record album Itch's wife Joy had bought. On the cover of it was a man holding a mask which was looking back at him-self. The album was a Billy Joel cover entitled 'The Stranger'. Curiously listening to the lyrics over and over and it began to play in my mind about whom and what was Billy Joel talking about. I asked Joy what she thought it all meant. She replied saying that people sometimes live behind a mask, and when one day they eventually find their real self staring back at them, it seemed as though it was like meeting a stranger. She went on to say that it's not until you know who you really are is when the beginning of your life's journey truly begins. That was a poignant aspect which I carried for many years after until the answer to what Joy had said came to make sense. Until then, my strife, contrasts and lessons were about to gain momentum. A pure innocent soul in time, slowly and surely, blemished by nurturers, tainted and festered souls, and trusted ones too. Like a seabird unknowingly landing in an oil slick on the ocean, each drop feeling like lead, each step closer to the bottom of the sea of despair, struggle, and fear. Believing there was a mask and yet seeing masks on the world outside in my newly purchased arrogance as though the world owed me the happiness they stole in the first place. Why leave this world and this reality without giving up the mask, and worse still, without your song being heard? It didn't matter to me it seemed for so many reasons, all of them innocently and pathetically defunct.

Years later a keen interest towards classical, pagan, cultural, ethnic, aboriginal, and spiritual music evolved and was to be a precursor to what was to become. Not understanding back then why I was so drawn to these styles, nor was I going to know so alarmingly.

Memories of growing up on the farm are just as vivid as they were yesterday. Strange as it may seem now, my short term memory now may have much to be desired. However, recalling my childhood, and remembering almost every cow by its number as though I just milked them that morning. As though it was like seeing replays of a familiar old movie.

We learnt a lot on the farm. In my mind, it was a university of learning that incorporated rural, town, and family life as well as having a deep reverence and respect for others, the land, spiritual and religious teachings. We believed that we got to experience a great deal than kids who were raised in the cities. By our teenage years we were adept and quite independent to milking cows on our own, plough and mow fields for hay and cropping, muster sheep and cattle the hills on horses, drive trucks and tractors, fence, fishing and catching eels, and fix most things. Nothing felt like work, it was the love of being outdoors, in the elements, amongst the animals, and seeing the result of a good days work completed together as family. It was always considered fun on the farm and whenever we were not at school, playing rugby or rowing in Wairoa staying at mums' house, or going to karate with Cousin Max who to us for a time was like having a real cool older brother, but mostly we would always be out on the farm.

One comical memory to make a mundane task like chipping thistles and weeds in the paddocks, or pulling ragwort, was a little ditty cousin David would sing and we would join in which went, 'Zippidy-doo-dah, zippidy-dee-day, pull out the ragwort and throw it away'. And at times it would become so boring and tedious that by singing little ditty's was a way that enabled us all to band together to make fun out of something dull. Some kind of sympathy and humorous self pity we imagined of ourselves was nothing to the struggles the black slaves in America endured watching on our black and white television.

There were lots of relaxation times too and during the summer we would always be down at the river below the homestead diving off the jetty or overhanging trees, or wading through the mud silt banks. Tennis was always a favourite past-time in the family and before I was born there were tournaments where local families and friends would don their whites and have a spot of tennis and eat club sandwiches and gin and tonics in gallantry style and panache. For us, we'd just play in our bare feet, jandals, or scraggy sandshoes and a pair of shorts that we had worn down at the river.

There would always be oranges everywhere from the trees near the tennis court, the same orange trees that my brother Denis and I were thrown into after Cousin Turi wacked our horse after returning from a day mustering up the hill. I can remember even now these two kids on this big horse, screaming and losing our chewing gum trying to pull on the reins with eyes as big as bowling balls and seeing the ground below flying under us and the tree looming up fast in front. We knew something was going to stop and as the tree was already at a definite stand still, we knew then it was going to be the horse. And it did. And like slow, slow, motion we were doing forward rolls, flying through the air as time stopped, and eventually, so did we, into the orange tree. How we came through it without a scratch and even worse a broken arm or leg is beyond our comprehension but nevertheless we survived the worst. Maybe there really was a God.

Someone was watching Over Us

There were many accidents where it involved Turi. Where ever there was one, he would normally be in it or the cause of it, and very occasionally it was both at the same time.

One time it had rained for days. It was very cold and yet being on a farm there was always work that needed to be done, regardless of the weather. After milking, Turi and I went out on the tractor. It was older one of the two the farm had, which had a roof over the driver's seat which acted as a roll cage in case of an accident. We loaded up the large home-made farm trailer with some hay to feed the two year old bulls in the Point paddock. All the paddocks had names. There was the two Riverbank paddocks, the Old Cowshed paddock, the Millet, the Old Stables, the Racecourse (which years before I was born Papa had it as a horse racecourse), the Woolshed paddocks, the House paddock, the Honey House were some of them.

The Point was a winding paddock which followed the main willow line creek which came from up in the hill paddocks and meandered its way down through the farm like a snake until it reached the Wairoa River not far behind the homestead. We loaded up the trailer with hay and off we went in the pouring rain, Turi driving and me on the back sitting on the bales of hay. As we entered the Point, the bulls came running, like they always do when there's not much feed and they see the hay coming. I began to cut the bale twine and started feeding out the hay as Turi drove slowly along. As we reached the Point where the creek almost turns back on itself and heads out towards the Honey House. Turi decided to drive down the gully a little so we could fed the last of the hay. The rain was torrential. Next thing as I was throwing the last of the hay out when the tractor and trailer lost its grip down the steep waterlogged bank and began to slide. The weight of the trailer and the load was too much for the tractor and Turi in it, and it jack-knifed. The tractor slid to the right as the trailers weight pushed itself forward and over the tractor went until one of the roofs forks stuck in to ground. Luckily, I managed to jump clear as the trailer went over too tipping the hay off including the dogs.

I remember feeling so sorry for him and not at all surprised when one day he was hit from his farm bike coming out of a driveway by a car coming down the hill at Kihitu at break neck speed. Unfortunately Turi, ending up with two broken bones, shattering one of his legs. He had two large plates with screws in them after that but it never stopped him. He was meant to take it easy but his desire to play polocrosse was too much and he crashed again badly breaking his leg again and bending one of the plates after his and another horse collided.

Turi's passion for horses was as strong as papa's. He was tough and took life much like as it came and nothing really stopped him.

We sure learnt a lot from Turi both what to do, and what not to do. I remember watching on our black and white television this guy called Evil Knieval in America and seeing him on a motorcycle jumping these rows of cars and sometimes buses in a single jump and once was amazed when he jumped across what the television said was the Grand Canyon.

He might have crashed a lot but I thought that he was either extremely brave or lacking an elevator that went all the way to their top floor. With horses, cars, tractors and motorcycles, Turi reminded me a lot about Evil Knieval but there was a difference. Evil Knieval seemed to succeed more times than Turi and I never saw Evil Knieval on anything else other than a motorcycle and where Evil Knieval looked for adventure, for Turi, it came looking for him.

Turi was a fine horseman and farmer. He was the eldest son of our cousins along with his sister, cousin Rawinia. It was where we learnt to ride horses and fall off a lot of times too. When he wasn't on a horse mustering, he'd be playing polocrosse, and when he wasn't playing polocrosse, he was breaking in a horse for the farm or for friends, and other farmers. He was so funny growing up, he might not have been that amusing to adults but I remember falling over in tears at the way he'd tell silly stories and ditties. I think that's why other kids enjoyed his company and that he was doing fun things like riding horses or taking us out to Mahia to learn how to dive for kaimoana. His methods may not have been standard occupational safety assessed procedures but we all survived. How, I don't really know, but thinking back how he taught us all to swim was quite simple. He'd get us to stand on the side of the jetty at the river or on a rock at the beach with a big swell and yell, 'Now jump, and kick!,' and sometimes you'd hear the odd 'you useless barstards!', but we knew we just had to kick a little harder and we knew also that he didn't really mean it. Turi always had a soft side too and until mum met Gerry, he was like a dad in many ways being the elder role model.

Standing Tall

When a bike gang from Hastings was on its way to Wairoa word got around pretty quickly and many of the whanau drove into town to ensure no-one got hurt. They had apparently ram road a Police cordon half way near Raupunga and were only thirty minutes away from town. We were too little, too skinny, too nosey, and too scared to watch this showdown go down on the 'High Chaparral' however it was comical to hear the next day that when the bikies had turned up and parked their Harleys in the main street. The main street has shops on just one side of the road with the river on the other side. There was some threatening behaviour and whilst they were bickering and getting something to drink from the pub across the road, and a bite to eat, the locals simply walked over to all the bikes and pushed them into the river. That's how protective and passionate the local whanau are about their town and even though Wairoa has had a long period of its own gang issues between the Mongrel Mob and The Black Power, back then, we didn't see them causing trouble to little kids like us, nor us to them. We were chicken feed really and deep down we really had better things to do.

Mother Mako

Mums sister, Aunty Mako was an angel. After papa passed away, she serupticiously took charge of Huramua. Her, and Aunty Kui were like a team when papa was alive and they kept a tight ship of the homestead. After all, cooking and feeding a large family from sunrise to sunset was a mammoth task and reminded me of a cross between a school boarding house and the army.

Aunty Kui was a legend in the kitchen. Her baking and puddings were always a special treat each night especially her Roly Poly, Bread, Sago, Rice, and Steamed Puddings would be delicious particularly when we had preserved fruit from the orchard and fresh cream from the cowshed.

Growing up, I remember trying to convince Aunty Mako that Peter Frampton was the first person in the world to be so connected to his guitar that it could actually talk back to him. Imperturbably as usual, she'd reply with a 'yes dear!", 'oh, really?', 'That's nice dear', 'now go and pick up those weeds in the wheelbarrow please dear' with her mind firmly on her beloved gardening than listening to some eight year speaking such drivel.

Mother Mako was the matriarch of the family. She was slim like her mother Parehuia, and in spite of that she carried no virtue of the fact that she ruled with an iron fist, a cheeky grin, and a compliment for almost anyone she met. If someone did something good like her boys, cousin Max or David had done, like fix the tractor or helping to shift a big load of firewood down the back, you'd hear her pitch in with 'Good on ya Maxy-boy (which sometimes sounded like Mugsy-boy), 'comon in and have some kai!'. Or,' my Davey-boy, Johnny-boy, Marty-boy', and you always felt like you were part of a team. A family team really.

Remembering back all those years, that family now could cover almost the entire state of Wyoming because of the love mother Mako had given to us kids. Just amazing how just one couple like my grand-parents could have now such a large tribal lineage of three generations, just shows the power of that equation they called at school the 'multiplier effect', and then again, I don't think they were all applying the concept of the multiplier effect from what they had learnt at school when they had that in mind.

Matinee was Makos preferred cigarettes. Can't quite recall when she did give them up but everyone smoked back then, and if the sheep dogs knew how to hold a cigarette they would too. Mum was just as 'classy' back then but menthols was her choice and she would do this french drawback inhale where shed inhale and then exhale out in back in through her nose and then out again. Aunt Mako would always look like she could drive a convertible automobile down Ventura Highway with her dark horned sunglasses, multi-coloured scarf over her head and her trendy handbag clutch. Sometimes she would have these silky looking gloves which came up to her elbows or those short ones that went past her wrists and with a Matinee in one hand and handbag in the other, she was ready to head off into the sprawling metropolis of Wairoa and get her hair done at Shands.

Aunty Mako was an institution of majestic grace, wisdom, great humour, and herself, a matriarchal inspiration which she bestowed upon her children and her mokopuna. Another moment of spiritual influence came from her just before her tangi when she passed away only a few years ago. Itch and I were digging her grave at our whanau Urupa at Matiti. We were almost complete deep at the bottom of the grave hole when all of a sudden we get a whiff, an overwhelming fragrance of Freesias fill the air. Itch and I looked at one another and I pull myself up on the edge of the grave to see where the fragrance was coming from. There were no flowers and definitely no freesias to be seen, yet the aroma was intense. They were her favourite flowers. We just sat there for a moment in the grave and acknowledged that it was Mother Mako saying 'thank you my boys, I love you all and I am ready to go into the arms of God, my mother and whanau, and my new exciting journey forward.' That made our day rekindling, resolute and peaceful.

Mother Mako.

Mother Earth,
As ever present,
Works in the house of God,

Flowing gracefully,
She dances to the music of love.
Grooming and planting,
Pleasantly proud of the joy in her heart,
Waiting for the brushstrokes she painted,
To dry,
Like wisps in the clouds,
Feathering the sky.

Under the Ti-Tree gazing high,
On a carpet of clover,
As the hawk glides beneath the moon,
As angels caress the sun,
Into rays of light shining down,
And the hawk flinch's its head,
Climbing forward and upward the ridges high,
To the valleys below,

God resides in His creations,
Among the hill-song of insects and birds,
Filling our souls with earths glorious fragrant,
The fragrance of love,
As he gives grace and impermanence to his heaven below,
Whilst closing thine eyes,
To see the stars and the moon,

This land is an offering, a gift just to you,
An angel from heaven, Mako,
Placed here upon this soil,
As long as you want,
We can play here forever more,
For this land is our home,
It is our mana and pride.

For many workers have lived here,
In rain and the sun,
Like the thickness of leather,
Strapped round the saddle he rides.
One kick and they're off,
Beyond hayfields and streams,
Whilst cattle and sheep graze peacefully bliss,
Their tails flicking like a whip,

Amongst walnut trees and the crackle,
Of shells on the ground,

He rides toward the whare with the orchard he see's beyond.
He stops on the earth,
Letting the reins fall from his mind,
Quenching his spirit, reliving the tales,
Gazing at the walls,
The history never ends.

Of wars and of flight,
Of conquering and of the time,
Wallpaper and news faded but there.

Te Wairoa, our river,
The willows touch its rippled mirror,
Sun glistening serene,
As the lazy tide reaches,
To the heavy sea beyond,

As monuments over our ancestors who still ever live,
Their love and their hearts,
Embedded in each one of us,
With every breath we feel them,
From Matiti,
To our hearts,

The spirit of Mother Mako reigns forever strong,
The matriarch, our angel of love,
Fragrance and sound,
Te ihi, Te wehi, Te manawanui!
Kia kaha!
Huramua!

Farm-life at Huramua

We grew up with lots of animals, horses, cattle, dairy cows, sheep, wild goats, dogs, pigs, our black tomcat cat named Tane and Papas dog, Timi, and his draught horse called Blackie. My brothers and I learnt much about animals except how to shear sheep. Perhaps it was because we were too skinny and maybe our older cousins knew we didn't yet have the strength to flip a sheep over let alone shear it without skinning it alive. I thought that was a good enough reason as Id seen many sheep get cut and seeing all that blood on the shearing shed floor and those bits of hanging skin, I felt more for them than I did for the person who did it, even if it was just a careless accident. It was horrible, poor sheep and little lambs.

Down in the whare paddock was the orchard. It was also where the horses would be kept, which they liked as they would eat any apples that had fallen on the ground and would be able to run around and up the gentle slope which led down to the creek below where the whare was. The whare was the original house. It was very old and was falling to pieces. It was used to store any old equipment that wasn't being used on the farm, much of it could have been restored and put in a museum like a lot of old equipment on other farms. In the whare, it was like stepping into another world. On the walls were old newspapers and photographs from a long time ago. Horse drawn carts, surreys, old planes, and old buildings, which were new at that time and it had an enormous amount of spirit and memories in there as you wandered around the little rooms imagining what life was like way back then. It was always a place to go and relax amongst the memories, of papa and nanas lives back then and all the good and tough times they had before there was electricity except for the big brick fireplace which stood in the wooden floor lounge.

The orchard grew a lot of different fruit. Mainly apples and pears, and there was an apricot tree which I loved, and a big fig tree with its crawling branches like a sea creature, and a couple of delicious peach trees. Around the tennis court and the drive were the orange trees and below the farm by the chook house was the lemon, grapefruit, and lime trees. The cooking apples were used each year for preserving and so too were most of the other fruit. Annual preserving was a big project with the aunts and because there wasn't enough peaches Aunty Mako would gather Ra, Bub, and us kids into Uncle Reays big Ford Falcon station-wagon and off we'd go down to Hastings to pick golden queen peaches by the box and car load and bring them back to the farm for preserving. That was fun going to Hawkes Bay except for having to stop once or twice to throw up on the side of the road with car sickness.

Growing corn and milking cows on the farm was the staple income, along with wool, sheep, bulls, and cattle. Uncle Reay would be finding plants which didn't quite look like corn growing in there too so he thought he was doing himself and the whanau a favour by making notes or removing them to help the corn grow better.

Huramua, was mostly flat alluvial land. It was tethered by rich topsoil which was once all lowland swamp and marsh areas over 1000 years ago when there were mighty native bushland of Totara, Kauri, Rata, Kowhai, and Rimu trees with an abundance of bird and wildlife. The Wairoa River was Huramua's water source for irrigation and for the farm. The water was used for the gardens, the sheds, and cowshed, which was often for the pump at the river to require fixing or repriming especially whenever there was a flood. That was normally Reaymonds' job and he was Mr Fix-it. If there were any split hoses which would rise up along the fence lines or in the middle of a paddock like a majestic fountain he'd arrive with his gas burner, butchers knife, spanner, and new couplings and the rainbow fountain that once was, was now asleep again.

It was cows, cows, and more cows. If there wasn't milking, there was feeding out to do, and if not that, there were calves to feed, repairs to be made in the shed or shifting electric fences. That was exciting seeing the cows enjoy some new and lush green grass for them after milking and they would be straight into their new pasture meal with impudent lust and fervour. I enjoyed cows and cattle the most. They always seemed friendlier and wanted to be friends with you unless it was a bull. They smelt good too and never minded what the townie cousins used to say when they'd come down from Auckland holding noses going 'Poo they stink!', especially when they shat close to you whilst washing their udders or removing the milking cups.

The cowshed was like a small factory. A working symbol of New Zealand dairy farming, supplying milk and cream to what I just thought was to our town. As kids, we didn't care where it was going, never gave it a thought. Just that it was off to become some family's butter to put on their toast or new potatoes, kumara, or as whipped cream on a cake, or a raspberry or lime milkshake which were my favourites or to drink straight out of the milk can.

The old cowshed was by the river. Remembering how each cow used to come in each stall one by one was the way it was until the more modern two race system came along where we could milk 20 cows at a time much quicker. We learned much about what was going on in the world in the cowshed and sometimes we would use the hoses as mikes to sing along to Gene Pitney, the Moody Blues, or Elvis, or we would be listening to the news. Vietnam would seem a million miles away yet imagining what was going on there, to me seemed sad. Hearing Martin Luther King and John F Kennedy's speeches over the song, 'Has Anybody Seen, my old friend Martin', got me thinking about why these good people were being shot for doing so much good. Wondering how, in some way I could find a solution to all this trouble, and then realising like so many others in the world that maybe we were too insignificant to make a change and hoping that it would all work out somehow. Nevertheless, things weren't adding up properly in my mind and looking at how hard we were working and feeling so blessed that no bombs or napalm was being dropped on our farm yet strangely; it stuck with me with haunting despair.

'Destructive minds are the most rewarding educators in developing a humble state of tolerance' ~ JahAnanda

Baking rewana was always a weekly task done by the women. The best was Aunty Here and Aunty Kuis'. The smell of it cooking was divine. Watching them kneading the dough and how strong their arms must have been all those years of baking was an art to see, smell, and admire. The dough would be placed into cast iron pots with legs and a lid, and placed out in the sun to rise for a few hours. David was the Maori bread lover of all of us. He always used his blue-eyes and cute smile, like a purring cat after a dish of milk to entice any mother or aunt to let him have the first slice of a nice fresh crust out of the oven.

Parehuia, or Bub as we call her, had control of much of the house and of all the men and us kids who would walk inside smelling of cow shit, or in farm clothes and socks that hadn't been washed for almost a week. I remember sometimes having a competition with myself to see how long I could go without a bath but after a week Id give in. Sometimes we just go down to the river with our soap especially if there was no hot water left and it be Bub who would say enough is enough if we either made a mess in the kitchen or 'ok, you kids, out!', and she had no hesitation in shooing any of the men out of the women's domain. I remember Bub tap dancing and thinking that she'd be a professional tap dancer and that she might even become famous and star in the movies and dance with people like Fred Astaire. There was always something about Huramua, I saw that she saw also that Huramua was everything anyone could have. Turi was the next best thing to Fred Astaire. He would come in after being on the farm in his stinky farm clothes, grab his mother, or Aunty Kui, or Aunty Here, and dance around the kitchen making a big racket whilst they're trying to get kai ready. His conniving would only fluster them, making them all either laugh or cry, almost flipping over in the whole process on the linoleum floor with his smelly woolly socks on making them almost lose their false teeth.

Cards and Scrabble

A long standing tradition on Huramua, after all the work was done and the kitchen was cleaned, was playing cards and scrabble. Cards would always be poker, 500, or Iuka and it would start off with the blanket laid out on the big dining table. The dining table was the place where we'd all eat. It was big enough to seat twelve and sometimes there'd be two sittings if there were more for kai. It was always a mass project and once breakfast and cleaning was done and the workers were off on the farm, the next job was preparing lunch, and after lunch it was preparing kai for dinner time. Puddings were a daily inclusion and consisted of a baked pudding like rice pudding, sago, steamed pudding, Roly-poly, pastry circles, apple and apricot crumble, or mixed fruit pudding. Fruit and cream we had for each pudding course and sometimes ice cream. The dining table was a wonderful time for us all to get together and share the day, who's been doing what, and organising work or who was having time off from milking the cows to go diving at Mahia or play rugby. The dining room was more than just eating. It was about sharing, laughing, protocol, and whakawhanaungatanga. Even after pa passed away, the family traditions remained and it was in this arena of sharing that the dining room is such an important part of coming together as whanau. What I didn't quite understand back then was the effort of saying Karakia or grace. That was about to dispel quickly, my partisan and innocently brash ignorance exactly why we did Karakia and the holy sacredness surrounding kai being more than just physical nourishment. There was Eat, Pray, Love, and there was Eat, Pray, Love and Eat again, and food was and still remains, a large part of Polynesian culture.

Everyone looked forward to cards and scrabble. Cards weren't really my thing although scrabble was fun, but it was always fun to watch the faces and the hilarious one liners and inciting remarks of skill and tact that went with cards. By 10pm the small change would come out and those who didn't want to play for money dropped out to watch television or go to bed. The more serious players would settle in with their beer or smoke in one hand, with a squinted eye from the smoke wafting up in their faces, and their hand in the other while someone in the background would be strumming the guitar or playing Elvis on the record player. By midnight it would be getting quite serious as they blue haze of busy smoke filled the air. The money stakes would be getting higher, the noise of excitement louder, and the air tense like Las Vegas. The aunts would always be the loudest, their crackling laughter you could hear outside even down by the tennis court or the chook house.

Den being one of the youngest on the table picked up the game and the skills very quickly and I could see that he was learning not just the game, but also the art of being ruthless by observing the eye of the older players. Poker and 500 are games where the skills depend on not just knowing how to play, but reading body language of those playing. And Den was doing more than playing it for enjoyment. Like a circling shark on the table, here was a kid who was gaining a sharpness to cause a quiet death to unsuspecting opponents who found their pile of cash was being vaporised by someone who should really have been in bed.

Remembering one night, Marty and I being woken at 3am in the morning from outside in the bach there'd be an almighty yelling match going on which somehow moved outside. It was some whanau and their townie boyfriends who had come to visit for a few days from the city who thought they were sharks and found the beer, pressure, and realisation that their savings was disappearing before their eyes. Accusations of cheating started to fill the early morning air, the rooster started cock-a-doodle-doodling, and it become all too much and Aunty

Mako and Den, as skinny and tiny as he was, trying to break up two festering drunkards, knowing inside that his mission was complete as he quietly went to bed, smiling.

Connecting and Luck

Animals are incredible teachers in teaching us about love and compassion, of devotion, and free spirited joy. I remember growing up on the farm being part of two separate incidences which made me think how my own actions had towards the lives of ducks. The first story was a time, where I held a deep sense of deep regret and guilt for a very long time.

Duck shooting was an annual tradition like many parts of the world. We would have been quite young, perhaps 12 or 13 and my brother Den and I had finished a day working on the farm and thought it'd be nice to go for a walk around the winding creek and go duck shooting. Next moment we spy two ducks about to land into the creek below and I took a shot and one duck as it plunged down into the water below. It was the hen. Her mate, the drake flew away and as we were about to retrieve the duck from the water I noticed the male duck had circled and was flying in to see his injured mate and upon seeing her I unconsciously took my gun out and shot him also and worse, in my enthusiasm, I almost shot Denis. Poor Denis, I thought. That was the second time I had almost killed him. The first was when we were down the river bank below the farm house. Aunty Mako had us take some garden leaves and branches down to the bank to clean up and burn. Once we had raked it into a pile we tried to light a fire with some matches but there wasn't enough kindling or paper to get it started so one of us had an idea to go up to the diesel tank and fill up a small paint tin and use that to light the fire. As expected we had no idea about how to light a fire and especially with diesel or petrol.

As I had the diesel and as I was the eldest it would be better if Den lit the match whilst I poured the diesel. Gently, I pour, he lights the match, and up goes the flame squirreling up into the paint tin. Next split second and in shock, I throw the tin, anywhere, not thinking that I'd just thrown the burning diesel and the flaming tin all over Denis. We were so lucky and knew to roll and quickly smother the flames but his screaming brought down Uncle Reay and next minute I was wishing I was on fire rather than having a hefty size 10 boot in my backside. Mischievous kids!

After all these years of duck shooting that I would finally feel such guilt and anger at myself for doing such a thing and from that moment onwards I've not shot an animal since. Not only had I had shot these animals but I couldn't help but feel so ashamed for ruining and even destroying such a loving bond between life-long companions even if it was food source.

On the same stretch of water were three ducks, two males and one female. The males were fighting and squabbling perhaps, it was over a female duck. When they saw me, they immediately forgot what they were doing and flew off. One duck flew away and the other two ducks in another direction. I thought to myself that would be it and they'd be feeling quite hostile and shaken by the incident and go their own way. However as I reached the pond where the creek split into two, I noticed the same three ducks again just swimming around together like nothing had happened. They appeared to not hold a grudge about what had occurred an hour earlier and I began to think, that doesn't happen in human lives? Wondering why animals, and ducks for that matter, forgive and just move on with their lives regardless of any outcome. It demonstrated to me that their love came with no conditions or criteria in which their love was given. They just simply forgot about any indifference and just moved on.

The Cats and Dogs on the farm had their own unique and particular ways of showing love. A dogs master loves his dog and the same affection is given to the master by his companion. If the master dresses in different clothes, his dog will always recognise him. Even if his master wore a mask, or a disguise, or if he was maimed in an accident so he would not be too easily recognisable, his dog will always recognise him. And, I began to think how we as spiritual beings can recognise Gods spirit present, whether it is in the eyes of a baby or a loved one, or when we hear the wind blowing through trees, or when we hear the waves along the beach crashing, or a flower bud opening, or a child or baby animal being born. Feeling its grace and presence is beautiful to behold, to cherish, yet those moments at times life tries to snatch it away from us, or so it seemed according to the mind, and 'snapping out' again. That no matter what scenarios that played in our lives, no matter what form they may take, we sense immediately the beauty and presence of God over and over again growing up. And like the dog or cat that will always recognise his master, we too know that our master is something beyond our lives. Something invisible, but nevertheless, more powerful, and present all the time. Accepting that this unquestionable force is real, the essence of love, affection and devotion is inherent in that this energy resides in all things including our own heart. Not implying that the force was God or not, or that it was in fact a he or she but knowing that there was something greater. A powerful spirit force of wondrous and divine quintessence of creation was always around on the farm. And, to look upon that same affection, love, and devotion towards this energy in a distinct and personal way as a dog and his master have towards each other.

For some unanswerable reason there was this understanding of things spiritual on the farm but on the other hand it seemed like so much working out, so we just trusted and accepted animals and their instincts and mostly it was quite amazing seeing Mother Nature and God work their magic.

Mothers are indelibly protective of their calves, piglets, and foals. We knew that getting too near them was going to be foolish so we always kept our wits about us. Once they were weaned off their mothers, the mothers would be relaxed and nonchalant and forgot how protective or how angry they'd be when they did have their babies with them. They never held grudges after that. They just forgot about the past and just moved on.

Birds were everywhere around the farm. When it rained, seagulls from Whakamahi beach would shelter inland and feed on the pastures. Magpies too would be like alarm clocks in the morning waking us up with their serenading warbling perched high in the macrocarpa trees and orchard paddock and in the bush beside the river as would the Tui. There were plenty of native birds in the bush beside the homestead along the river.

One day Den and I decided to climb the Rimu tree below the porch. It was a brilliant sunny day as we made our slow climb to the top. As we neared the top, it was quite dark and thick with trees all around us and as we looked up to take hold of another branch, there were these two large eyes peering down at us. I'm sure they weren't as big as they appeared but to two adventurous Maori kids, they looked enormous. It blinked as its eyes shone down at us in the darkness and we froze in horror not having a clue that it was a Ruru, an owl we'd disturbed having a sleep. We first thought that it was a ghost and we didn't hoof it down that tree fast enough, terrified as our hearts pounded through our chest at what we'd seen. I think it made Aunty Mako laugh when we told her what had happened and she knew exactly what it was.

Sometimes native fantails, or Piwaiwakawaka, would fly in through the front door of the homestead. They'd be chirping away, their tails flicking like taiaha as they darted around the front room and landing on the light chains or on the piano in the lounge where Papa and his friends and visitors would have hui and wile away the afternoon and evening having a spot (as it was called) of Scotch and cigars. We were told that when Piwaiwakawaka came into the house it meant that it was tipuna, our ancestors coming to visit to say hello and some used to say also that it was a sign of death but we never believed it as they were such happy and playful birds.

Kupe

The tale of it being connected as a sign of death came from the legend of Kupe who first discovered Aotearoa many years ago. It was his grandson Nukutawhiti who also came to Aotearoa with him, and was met by the Piwaiwakawaka. Its tail flicking like that of the traditional fighting weapon known as Taiaha, the Piwaiwakawaka was considered along with the Ruru, or native owl, as the children of Tane, God of the forest. There was a great battle between the seabirds and the native forest, or Ngahere birds. And, it was the Piwaiwakawaka who danced and skipped from side to side in the air, dancing and gesticulating glaring at them, its tail flicking confusing and mesmerising the seabirds into a retreat and winning.

The Piwaiwakawaka had a more significant role much earlier in Maori mythology. It was its ancestor, Mahuika, the ancestress God of fire whom the Piwaiwakawaka protected from the great explorer Maui, who wanted to know where Mahuika kept hidden the precious fire that she had created. This got Maui so angry that he caught the Piwaiwakawaka and squeezed it so tight its eyes popped out and its tails feathers sprouted out behind it and to this day hence explains the way it looks and uniquely flies today.

The fantail did finally get its revenge on Maui for his rough treatment by not obeying his instructions when it accompanied him on his last and greatest exploit to the realms of Hinenuitepo.

In those far off days Hinenuitepo, goddess of night, goddess of death, lived, as she does today, in the underworld of spirits. As mother of mankind she has decreed from the troublesome earliest days of creation that man should live one cycle of life and die. Maui wanted to give mankind everlasting life. He sought to kill Hinenuitepo and by doing so abolish death forever.

When Maui asked his father what Hinenuitepo looked like, he replied: "you will see that her body is like that of a human being, but is of a gigantic size, with thighs as red as the setting sun. You will see eyes of pounamu, flashing like the opening and shutting of the horizon in summer lightening. You will see teeth as sharp as flaked obsidian and a mouth like that of a barracuda, and hair like a tangled mass of sea kelp".

Maui chose several bird companions besides the fantail to accompany him on his great quest. Because he had the ability to change into many life forms, he was able to travel with these birds to the underworld as a sparrow hawk.

Maui's objective was to enter the womb of Hinenuitepo when she was sleeping and by passing through her organs to her mouth, to destroy death. He said to his companions, "My command is that when I enter the womb of Hinenuitepo, you must on no account laugh."

So Maui, having taken on the form of the Noke worm, then entered the womb but as he disappeared within, Tatahore, the whitehead, burst out laughing whilst the fantail rushed out and began dancing about with delight. And then was roused Hinenuitepo who closed her legs and strangled Maui and killed him.

It was listening to tales such as these that it dawned how revered our animals, birds and mammals have and the connection both spiritually, and in mythology, they have in our lives. We take certain stories for their fluidity and literally, and underlying messages of which many stories share. As kids, we knew that they did have a spirit, and they also have an affection and drawn instinct towards being loved, showing love, and expressing love in an affectionate and devoting way towards one another, themselves, and to humans. They enjoyed being patted and even talked to, and especially fed grass or a piece of hay or straw. It was a mutual understanding towards each other and that their love was always unfettered to the point that they show such love so powerfully devoted that it supersedes the love their master has for themselves.

'Days when buying the weekly 'Rugby News' was mandatory and like reading the NZ Farmer and Dairy Exporter monthly magazines, they were like our bibles. I did feel sometimes a little abnormal going to school thinking why the other kids at school didn't talk or share their favourite articles or stories from the farming magazines and so I just kept it to myself. The town kids didn't read them and the rich farming families kids went to private schools. Strangely enough the bible was always the least read but has lasted longer on the bookshelf probably wracked us with guilt should anyone toss it out or store in an old suitcase under a bed but I'm sure someone in the house read it at sometime.

Punch

A favourite Huntaway, a black, tan, and white dog of ours belonging to cousin Itch, was a dog called Punch. He was an extraordinary athletic and very clever animal who was the leader amongst the pack of working dogs the farm owned. Itch and Punch had a very close relationship and they went almost everywhere together on the farm for many years. Sadly though, late one night and from the outhouse bach we heard him yelping down under the large macrocarpa trees below the farm house. After a while it stopped and we fell asleep not thinking too much and that perhaps everything was fine and maybe a rabbit or sheep might have excited him. The following morning we were shocked to find that he had tried to climb out of the shed window whilst he was still chained and he had hung himself. That had come as a big shock to us all and for some time I, and I'm sure all of us, carried a great deal of guilt for not realising that he was in trouble and that he was calling out for help.

Some weeks later whilst driving the tractor back from the old cowshed after feeding the calves. In the pines near the river seeing this misty white figure of a dog running through the tree's towards the farm house as though he was running along with me back to the house. I think both Itch and I, even to this day, have a deep admiration for Punch and the respect we had for him as a very clever, instinctive, and fine working dog but also as testament to the incredible work him and all working dogs do on New Zealand farms.

Pine

A life-long friend of mine Pine was another who came into my life for many reasons. Someone Id known since birth and throughout those years, we laughed, played, cried, and fought together, like soul-mates side by side. After leaving school, we lost contact for many years and when we connected again here he was doing the good work, sharing and showing the love, making life good from pain, against the odds. Having this inherent desire to teaching people about our earth mother, and about her plants, and creatures, about her gifts and joy she gives to us in return, if we treat her with respect us our mother. To us, life was no different in other lives that we shared many lifetimes before. Attuned to life, aligned to the land and its people, and looking at deep wonder and reverence to the mighty stars, galaxies, and moons which serve to bring us hope and spiritual understanding. Learning Te Reo became a path he wanted to develop more strongly for himself, his identity, his Tamariki, and how important it was to opening up the myriads of doors in the domain of spiritualism, Tikanga, Kawa, and Kai, particularly vegetarian Maori cooking. Other than Kaimoana, the small supply of Kiore, Kereru, Maori were predominately vegetarian as there wasn't the plentiful supply of meat available as there was the range of vegetarian delicacies. These were doorways for Pine, his new found rekindled path.

His parents, Pine, and mother Tilly, were teachers so it was a progression, bringing together his passion with hereditary accustom to helping not just all Maori but anyone who themselves wanted to learn about Te Ao Maori.

The same is known of Itch. Like Pine too, a quiet and maliciously intent achiever. Who speaks more with source acknowledgment seeking to attain his own wisdom and guidance, than taking on board the fallacies of thoughtless men and their ways. People whom have formed for many generations, a deep desire to seeing things through, to following their heart, and trusting wholly in the power and guidance of their Tipuna knowing that it is through their Godly intent, is provided in which both Itch and Pine knew well.

School Days

Den, Marty, and I were farm kids but through the week we'd be staying in town at mums in Osler Street. Osler Street was a quiet dead end street with only twenty or so houses. We lived at number 7 next to the Campbell's whare. Pine and Aunty Tilly (if they were friends of the family they were called aunty). Pine and Aunty Tilly had two sons, Pine, who was the eldest and a year older than me, and his younger brother John, whom we called simply as JB.

We learnt to be racist too which I think we got from other kids in the neighbourhood, on television, and at school. We didn't know what it

really meant other than just having a dislike to certain pakeha kids who
didn't toe the line, whatever that meant also. I felt so sorry for Lawrence
who was quite pleasant, wise, and extremely polite boy in our class who
wore thick glasses. He was a little chubby but he did play soccer quite
well also. Some boys thought he was worth picking on and when they
did they laughed at him because he cried strangely so they gave him
another slap so he'd cry again and I took him aside and sat him down.
It broke my heart the sad and poignant moment seeing someone being
bullied just because he looked and acted differently to all the other kids
and it had an important impact on me.

That was the difference between town schools like Hillneath compared
to Turiroa School which was where mum went to at Huramua. Turiroa
was a kilometre from the farm homestead over the back and got its name
after papa. Mum could either take the bus the long way around to get to
school or she would just walk across the paddock where the whare was
and cross the tree over the creek and then across another paddock and
she would be there. I remember one time her telling us kids the times
she had to cross the paddock and it was full of bulls. She said whenever
she wore red ribbons in her hair they would run straight towards her so
she'd hug the fence line and if they charged her she could hike up her
dress and jump over it FAST! She hated those bulls. Turiroa was also the
school that Ra, Turi, Reaymon, Max, Parehuia (Bub), and David who
was the youngest, went to also.

In town we had many other cousins going to Hillneath also. Mum
after all came from a family of 16 children and they in turn had six or
seven children each so it was like a small African nation eating, working,
breeding, and living together. The only contraceptive they had in those
days was the television and playing cards. Aunty Nyras kids went there
too and I remember Cousin Johnny was an awesome singer. When he
left high school he liked only Reggae and Black Sabbath but when he
was at primary school he sang 'Guitar Man' and 'I Wanna make it with

You' just like the white guy in America sounded. I liked Johnny's songs back then and whenever he had a song to sing Id try not to spoil it by joining in. I learnt that from mum.

My first day at school, my teacher was Ms Thompson. It was also my first time I had to stand in the corner facing the wall too, for making too much mess finger painting. Mr Postlethwaite was our principal and he had a moustache like Adolf Hitler and he walked much the same too. He lived right next to the school so his house was always getting biffed at or trashed by upset kids whom he beat up in front of the school at assembly. West's Orchard was right next door to the school. They grew oranges and mandarins, lots of them. I don't think it was a very good idea having a school next to an orchard. I remember saying that to myself whenever Id see kids running across the ditch and through the pine trees quickly fill their school jersey and walk real cool across the field, eyes tracing left to right watching out for the teachers, sheepishly looking innocent with a sneaky grin on their faces.

We were quite lucky in a lot of ways compared to kids these days too especially if you liked space craft's. There was a lot of Apollo missions into space and to the moon, and for some reason a different spacecraft would come to Wairoa almost each year after they'd been to space. It was quite amazing how they thought of us that much and I thought maybe the world wasn't really that big to come to our town all the way from America. We couldn't touch it in case we got infected so they'd say, or the craft got infected, and even though it really looked just like a tiny grain silo with legs and lots of aluminium foil wrapped around it and an American flag, I couldn't work out exactly how that piece of junk got off the ground let alone fly around space and back again. Nevertheless, mum would still wake us up in the middle of the night to tell us that it was going to be on television and that the man in the rocket was on his way to space and he was going to walk on the moon. Well, he did. Well, that's what the man on television said so we better believe it so we did and that was it. I did begin to wonder later why they never went there again though. Was it too far to live there, or build a house there, or breath?

The Masters sisters and the Cotton sisters were the most beautiful girls at school. It would be good for sport at our school as both the Masters and Cotton sisters loved playing sport. In the summer they'd be in athletics and softball and strange how all of a sudden the boys wanted to be in athletics and softball. It was quite good during that time at Hillneath because a lot of records got broken mainly in the boys events and mainly because every boy wanted to try their best to win for the Masters sisters and the Cotton sisters. Most boys played rugby in the winter but when the Masters sisters and the Cotton sisters chose to play hockey, well half the school wanted to play hockey too, so really having them at Hillneath did wonders for sport in general.

Intermediate was no different really. It was a brand new intermediate school and Mr Jones was the new principal. There were three main blocks, A, B, and C block. I think it had the same reference names as some prison in Auckland called Mt Eden. Some of the kids from gang families thought that they were cool names because of the similarity. A, B, and C, Cool? If they think three alphabet letters are cool then wait until Sesame Street comes on television. They'll think all their Christmas's have come all at once and then they'd be able to learn how to get from D to Z then they may realise how hard school will really be. So, I just went along with it all saying, 'yeah cool alright' just to make them happy.

I was accused for stealing twice at school, once at my high school, Wairoa College. It was for stealing a headphone cassette player and I was prefect too which meant having senior responsibility with other prefects at high school to uphold and an expectation to be a leader, truant officer, and an advisor to any student that needed guidance and support. Mr Braemer was the principal and he lambasted me to the letter in his quiet yet demeaning manner, feeling obtrusively authoritive and zealously intent on finding any reason to end the matter so he could go back to being a whip for the more domineering teachers who really ran the ship. By the third lashing of the cane on my butt it didn't hurt after that as it was already numb from the first two. Little did he know that night was the high school disco and prefects at discos were considered a pretty cool catch and I couldn't believe how I was still allowed to go. Cool!

The next morning, like most mornings, was the high school assembly. The whole school assembles in the school hall at 9am and the school stands as all the teachers and staff, followed by the deputy principal and then the principal wade onto the stage. This is followed by the school singing 'God Save the Queen', that in itself was another issue I had, why should God save just her? I thought. Afterwards, a prefect is selected the day before to read out the morning quote. Guess whose turn it was that morning, the day after the 'six of the best' from the principal, and the day after the school disco?

It was the middle of summer, a stifling hot day already and I come forward onto the stage wearing a scarf and my piece of paper to read my inspirational quote to the school. The school goes deathly silent. Stepping onto the lectern Mr Braemer gives a cough as my head turns to him and he's motioning me to remove the scarf. I swallow deeply and slowly remove the scarf which reveals half a dozen love bites on my neck which stood out like dogs balls even from the back of the school hall. The whispers in the hall increases as Mr Braemer and the staff are all standing behind me but don't know what on the earth has just happened. I give a wee cough and start my quote for the morning thinking at that precise moment that I should have chosen another quote.

'Never trouble trouble til trouble troubles you, because it only doubles trouble and troubles others too'.

The laughter was deafening. And as I turn to walk from the stage Mr Braemer catches a glimpse of what the melee was all about and you could have seen his stern look as the blood rose up his steaming face through his glasses. A tiny smile triggered the corner of my cheek. It was the only applause a prefect had ever received for a morning quote of the day!

Mr Braemer wasn't too bad as a principal really and after our 6th form party there were sirens and fire engines roaring and into the school grounds. The following day we had heard that someone rang Mr Braemer and told him that the school was on fire. Phone pranks were common back then. We had teachers with names such as Miss Glass, Mr White, Mr Brown, Mr Black, and Mrs Green. As you could guess, an annonymous phone-call would go to Miss Glass's house, 'is that Miss Plastic? No, it's Miss Glass. Oh sorry I've got the wrong window, And, 'Hello, is that Mr Browns house? 'No, it's Mr Whites'. 'Sorry, I've got the wrong colour' the demeaning and gloomy nature at that time of student skylark and peer pressure.

> "What happens is, when I perform, I'm somewhere else.
> I go back in time and get in touch with who I really am.
> I forget my troubles, my worries."
>
> Etta James ~ Blues and soul singer

Being relatively shy at school, I hid behind a mass of hair which wasn't allowed to touch our shoulders. Mine went further so Marty and I had a great idea which we used mainly at school inspection. Using handfuls of mums cooking oil which made our hair go like greasy hair gel, mine would curl up in ringlets and we stretched our necks up and forward so Mr May would give us a mean 'just pass' look in his eye, and a cruel sniff. Half the school were Maori and many of them had curly hair so the trick worked well for inspections and cooking oil became a fashion unique to Wairoa. I think Mr May was in the army and he looked like an army sergeant too. One day Peter Karaitiana spat on the ground as we were standing at attention which Mr May saw. He marched toward Peter and gave him a stare that would wake Sleeping Beauty and yelled loudly, 'pick that up!', which poor Peter did. 'Now put it in your pocket!'

One day I felt sorry for Marty. It was another scorching hot day and we'd be standing for quite some time waiting for inspection to begin and end. Next thing crash, he fainted and he hit the ground. The same thing happened at Pa Sonny's tangi at the church. It too was a hot day and we were late arriving as we were coming into town from the farm. The service had already started and the church was full and there was nowhere for us to sit so we just stood at the back as the congregation turned to see who had arrived late in the sombre silence. About twenty minutes into the service we were feeling really hot and still there was nowhere to sit. Marty whispers, 'hot eh? I nodded agreeing, next minute down he went in big heap in the church aisle as what seemed like a thousand eyes turned their attention to the back of the church at what had just happened.

School Excursion Glee

School trips were always a lot of fun. We would visit high schools in Gisborne, Ruatoria, Te Karaka, Napier, Te Aute, Taradale, and Hastings, to play in sports exchanges and sometimes we would go on school camps. The school camps were fun as we would visit places we'd never been too like certain tracks in the Urewera National Park and practising putting up tents or staying at Camp Kaitawa. Mr Laughlin was our rugby coach and he was always a fun teacher to go away with and he always got on well with all the students with his dry and sometimes very witty humour. He was also a real character and most times a 'bloody typical Maori' as some kiwis would also say, as he would enjoy wearing, when he could, a pair of walk shorts and a singlet which sometimes was two sizes too small over his buff physique. He used to come out to the farm sometimes and one particular time he had dandruff. There wasn't anything that he could find in the medicine cupboard to help him at the farm but decided to try something he said he saw being done on television. It was using a disinfectant antiseptic called Dettol and read on the label that it could be used for dandruff. I don't think he read the instructions carefully because when he came into the dining room where twelve of us were sitting down to eat his whole head looked like a big tomato on fire. I don't think he got dandruff after that and better still, I don't think he had much hair left either.

Our swim team was heading away to Gisborne which took about an hour or so to get to Gisborne you travel into the Wharerata State Forest which winds up into the hills through bush and when you get to the top of the summit, the views of Gisborne and Young Nicks Head are quite spectacular.

Mr Laughlin was a keen pig hunter and he was always on the ready, even driving a bus full of high school kids. Next minute he slows the bus down and the kids are wondering what on earth is going on. He whispers to some of us at the front of the bus, 'I saw a pig here last weekend we'll keep our eyes peeled'. Sure enough he spies it and quickly he stops the bus reaches down takes his 303 rifle which we had no idea he had a gun on the bus and off he goes firing bullets into the bush. 'Whoa, exciting stuff!' we say to ourselves, 'Mr Laughlin's cool as!' I don't think he got it because he said, 'I'll see if I can get him next weekend' and off to Gisborne we continued.

CHAPTER 3

Papa

Life on Huramua was extraordinarily pure and free. It was like it was a world within another bigger world. I didn't really care for what lay beyond the distant hills, or what the world was like across the oceans. All that mattered was my whanau, mates, the totara, rimu, the tall poplar and willow trees, the eels, whitebait, and fish, rivers, and miles of land and hills, farm animals and pets, the songs of the wind. Feeling free amongst nature and the animals; and with my tipuna who had lived at Huramua and passed on who now resided at Matiti. Huramua certainly had a soul connection. It was a place where I my mother Amiria, and my siblings, cousins, aunts and uncles were raised. It was full with history, hard work, extremely fun and happy times, and it was also a heavenly reminder of family who had lived, worked, raised their children, and who had passed on their legacy to the next in line.

Nana Tangi was another kuia I adored. She spent her days playing golf, weaving harakeke, and white-baiting down at the river below. She would take whangai of the eldest male from each whanau to raise and lovingly spoil for a time. In this case it was Turi, and me. I remember being taken around town as a child in her little car, then off to golf and spending many days white-baiting down the river below the farmhouse. I loved nana Tangi, her beautiful dark skin, deep warmth in her eyes and soothing peaceful smile. And the beautiful traces of wrinkles which only made her even more striking as they were like indelible pieces of her past woven like a moko on her chin. She was a fine and gentile lady who embodied presence and peace in everything she did, it was as though I had finally understood that she hadn't arrived to anything she was doing, she always was arriving and thus perpetuated her blessedness of each breath, each task, each ounce of love she gave and received she remained fully captivated by what she was doing in her moments of her space, time, and her own grace of living truth timelessly.

Whitebait though scarce these days my kuia hauling by her-self two five gallon tins full with the tiny silver fish she had caught that morning with the set net and the scoop net further down river. Having her transistor radio with her, I'd be there with my own fishing rod made out of bamboo and a twisted wire spreader at the end of the line which held two hooks to catch herrings. Shrimp was our bait and we always had plenty from the scoop net where Nana Tangi would empty into the tin bucket the delicious tasting delicacy. It was so plentiful we never thought anything about feeding it to the pigs if there was scrap food left over. And if we got sick of whitebait fritters we would have it in a big pot just boiled with salt and scoop it out with a strainer with barracuda bread, salt and butter.

Farm–life at Huramua

There was always plenty to do at Huramua and in the heat of the summer after haymaking or shearing, or after tennis or swimming down at the river we'd siesta in the batch outside with the windows wide open hoping the blowfly buzzing in the room would just buzz off so we could sleep during the hot afternoon sun.

It was fun to feed orphaned lambs which we always had a few during lambing season. They were eager, hungry, and happy guzzling as I used to watch their wee tummy's grow through the sound of the slurp slurp on the teat, their mouths foaming from their bottles until it dropped onto the grass below.

By six o'clock in the morning, there would be a large pot of porridge simmering on the stove. In the early days it was Papa who would be preparing it but when he passed away it was Aunty Kui, Aunty Mako, or Pa Dixie would get breakfast ready for the family and the boys who had been milking the cows at the cowshed. There was nothing like trim milk or low fat milk like we see these days, it was always fresh cream from the cowshed, a race to scrape the thick gooey cream from the top of the milk for our porridge followed by a good spoonful of soft brown sugar. It was always delicious and satisfying and like the lambs I'm sure our tummy's grew too, to the sound of our slurp slurps from our spoons into our own hungry mouths.

Outside in the still morning air, the expanse of the sultry mirrored river just below Huramua homestead would be swathed in mist which would wind up and along the willow lined creek from the rivers mouth up towards the hill country to the west. At the rear of the farmhouse were tall, thick gnarly pines, some bent over under their massive height and weight as the land slid down to the river below. They looked like big skyscrapers and sometimes like giant old men bent over from their years of work and toil on the land, their branches depicting thick arthritic arms weathered by the elements and the years gone by. The sheep dogs would always be awake early barking and yearning to be let go to help out with farm work or to just stretch their legs and play with the other dogs or chase magpies and other birds down by the whare or near the tennis court, or in the pines near the creek.

Papa's bedroom was in the centre of the homestead. It was always dark and silent except for when he wanted to listen to the concert program on the big wooden radio beside the wall he would have his bedside lamp. He always smelt good, Old Spice it was. And much like many of other things he had, I remember his beautiful Maori carved cigar box in the formal room at the front of the house, and carefully taking out one of his cigars and without tearing the wrapper, picking it up in my fingers and sniffing along it and thinking how special they must have been and how delicious they smelt. Even the aroma of his favourite Johnnie Walker, which must have permeated the beautifully carved old oak side tables and coasters for which Papa and any of his visitors who would join him for meetings, get-togethers for a 'spot' or two as it was called back then.

Papa's room was filled with books, mainly parliamentary books and journals which he seemed to be always reading either in bed or on his wooden oak slide and his leather and wooden desk which was covered in letters and minutes from meetings. I had no clue what they were but knew it was his work, his love, and his passion. At night after his bath, which overlooked the river below, he'd be tucked up in bed and most times still listening to parliament in session on the radio half awake. I would take a peek in his room and snuggle up next to him, his glasses by then would almost be falling off his nose and with a short grumble and sigh he would close one eye and drift off to sleep with his hands clasped over his cheeks, papers sprawled on his lap on the bed. I knew his other eye was a glass eye and when he went to sleep it never closed, so I would gently close it for him. I knew that he was shot in that eye though I didn't know if it was from the First World War or what it was but when he was awake you never knew he was blind in that eye because his glass eye was exactly the same as the other.

The time I enjoyed most was taking Papa for walks around the garden. He never spoke that much, but neither did I, but I don't ever recall him talking idly or gossiping but when he did, it was worth listening. Never would I have imagined that some forty years later we'd be walking together again in heaven, talking and sharing like we did all those years ago.

I learnt this from my Papa that in life, if you wanted to get along with people and relate to them, the secret was quite simple, it was always being polite. We were all brought up to be polite, courteous, well mannered, and obliging. I never felt comfortable even swearing, even now going out for a meal at a cafe or restaurant, not feeling comfortable leaving my plates, cutlery, and glasses on the table expecting someone else to clean it up. To always take our own dishes up to the kitchen out of courtesy and gratitude. No matter whom you met in life, if one showed decency and respect towards another person, that would always reflect on their response and the way you wished also to be acknowledged. No matter whom they were, Papa ensured we maintained our respectfulness and dignity whether it was saying karakia at the dinner table, to greeting visitors, or talking to neighbours over the fence, or people you played sport with, whether you are treated in kind or not, dignity and kindness always serves its purpose by treating others how you wish yourself to be treated. It always prevailed and these days with many of our leaders of today who should set an example from the front, including parents, this feature of life has no reason to suffer fools.

Papa had a very extraordinary and illustrious life. When he returned from the war, he had a vision for the people, his people the Maori people. He was well educated and excelled at Te Aute Boys High School and Feilding Agriculture College and then went on to study at Lincoln University in Canterbury, though he did have a tutor with whom he was picked as a future Rangatira, or chief. Papa was influenced through his own childhood by his uncle, Sir James Carroll. He wanted young Turi, as this became Papa's name from Alfred Thomas, to be a future Rangatira and this meant for him to have a deep entrusted understanding of what it took to be in charge and to be a respectable and responsible leader. Fluent in Te Reo Maori, schooling was very much a big part of Papa's path in his early years along with working on the farm and learning as much as he could from esteemed leaders before him such as Sir Apirana Ngata, George Nepia, a famous All Black and Maori All Black, and NZ Rugby League National Representative; and his uncle, Sir James Carroll. Uncle James himself was a fine orator, an instigator, and esteemed tribal leader. My great-grand uncle entered politics at a young age, he was noted to have been Aotearoa, New Zealand's first ever Maori Acting Prime Minister and I could have imagined Pa as a child, clinging to his wisdom and notoriety to following in his uncles' footsteps to forge his own path for the good of his people.

Papa was decorated in the war, and played rugby for the Maori All Blacks but his greatest achievements was in politics, public speaking, and being involved with dozens of tribal, sporting, land, political, church, and farming boards, groups and councils. He was knighted by Queen Elizabeth II, and even though people referred to him as Sir Turi, to us he was just simply papa.

Papa always had visitors calling around. We knew when important people came to visit when they would arrive in flash shiny cars, some with New Zealand flags on the front with a driver who just sat outside waiting. They could have been ministers and their wives and they dressed like they were about to go to the horse races.

You knew that they were his visitors coming down the road as they would take forever to drive towards the house along the two mile gravel drive from the mailbox down the driveway to the homestead. If it was anyone else's car, it would have be flying down the road as if being chased by the cops, or a car rally, or imitating 'Starsky and Hutch' Maori style, with trails of dust billowing like planes spraying flaming chem-trails in the sky. It were as though Papas visitors were trying their best not to get any gravel dust on their car, overturn any stone or avoid worst still, falling into the myriads of scattered potholes dotted along the road.

Some potholes were so deep when it rained ducks and Muscovy's would wash themselves in them as though they were bird baths. When they came through the front gate past the tennis court it was like watching a painful movie in slow motion, but nevertheless they were Papas friends and guests.

We knew that children were to be seen and not heard. The older cousins, Turi, Raymond, Max, and David made it even easier by just vanishing completely though us kids including David would always somehow find a way to creep inside the house from the bach outside and sneak into the kitchen begging from cousin Bub, Aunty Kui, or Ra for a cheese and cracker biscuit, or a piece of Madeira cake, or the delicious sandwiches with curried egg, or tomato and cucumber, the ones with the crusts cut off them. We always knew though that it was mischievous but at least we kept away from the front room where Pa's manuhiri were and that room was definitely out of bounds. I began to wonder over the years whether any of Papas visitors even knew he had grandchildren as it would be so quiet hiding away.

CHAPTER 4

Life at the Foot of the Tararua's

Linda and I met in the Wairarapa. It was love at first sight and all her
university friends from Otago where she grew up called her 'Spindle.'
I was working for the government at the time enjoying three to four
months off each year to do triathlons which became an obsession. Linda
was in charge of the YMCA gymnasium after having a break from
being a school teacher for several years. I had no idea at the time what
a spindle was and had never been inside a gym before either other than
at Wairoa College. It was a little old fashion yet it had a vibrant small
town atmosphere. It served a wonderful purpose to helping get people
into shape and losing some extra kilos and an opportunity to having fun
at the same time in the very quiet inland town. After five years working
for MAF as a meat inspector, the job was beginning to become tedious
and unfulfilling and mastering the art of flicking lymph nodes also had
lost its appeal. Believing that government work was the 'be all and end
all' of career accomplishment and that you would be taken care of for
the rest of your life, I began to realise that earning good money and yet
having copious amounts of time off was appealing so I could train. It
didn't take too long before I began to feel dissatisfied with my work and
the common apathetic hierarchical nature that a government department

held began to highlight a desire to wanting to find something more satisfying. Hollie was born not long after Linda and I had met and seeing this new phase where it involved inspiring others was beginning to open my eyes in a big way. It was through Linda's direction that focussed my attention to helping other people get fit and having fun doing it at the same time.

I lived on the top floor of an old disused hotel which was in the main street of Masterton. The town itself was slightly larger than Wairoa and even though it seemed miles from where I had been brought up near the sea it did have an appeal in which to create a new life after working for the government. Tony, Bob, and I were flatmates and we looked after the hotel ensuring that it was secure as it wasn't being used. Later it was turned into a polytechnic for a time. Rent was very cheap and the power was free, and it had great views over-looking the town and towards the Tararua ranges which in winter looks impressive with its snow capped mountains radiant against the blue sky.

Tony was an accountant, very polite and a great guy, and although I kind of thought he wished he were a royal aristocrat, his background certainly wasn't, he was nonetheless pleasant. He appeared to have a deep fondness for things British like cricket and gin and tonics, and laughing with a stiff upper lip and being very 'oh so polite' and he was quite fun to have around. Bob on the other hand was quite the opposite. He was a DJ in the pub below and everyone called him Dr Bob. He was indeed the life of any party and even though Tony and Bob were quite contrasting, they became relatively good friends. Bob was often messy and dreadfully carefree. He would come home from work when the sun was rising and I remember the putrid odours that would waft out of his bedroom door which had a blend like swamp, road kill, and old socks. Once, Tony and I had an idea that we would place a piece of meat under his bed to see if after a few days he would smell the rotting odour. After 3 weeks the odour was too overpowering for Tony and I, but not Bob. He hadn't noticed a thing so we got under his bed and got rid of it ourselves as it the foul odour was rampant through the whole apartment which made us dry reach walking past his room.

I had no idea what being unconscious was yet I was living it. Life became one phase from another, forgetting for a time, my roots, and being a typical kiwi bloke with a 'Steiny' in one hand and a swimming cap in the other.

Triathlons became my life after a while after becoming dissatisfied and sometimes bored with the drinking culture that rugby and drinking beer had. It was a lone sport, one that didn't rely on being part of the team and doing things on a specific day and time as I had become accustomed too. I could set my own times to train and found either being on the bike, or running in the beautiful Wairarapa countryside. With swimming, I could 'switch off' to think and challenge myself to going further beyond anything else physically that I had done before.

After several years, I had this flashback to Huramua. It was on television, this race of an event called 'The Ironman' Id not seen before, being run in Hawaii. I remember thinking how crazy and stupid these people were swimming at dawns light in the open ocean for what seemed like miles and then ride a bike through hot searing sun and volcanic plains for 180 kilometres and then running a marathon afterwards until sunset. It seemed so ridiculous and I thought to myself, why in the world anyone would want to put their bodies through all that pain and torture when you could just lie in a hammock by the beach under a tree and enjoy life instead. My mind recalled that time as I was half way through the marathon leg of 'The Ironman' in Auckland, and it hit me thinking how crazy they were, and here I was doing it myself. Karma sure works in mysterious ways I thought.

It was only months earlier whilst training for it that I had come off the bike and had torn a ligament in my knee which needing reattaching, and being stubborn and defiant, continued to keep training after the operation determined that I was going to do this event come hell or high water. My knee still wasn't completely healed and I decided to sticky tape a strip of pain killers under the seat of my bike once the pain started which it did near the end of the bike. My face covered in stings from jelly-fish from St Helliers beach and by the time the run had started it was at that time all those years earlier my intuition or fears were telling me something which I chose to ignore.

In our apartment, there were so many doors to unlock and lock to get to the 4th and top floor where we lived so we instead used the outside fire escape to criss-cross our way along the narrow railings until we got to the top and we then simply opened the lounge window and step inside. Not long after we met, Linda had earlier planned to travel overseas to Australia briefly and then onto Asia and then Europe. We agreed that we would stay in touch as there was no determination as to when she would return. I remember it being a Saturday afternoon some 8 months later, seeing this strange and colourful, and tanned figure standing at my window. It certainly wasn't a Masterton local as they tended to dress in very plain unobtrusive clothes, and when I realised who she was, it was more than a shock.

We decided to then buy a house and settle down, whatever that meant, as was the dimension of being young with a free and grand disposition and coddling the regular mainstream expectation to follow the usual traditions of settling down with children, a business, and a picket fence.

Before Linda had left to go overseas she had taught me to teach aerobics. I enjoyed my time doing classes at the YMCA, the numbers were definitely growing and it was a lot of fun. The money was something like five dollars, before tax, per class. It wasn't the career that would make anyone a millionaire and even though I had a great time getting fit myself but it was helping other people get fit too that inspired my desire to serving people instead of farm animals all these years. There was some dissent as to how much we as aerobics instructors were being paid so it was then that I decided to go out on my own a teach as an freelance instructor. That was immense fun and whenever I wasn't teaching at the 'Y', I began teaching in school and country halls around the district. It was a great way to make a little more money and to meet the locals and new people too and it was extremely satisfying to be welcomed so hospitably and then being invited to their nearby farms for a drink and sampling their home baking over a cup of tea or cold beer.

Being paid to stay fit seemed to suit this new life and I remember seeing what had got me into the fitness industry in the first place. It was only a few years after leaving high school, I wasn't rowing or playing anywhere as much sport, or working on the farm as I was back in Wairoa. It was now flatting, drinking, and partying, and when you're flatting you got to cook whatever was easy, tasted good, and fried food was the staple diet. Over three or four years I had put on around 30 kilograms and it wasn't until I saw a photograph of my cousin Colin and I drinking out on the lawn at Huramua, the disgusting belief that I was this fat faced, over hanging stomach of a kiwi version of a blimp looking back at me in the picture.

Back on the farm we loved porridge with lots of brown sugar and fresh farm cream for breakfast, and butter on almost everything, and roast lamb, pork, or mutton with roast potatoes and yummy rich gravy was normal farm food. But we were also young and active and we were always on the go, running around at a hundred miles an hour working, playing sport, tennis, or swimming down at the river. Being in a new town away from family, cooking and having the freedom to choose whatever you wanted, became a despised nemesis for a while and I too, became 'Mr

Caruso,' and it made me feel disgusted, so triathlons and aerobics saved me, to a point.

Linda and I started Body Rock, our first business venture primarily as an aerobics centre for a couple of years and then afterwards, a gym. It was a fun time, and the boys were born during that time and they grew up seeing mum and dad taking classes along with a number of other staff. Huramua and farm life became a distant memory for a time and living in the hustle and bustle of a town like Masterton was an ideal landscape which was a perfect environment for raising children. With vast open spaces and a number of beautiful rivers to swim and have picnics under the Tararua Mountains during the summer and the wild coast of the Wairarapa, we enjoyed immeasurably our time as a family.

They were memorable fun times teaching classes and working and decorating our large old villa which was only five minutes away from work. They were prosperous and sometimes understandably challenging periods, and yet as a family we took everything in our stride and readily took any opportunity to visit Wairoa or seeing the awesome beauty of Te Wai Pounamu to visit Linda's family in Otago. The beauty of the Southern Alps was normal for Linda as she grew up in the south however for me it was simply breathtaking for a Maori boy from the East Coast. Remembering how high and how contrastingly different they were to Te Ika a Maui, the North Island, with the captivating and sheer broad length of the vast landscape just took my breath away. Driving down through to Tekapo and asking Linda 'Is that Aoraki?' Aotearoa's highest mountain, she would calmly say, 'No, that's not it.'

'Is that that Aoraki?' Again, she would say 'No, that's not it.' But as we headed around another mountain range there it was, gleaming and glistening just as I had seen in pictures all those years ago. This incredibly beautiful mountain, Aoraki, reaching up and up into the sky, a towering rocky and majestically commanding looking God like in its structure blanketed in snow, and either side of Aoraki the southern alps as far north and south as you could see.

Feeling proud to be Maori, a kiwi, a New Zealander from Aotearoa and Tangata Whenua, tracing back in my mind of the great migration several centuries earlier when stories of our tribes who had migrated from Tahiti and Polynesia to escape the famine, over-population, and warfare. These were made of the great legendary canoes, the best known Aotea, Arawa, Kurahaupō, Mataatua, Tainui, Tākitimu, and Tokomaru. Various traditions name numerous other canoes. Some, including the Āraiteuru, are well known; others including the Kirauta and the sacred Arahura and Mahangaatuamatua are little known. Rather than arriving in a single fleet, the journeys occurred over several centuries. These were my ancestors, the noble and courageous Rangitira, tohunga, wives, warriors, and their children.

Of their amazing courage and tenacity, to venture off thousands of miles into the far reaches of uncharted ocean by following only the stars, to a hopeful new dream, a new land, and a new life for their families. If it wasn't for their faith and their belief, their trust, and the knowledge that they were going to be safe because of how much they had put their ultimate destiny in the hands of something much higher.

Looking out over Nga Maunga Ataahua o Te Wai Pounamu, and the story I heard as a child, of the man who had found a mighty Kauri tree, the most supreme of the forest. 'This will be perfect for my waka, my mighty canoe! He exclaimed excitedly. And without haste he began to chop it down. It took him many days to finally bring the tree down and with a mighty crash, it fell among the bush and onto the earth below. The man feeling tired but pleased with himself decided to rest for the night with the object to waking up early the next morning began building and making his fine waka.

When he woke, he walked towards where the mighty tree lay, it wasn't there. It was standing back up again. Every chip, every piece of wood, leaves, branches, and bark had been returned. What he did not know was that he had made a terrible mistake, and he sat down on the ground feeling very sad, angry, and confused. 'All that work. All those many days of sweat and toil,' he lambasted to himself, 'for what? For nothing and someone knows why this tree is standing back up and I want to know the answer!' he lividly demanded.

Not long after a beautiful Piwaiwakawaka, a fantail came and sat next to him. It was flicking its tail and singing a song as beautiful as any other bird in the forest. The man looked at the Piwaiwakawaka and asked, 'Why is my tree standing back up again beautiful Piwaiwakawaka? After all the days I worked to cut it down and now its standing back up again. Why?

'The reason you came back and found the tree standing again is because it is one of our children', the fantail replied. 'You took one of Tane, the God of the forest, one of his children, his creations, without first asking permission for it. And when you slept, all of his other children, the birds and the insects all came together and worked all night to put the tree back where it belonged and that is why it is now standing back in its rightful place again.'

To this, the man felt remorseful and so sorry for what he had done. He realised that taking something that wasn't his was wrong. It was a lesson of learning respect for the things we have and the precious gifts that nature creates and there are certain Kawa that must be observed always before anything that belongs to another, can be used, taken, or removed with first seeking permission.

Flickerings of the past and the teachings from my mother and whanau, my koro, aunts and uncles, of holding close to our hearts, the values and precious gifts we have as Tangata Whenua, as Kiwis, not just Maori, not just settlers to this great land, but all people. So too was to the children. They too must know the history of the land, the whenua, and about their parents that brought them to this land. That there must be something greater, more powerful, more revealing, and more loving than what I started to see, even remotely consciously, nevertheless, there was a duty to pass this knowledge onto them.

It wasn't too long after that, Linda and I decided that the children needed the same opportunity, and how appropriate it was to settle upon them attending Kohanga Reo, a pre-school for children who wished to learn about their roots and all aspects of being Maori, and Tangata Whenua. We as children weren't given the opportunity to learn our language yet our mother would be beaten and punished at school when she was a child for speaking Maori. It was now the time to regain our tribal and traditional sovereignty back and the boys were enrolled at Kohanga Reo.

I found it somewhat embarrassing sometimes looking Maori but not being able to speak the language when we were young. It was like looking like a duck, flapping our wings like a duck, but sounding like a chicken and feeling like one, the shame was inebriating.

The beloved offering by Papatuanuku, our Earth Mother and her creations were reason enough for naming three of the children Hollie, Rata, and Tane, who is God of the forest. Riki was more towards our musical tastes at the time which was Steely Dan's song, 'Riki Don't Lose That Number,' and Rikki Lee Jones tunes 'Chuckee's In Love', and 'Company'.

Tane

I could remember numerous such contrasting occasions. For Linda and I losing our eldest son and twin Tane, to an autonomic brain condition similar to my own which caused my NDE was one of the most difficult.

It took us almost two years of tedious frustration of trying to have a baby and then be shocked and surprised to find out that we were expecting twins, and later on finding out that one of them had a condition, at the time we both didn't think would be as serious as it eventuated. In spite of a trying and emotionally painful period in our lives, we learnt a great deal about having faith, and how having a perspective reproach was important to see the context of another's suffering apart from our own. It also helped us realise that windows of opportunities would arise and that darkness would always give way to light if we look at Tane's short presence and life with us as a gift. One that we would always have in our hearts and treasure forever and knowing intimately that he remains with us still as much as we do with him yet for me losing my own flesh and blood was and began to become a painful noose I chose to hide.

Not long after, we met a couple who too had lost their son around a similar age and in similar circumstances. We had time to mourn, well more so Linda, and get our lives back on track again and to be witness to someone else's suffering, it certainly exemplified to us just how much we had come towards our own healing and having enough love and compassion replenished in our hearts to offer to someone else knowing their circumstances.

Unbeknown to me however, I was living a lie. Id hardly shed a tear when Tane passed away which I put to childhood memories that had become a block to being able to show emotion and in particular, grief. Unrealised to the truth that we are born into two realms, the place of our birth, and more relevant, the birth of our existence. I was caught up in the mindful physicality of beliefs and perception all wrapped up in thoughts, a result of being caught up in being humanised instead of holding true, my spiritual connection of mauri. Back then there wasn't anything close to what flowing and allowing was and should have been, knowing what the conscious awakened state of the higher dimensional plain of the soul and understanding was, and meant. I was a million miles from it, unprepared and under nourished. Nevertheless, and gravely rasped in the heady and reminiscent years of a childhood, attempting to hide behind being a tempestuous and brave Maori warrior on the hill protecting his whanau, crying or showing emotion was pre-empting weakness or that what a meek and vulnerable child was meant to believe anyway. Deep down, Linda and I were in pain, reliving how beautiful he was, how strong and how brave he was, and feeling so much for Riki who hardly cried, he was a model, peaceful, and obliging soul. It was as though he knew that Tane was not well and he wanted Linda and I to have as much time with our boy as long as we could spend, that we certainly both knew and respected both him and God for giving us such grace an opportunity, yet Tane was his brother also.

The night when he was taken off life support was a heart wrenching and poignant time in our lives. We had some close friends and family with us for Tanes last remaining hours and Riki still being his smiling, quiet, playful self. He was giving Linda and I consideration and to his brother in his last remaining few hours for us to say our goodbyes. We talked and shared the times we had together summing up life, its good times and its challenges upon young ill equipped parents. This challenge was one for us all, and trying somehow to dig deep, remaining faithful to what Gods plan was for everyone, come what may. We believed that Tane already knew what that was going to be, and he bore this mournful period with so much strength and courage beyond any suffering we had seen before in our own lives. However, the moment Tane passed away in my arms was apparently fluid, peaceful, extremely sad and heart wrenching, and in another way we fought in accepting that all was well and how beautiful this moment had become both spiritually and emotionally.

The moment Tanes heart stopped beating Riki unexpectedly let out an eerie and painful scream, something both of us had never heard from him ever before. It was a moment in time, a precious time, and a revelation that spelt to us all in the room that spirit was most definitely evident and Tane's departing spirit broke his twin brothers' heart deeply. As much as we felt for Riki and his pain we wanted to spend some time with both boys nevertheless his screaming was too much for us and we asked one of the nurses if they could take him away to another ward. No matter where he went, we could still hear his screaming on the hospital floor above us until he cried himself to sleep whilst we spent the night with our boy in his room.

I called Marty in Auckland, shivering and trembling, to tell him the news. It wasn't until then that my emotions poured out and how lost and sad I began to feel for all of us. Pushing through the tears and feeling like my heart was going to explode telling him and feeling so consecrated that I had a brother who understood and never tried to make it something that it wasn't. He just let me decant it all out and I felt his love just by his presence and support that fateful solemn night.

As time went on after that my tangled ego began to rear its head, and like an unconsciously ugly demon, the past of being taught to be the brave Maori warrior began to take over and trusting in what I was taught all the years ago began to take hold.

Thus was the armoury, as fake and unseen it was, the visions of the warrior protecting his hapu, his village, with flaring nostrils and the storm at his chest began to melt and crumble. Long hair blowing in the wind, with squinted eyes stern and cut, standing proud with his hand firmly clenched to his taiaha like a defence wall built of stone, and of marshmallow, but no-one was never to know.

Buried under a veil the memories and scars of child rape at age seven by the friend of the family on the settee at my mother's house in the lounge, was blamed upon by the perpetrator by alcohol as his alibi. Keeping the secret of it out of shame and fear of being ostracised and ridiculed by adults whom I felt would take sides or sweep it under the carpet as a dream or harmless fun. Experiences that forsake and demean a child's innocence and benevolent purity to becoming withdrawn, desensitised, and devoid of confidence and esteem propelled my shame beyond ever being a happy free child again. So are these crippling and soul destroying ramifications towards children who are left alone with an unassuming and unlikely predator to become a victim and being clever at being adept at hiding ones emotions, like a prisoner in a concentration camp told to not speak or else.

Thereafter, carrying the indignity and guiltiness from a dark stolen childhood, an even darker veil loomed from that day onwards. Being happy 80% of the time was better than none, and concealing my weakness and fear formed an art of which a child, just like most any other would I thought. I was too innocent and too fucking scared to know any other resolve, nonetheless, an art form to conceal it, it became.

Sincere to beliefs along the way, I thus became acquainted with matters of heart. Whether this was a symbol of self mourning for having to witness seeing my mother toil and labour on her own to give her children the best life she could give, or of my brother suffering through asthma, or that experience, our bond would never be broken. Having a penchant and escape, so to speak, listening to music whilst being influenced by my older cousins whom we were exposed to through the Beatles, Rolling Stones, and the revelling Woodstock era. Another was Elton John. His music flowed and oozed eloquence, flamboyancy, style, passion for being who he was however it was his hit single, 'Daniel' hearing the lyrics, 'of the scars that won't heal'. Those few words further cemented that dirty little secret and all I had to do was simply throw away the key. Little did I know by holding myself to these beliefs presented a cataclysm of contrasts and repressiveness which ensured the periods of my life thereafter would have been easier to resolve with a braver heart. Lying in bed imagining through the transistor under my pillow, was there really a yellow brick road, was there? Beyond my thoughts I knew somehow there really was, a life of journeying, adventure, colour, and peace. A place where you never felt scared, always had dreams, and hope, and surely if you kept to the winding yellow brick road you would be safe, you and your friends.

By the time I had my own children I was further reminded of a horrible night and when I heard of a child near Hastings who was taken from his bedroom when he was asleep. The kidnapper had climbed through the open window leaving the parents suffocatingly distraught, distressed, and heartbroken. How I felt for the couple and their precious innocent baby child particularly knowing that we had our own children and lost one. I wasn't going to allow my babies come to any harm and I became at times an over protective parent. In hindsight though, if not being a victim to a child sex offender, I could have become a less fastidious parent but that wasn't the case so it was lost bearing the thought.

The love affair with life went without suffering. For no longer having Tane's physical body with us, the presence it seemed that we both knew in our own internalised way that something more powerful out there in the mystique vastness of the unknown, its invisibleness deeply woven so tight like the fabric of silkiness of a pashmina shawl and how it was made was irrelevant yet the softness and strength kept us warm and content. It didn't always seem so and living this spiralling new life over and over again was laced with reward and the reoccurrence of heartache that he was no longer with us and yet looking at his brothers peace and contentedness each day. Realising that perhaps he knew of peace far beyond what were struggling to deal with after years of a fabricated conditioned mind and wretched beliefs along this journey had strangled more mine, it seemed, than Linda's. Like life was filled with joy woven among the vast void of dark emptiness and pain, and the vision to always being the proud warrior on the brow of the hill to stand strong protecting no-one but his ludicrous self and holding defiant yet again with the mask of the stranger, not knowing too much inside its empty head. Ravaged and succumbed by this tortuous mind for so long, like an obedient fool thinking that believing 'out there' held all the wisdom to know and to heal, and the soul knew nothing worth considering as though its job wasn't needed for this life at all until death.

But bearing down on me day after day, month after month, year after year, the dirty secret of the little boy molested never left my mind. So much so that eventually Linda could take it no more, my emotions became a block of wood, a mass of solidifying lava. Proud of our children, what we gave to them as parents, and what I lost was their gain in every meaningful way possible, yet the combination of losing Tane only ensured that the brave Maori warrior prevailed to stand tall, defiant and unaffectionate towards Linda. Unobtrusively, and unconsciously manipulated. Goodbye yellow brick road, goodbye forever unconscious soul.

CHAPTER 5

Out of Body, Out of Mind

Passing of Time, Passing Away

'Like the setting sun gives rise to the moon's approach forming,
The night sky is born to the new day it too.
So do the autumn leaves whence falls before the winter chill arriving,
And the spring buds dawning,
Heralding the summer's sun glistening

Same to the precious new born infant,
Whose blessed life is full and wondrous

In all its glory and beauty beaming,
The time comes to close our eyes,
Upon our last breath

There is nothing to fear,
Nor sadness pervades sorrow.

Comes a time for the beating heart to sleep,
A time to say farewell,
And a time to say,
Welcome Home'

The Fall

No-one plans to die, unless by suicide or feted fate. So far from my mind, it wasn't even the last thing nor was it even a distant thought. But like a lurking lion, nevertheless, I was in its sight. On that hot November dusk it pounced, as my blood froze and so too this heart. To my knees, in front of Delwyn's eyes, falling like a high rise building with a basement packed with exploding tinder, sent plummeting to the floor.

Time stood still, this can't be true, I have children to care for, and I cannot go now! By then, there was no sense in fretting, or freezing with fear anymore, for the crazy oblivious world continued unobtrusively along its way, and me, caught in deathly slow motioned silence, laying there without a breath, pulse-less, glowing white, departed. An empty shell of which that body was for forty six years, used to be my home, now unoccupied and vacated.

This now lifeless body, a moment of sudden stricken alarm fills Delwyn's face in disbelief, of the sight confronting her own wounded heart. No pain at all, just as though Id stepped from one reality into another. And, as easy as walking out from a stifling aeroplane into another time zone, another city, a vastly inconceivable new world that was always there, like Id carried it around all these years and that something much higher orchestrated this scene by opening a door and into it and upon, I rose. Slowly and peacefully, ascending from the floor out of the *shell* and gaze down upon the body slumped on the couch in the reception area near my office, serenely observing her running to the telephone as she dials

111. For some strange reason, I wasn't panicking at all, just observing and staring at my body from a silent enclosed bubble, my face below so glowingly white like it wasn't mine at all. As if it was a manikin, an empty, lifeless, soul less case. It was so, so silent and peaceful up there and now I felt so safe.

Forgetting herself, she pulls my legs from the couch with all her might. To the floor, my head hits with a thump, observing a crack in the back of my skull like a coconut being split. Well, if I'm not dead then, I surely am now, I muse ruefully.

There is no pain, except observing Delwyn's calm methodical fortitude to which my heart poured seeing her enduring such steadfast determination, maliciously uninvited and yet her will, mercilessly unopposed. Her tenacity and quite desperation, slapping my face, over and over until the reminder from the phone commands her to listen to their instructions and telling her that help is on its way. Expressionless and motionless, and gone, my body lies still and in amity. Conscious by the sight of the glowing sheen of whiteness of my face, as Delwyn is directed to stay focussed to every word.

Seconds turn to minutes, in the distant sirens scream as the chosen angel pounds its chest and slaps its face amidst her heightening purpose and commanding resolve.

'C'mon, take a breath, show me a sign!', she beckons over her own systematic instruction as helpless frustration besieges her faith as she hears in the distance the sound of heavy footsteps bounding up the stairs from the tyres which came to a screaming halt outside.

Two by two and two more still, paramedics and fire crew rush in like precision, the years of expertise and appreciation to the angel giving life, the team take control, the measure of many years of training take over, like clockwork the masters of their years devoted to saving lives as if they were saving their own wife, husband or child.

The Glittering Stairway

There was peace in the room, the dim lamp to the left softly glowing in the stillness and silence of the night. It was like being at the entrance of a dark pitch black tunnel. Sitting from my bed, I glance over to my mother, my children, and brothers and sisters standing silently next to me. Not a sound, just their light and love, their tranquil unabated presence.

Way off in the distance above and beyond my feet, a distant dot of white light in the darkness, piercing like a brilliantly intense speck or laser it seemed. The bed upon which I laid appeared to move slowly like I was on an escalator. My family, my bones, my loved ones, slowly began to fade as I rose up towards the distant beam of light. It felt as though I was drawn by the light towards it. In time and patiently unfolding and revealing, it grew larger and more radiant, still peacefully transfixed to it, with my feet out in front and toward it. And during this slow procession journey to my left, like a speeding train of colour, the many lives like a movie being played at fast forward, being able to just simply stop each one and peer inside each life, gazing in wonder at another me on the other side, and then another and another, like a pictorial carousel flashing before my amazed observation.

I took one last glance down below at my family as they faded further and further away until they themselves looked like a speck, and then like a quick silent 'pop', they were gone. Perhaps that was their farewell.

'Time stands still, entwined in chains by the world's eerie crowd, and swept up through the tunnel of ebony crystal solitude, its silence surreal. No heartbeat, no breath, no voice, no aching, eyes gazing to the beckoning white . . . the journey from seclusion to joy, to this haven of love . . . yet no heartbeat, no breath, no voice, and no pain. I am, ALIVE!'

The serenity of pure peace, the darkness of the corridor, bathed in its own exquisiteness and bliss. No fear at all, just unobliterated stillness and tranquillity. Towards the light before me, growing brighter and brighter. The light was the brightest yet my eyes didn't hurt, and standing before me in its doorway was a shimmering silhouette, four shapes I couldn't recognise and beyond them many more figures. It felt like I was beyond space in the deep infinite darkness all around. No longer trapped in the limitation of mind and body anymore, feeling free, feeling released of pain and, strangely, feeling alive.

Feeling that my soul had come to meet me after all these years as though it took my hand, and through nothing but faith, like an inquisitive and exciting date, we took a journey. The pin prick of light was now like a hundred shining light houses, so bright though not straining my eyes at all. My feet first still before me, towards these four standing figures in the doorway, my Koro, Pa Turi; and Kuia, Parehuia; my Aunt Mako, and another. He was tall and momentarily, unknown, and then it began to disclose ever so slowly until eventually, and finally, it came.

Who was he; could he be; our son? Tane? Not as a tiny, fragile baby anymore, nor was he sick or suffering anymore, is that really you?

My heart filled with joy, here was this handsome young man all grown up perhaps eighteen years old. Like his Maori name sake Tane, God of the Forest, standing tall and proud, as the young guardian and protector, not that this heavenly realm ever needed to call for such offering. Tane was the name Linda and I had chosen for him, a name depicting his strength and unyielding courage to come to the Earth, the earth now far away below. He was born just four pounds, and his twin brother Riki just five. Premature twins, as small as can be, a sterile light incubator each, with monitors and drips attached to their tiny bodies, but all that seemed so long ago.

My tupuna all looked so young, healthy, light filled, radiant and beaming. Papas skin was smooth, his eyes warm and smiling, they all were. It was beyond belief, Tane had grown up yet my Koroua had become adolescent, as though they'd been, dare I say it, glowing and youthful. My heart sunk and at the same time filling with pride and joy seeing them all in amazement and wonder who exactly was the conductor, the creator of all this beauty and delight for all of us to embrace and behold.

Where the Heaven am I!

Papa slowly took my hand and we turned beyond and through the light as my eyes searched scanning slowly left to right, and back to left, gazing at this incredibly beautiful place, its beauty somehow I knew and recognised. All so plainly familiar, we walked this path as he talked to me, I couldn't hear not a sound but felt every word, as I took in the sight of the fields, the beautiful crystal clear stream, the fish, the hanging gardens to my right and bright coloured flowers. The birds, like swallows and white swans or herons on the water and in flight. Beyond in the distance snow capped mountains and the clearest blue sky.

I knew where I was, there was no doubt about that. Call it Heaven, Nirvana, Janna, Shangri-Lah, it never came, a name. It just was.

The earth seemed a lifetime away, a silent enigmatic journey, and millions perhaps billions of miles, a thousand worlds away. Yet, I was home.

Vulnerable Venerable Awakening

As my feet reached the top and gently placed onto the ground, I stood up to their smiling faces bathed in the light like Id walked in through a welcoming door. Tane stood behind them, his hand on his great nanas shoulder. They all looked so young, so pure, so happy, I felt like I had come home. Beyond them I saw other shapes, misty faces I could not recognise but I knew who they all were, I did not need to know through their disguise.

More than anything was this feeling so intense, so penetratingly captivating. Like Id sipped stagnant or chlorinated water all these years and it turned into a pooled bouquet of piquant mouth watering liqueur of love, oozing like heavens own nectar down my throat and into my quelling heart. A relishing, enveloping, and heart piercing feeling of something beyond any kind of love Id ever felt before. Beyond falling in love, dare I say, and far from catching a glimpse and feeling of that first moment upon when the dim darkness of morning is sheered by the sight of a thin red line on the horizon dawning and signalling the birth of a brand new day. Words could not describe the intense peace that surrounded and plunged my soul upon my decrepit once ego rabid body and mind. My soul was completely drowned in something it had longed for, for so, so long. And the stagnation of this vice was nothing but the stubborn will of my own sorrow and pain chaining and blindly wielding its authority to build a greater wall to protect from nothing but my own love and my own truth, which purely and silently waited patiently, for that moment to arrive. That moment, in which I began to pour tears and more agonizing tears, to be given this gift to feel something I thought never ever, and could ever exist, truly did. Bleeding with unlevered and unobliterated remorse, washed and cleansed in this shimmering all encompassing light, spellbound in my own self forgiveness from God; humbled that I could deserve such an honour, to be bid such a humbling savoured request, and cherished reward. Perhaps other souls who reveal upon this landscape of love came to this same place also, that, I did not know, but willingly sure they did, for I hoped they did no matter how horrid or loving they had been on the earth below, everyone deserves this annunciate of forgiveness.

Defining Moment ~ Sailing into the vortex beyond.

The tunnels end was now behind me.

There is no point to fear 'death'. I know, for that it does not exist. The 'shell', the body, this vehicle is death, but not that of the soul.

Further, there is even less regard to acquaint and compose ones thoughts with fear. Not fear of any pain or suffering. Even from your place you sit imagining the heinousness of your own 'death' or of your father, mother, brother, sister, daughter, or son. Death whether by sword, or fire, crushing or falling, electrocution or disease, bullet or explosion, or even less, by your body ceasing, giving up its duty. It should not be a concern to you. If I have to repeat this over and over again, I will. Just let it all go because once ones crosses the chasm from pain, they will eventually find the purest embellishment of peace and love.

There is nothing to worry or fear. Live life right now, live it pure, and live it full. That is all that you should concern, to the pure soul you wish to become, and endeavour to remain.

For now, trust and be present. To the disciple, just relish this moment, this moment right now, and then the next, now and always, that is all. Give peace to your soul and give rise to your desires. Set forth a compassionate heart, and journey with the knowledge and sanctity of your faith close to your soul and that of your worthy recognition of thanks for what you possess, and what you receive. Be grateful, serve fully, revel in your joy, your existence, your peace, your ability to know purist love, feel love, share love and embrace love, resonant love in all that you do. For when you do 'die', no matter how, when, and where, you will know that you didn't feel pain, none whatsoever, except on this earth where you ignorantly and blindly suffered and feared death. And yet all that it was, merely a doorway which you graciously walked through into the field of heavenly Nirvanic light. No reminisce of suffering or fear, no scars of the world to carry you through from whence you came. There are none. That was the old, the past, the lessons and sufferings. They do not exist here.

Here is Heaven, Janna, Nirvana, Ananda, Shangri-Lah, Pearly Gates, Arcadia, Utopia, Azure, Zen and Eternal Home. It may be written in scriptures and labelled as such, inspired by God, given through inspiration to, by, known as, and referred. Whatever its name is of no concern as it is what it is. Call it whatever you choose, you have the power to, like you did to the naming of your own child.

Let this be known and acknowledged from this respectful and humble place of the divine. Do not equate it to religion, or any religion. For the spiritual source, the celestial realm did not ask for religion to source it a name as important as to what it is.

'And to what it is, from the eyes of the travelled, and not of the read is your own truth'.

Beyond the Stairway, into Heaven

Papa took my hand and we turned away through the light as my eyes searched and gazed of this place, its immense beauty I knew of, like I'd been here before, was becoming and familiar. Bare foot, we walked the stone and pebbled path as he talked. There was no sound but felt every single word, like my heart was connected to his, and so I listened with patience and intent. I took in the sight of the striking gardens, some hanging, and the fields of green, and some gold like straw, and the beautiful flowing stream and the brightly coloured flowers. It was the colour, the immense stark radiance of the most splendid colour that pierced this soul as deep as it felt as though I too was part of heavens radiance. There were birds, some like herons and white swans, and swallows, some on the water and some in flight, too many to count. And beyond in the distance, snow capped mountains and the clearest deep blue sky.

I knew where I was, there was no doubt about that. Call it Heaven, Nirvana, Janna, the blessed sanctuary of love, call it whatever you like, it was more, much, much more, and all of that.

The aroma of roses and freesias was fulfilling and mellow. Aunt Mako smiled intently, full of love and warmth. She never spoke but she did through her love. It dawned how back on earth how most words are spoken without much thought, senseless and unconscious at times, as though words are needed to fill in and supplicate the lost connection of communicating through silence, through the heart. Perhaps this is why silent meditative retreats are beneficial. To awaken an innate skill of connecting that has been lost and having to say anything may make no sense to saying nothing at all and the compulsion to speak for fear of feeling through the mind rather than trusting the heart to feeling what it unashamedly desires. Sometimes the mind is best instructed to sit in the corner and just be quiet, which it certainly can do with practise and discipline.

I felt Aunt Makos heart, her love, her joy, and her soul. The power of communicating through a resurgent art thought extinct had been discovered in mine. And, if it had taken forty six years to understand and realise that feeling happy and embarking on a journey of bliss should not whatsoever be considered a crime or sin. This heavenly world was no different and the force that it operated on, in all aspects of ubiquitous existence was experiencing love of the purest nature. The solemn chaste of God given, God blessed divines love. Un-seeking and present, no matter from whence any unforsaken revolutionary mercenary of puffed up pride, or greed, or power, or hatred, even arrogance entered the palace gates of heaven, they will inevitably reveal their true self, their destiny, their pure soul to awaken. The faces of those who shared my life gleaming as if they knew how simple it was to just be, they would enter their next life a virtual truth of themselves as their hearts desired like a chorus of natures songs blissfully drifting downstream a soothing river. Oh how I wished for life to be like this back down on earth, how simple and easy it would be; a world with love in each breath of living breath, and the money on war instead gifted to feeding the hungry and impoverished souls of that land below. Oh how the world then would revel with euphoric enthuse on paradise earth; with peace so plentiful, a land that held out arms of love to one another how the pure soul defined was created to be.

Taken by this blessed Nirvanic paradise world, every sight and sound, the fragrance of nature, the height of pureness, on earth a place like this couldn't be found. The blossoms and trees, the willows being serenaded in the breeze, their branches and leaves gracefully trailing upon the whispering crystal clear stream, it all revealed serenity of the purist. Its reflection of deeper, far-away places, and to go there simply meant one could dive in and discover.

Papa spoke of being here, at home as if he'd known it for hundreds, perhaps thousands of years though this place was timeless. It was nonetheless their world, this paradise to themselves. There were many people, no not people, souls. Souls that themselves and God had chosen, to venture beyond the horizon, in their thousands, perhaps millions, yet there was still columns of wide open spaces. Papa shared his heart, his passion, his light. His wisdom flowed and with it he acknowledged his whakapapa, the lineage, his ancestry of his family back to Io, who too were all residing here. And that they chose to go off on other journeys themselves, knowing that it is this pristine domain of paradise bliss, their sanctuary of heavens retreat, and their home.

'Consciousness is not that with which is present because of the brain but the entity of the soul that it exists in spite of it' ~ JahAnanda

There was no sign of farmer's gumboots, or his brimmed hat he wore when I was a child. Nor did anyone else carry their past life back on planet earth onwards in this majestic and serenely enveloping dimensional paradise realm. That was all behind, but not forgotten, nor the love and memories of those close to their hearts. Perhaps they knew that it too wouldn't be long before they would see them all soon one day. Back home Huramua was theirs too, for all the family to enjoy. To learn about whom they are and never forgetting of their roots, their connections live forever through their lives and the next.

Tane let his koro Papa unfold the lives and will of their heavenly garden, and like a child eager to learn more, I too, obligingly let him share what he wanted to say, and what I wanted to know. In the back of my mind, there was a burgeoning dilemma, a question, that I kept safe for the moment, consumed and engaged in his wisdom, listening intently, as though it was his duty to impart, when he was the leader, the Rangitira, the chief, he was back home.

Too difficult to express into words, like to explain how a rose bud grows into a flower, or how silver is extracted from the ground and made into a watch or charm. Or how much sand it takes to fill a beach, or how DNA, cells, and matter come together to form a new born baby with the characteristics of its father and mother. That is how it felt listening to Papa, trusting his wisdom and believing that what he shared, he knew of the process and outcome. Through his own trust in God to him, his wisdom was passed on. His words, whatever language it was, this meek conscious soul understood, never dwelling to ask why, yet willingly accepted all that was being given and agreed. It felt as if the unconscious state, after all these years, was alive, for the first time. That who I was in the past was all an illusion, and wasn't who I really was after all. That it all meant nothing, other than a sprinkling of some, leaving the remainder completely erased for this awakened soul entity to receive something unknown. Perhaps it was a dawning insight for the next new journey whatever that may be. When one sees the light, and trusting in it that much, to the degree that one submits themself, to revel in its power and beauty, with another willing soul whom it shares, who themselves is agreeable to receive.

Hui in Nirvana

We all sat around in the garden, in a circle. There was a sentiment of source present, flowing through my tipuna, my family, through Papa, knowing that their faith in their own plan was accepting of God. Like-wise faithful deities, of the One, to the Oneness, their love and solidarity, reverence revealed, blessed, and commanding. Yet somehow, it seemed Id been here for what seemed like many hours in a timeless space, feeling more that this was home, but with one question unanswered, one that I'd put aside. Not having the courage at that point to raise, out of fear that my family, that their souls would be wounded. Seemingly at peace and immersed in the most indescribable essence of overwhelming love Id felt, my heart by Papa was heard. Too afraid to say, he looked at me and asked simply, 'what would you like to do?' Immediately, I knew what he meant, and he certainly knew I understood. With the silence deafening, the journey through the tunnel, pictures flashing past as though they were frames from a film, renditions of the period going back, not years, but millenniums. A colossal logbook of lifetimes, recalling events, struggles, pain, love, and joy.

In this deep, unanswered, new found consciousness, but always present state, the ponderings of life. The many lives lived, and in the next, and the next. A pagan farmer in coastal Brittany, France, but even back then it wasn't called that, but a small village farm called Montdeaux. I remember the coast in the distance and the rocky landscape of the farm I toiled and worked to support my wife and family with animals, cows, goats and sheep, fruit trees and a vineyard, as it were. Pheasants and quail were abundant for food and inside our stone cottage, a larger stone bread oven which had seen many years with its fire burning brightly in the kitchen, its hearth covered in soot.

There were two lives there and two more in England and Ireland, pagan through these veins, more in ancient Egypt, another in Sudan, another, an Inuit tribesman akin and at home in the ice and snow of the vast Arctic plains hunting whale, fish, and seal for his family and other villagers. There were many more. A blessed life in a town called Bethany near the city of Jerusalem, with my sisters, our home was palatial yet still held an air of solace and love. My dearest of brothers, soul brothers we were, exchanging our insights and listening to his undying love for the people of this earth and the journeys he undertook from the far off east and to those escaping the suffering from all corners of this land, Jordan, Assyria, Egypt, in bringing peace to the world suffering hate, greed in their hunger for power and rule. So young and wise he was, a travelled beautiful man, an undeniably determined angel of light, of Michaels estuarial body from heaven, we lived, laughed and cried together, the fondness and dedication to the path of doing the great work with the knowing that Gods love too was abound as His sovereign and supreme protector. Jesus, the Messiah had bestowed upon my family love beyond no other, that imparted sharing and fondness to one another had only sought to blossom over the many long nights beside the quelling fire. And with his wife Mary, so beautiful and so loyal to thee, we built upon this love, my home as a refuge and ours to pray, eat, and drink wine as I anointed his feet with oils of Rose and Spike Nard and incense he brought from the south and the east. He spoke of his short time on the earth yet lived and breathed the sacrosanct and divine will of his heart to end suffering forever more.

My sisters gathered and served our brother and fed upon his love as I did too, his warmth no longer, it seemed, omnipresent but availing to his disciples. When he spoke of his imposing death by the Romans upon him, he smiled and touched the tethered distress paining the faces of his beloved Mary and my sisters, whilst Martha trusted his faith with quiet discern and acceptance of his love and her own.

I looked upon him as not only my brother but as the great teacher to this ponderous earth. Though jealousy of him ruled vengefully amongst kings and rulers, priests, and the foremost ruler of them all, he loved me enough back in those times back then to save my life much like he too had a part to play in what further was to also come in this arrangement.

In Egypt, I was a doctor administering his people and travellers with an abominable distaste for the raging wars between tribes over land and religion. Near a town, a city it was, a city called Aswan. It was a time when I served and revelled in my love of science and the human body. The list of lives unfolds. Astounding it is the consciousness of the soul. It just is. The crushing demise and fires of Babylon, the tumbling towers made of rock, now of rubble. The rising tide and the rains upon Jordon, Assyria and beyond, and to the east and the west, the young Messiah my dearest friend and brother imparting Gods love, and His own to those who gathered round. His time to the furthest corner of the east ventured far to share in offering of his divine will and of theirs, and acquainting and observing the beauty of the pure soul and divinity of God's will as if holding a film strip capturing each segment of different lives in a certain space and time and then stepping in. The ever evolving awareness of the consciousness keeps flowing, like the eternal river, the stream, flowing constantly. The shell is but a human one, a vehicle nothing more. It serves the people well for their journey below but there are many more so everything is fine.

Seeing people from this life as soul mates from another time, wondering why after all these years why there was such a connection, a link, a correlation to the past to now and the future. They too had their journey and in some planned God given way, their journey was indelibly connected with this, and with those close to thine heart. The perceptive awakened soul recognises instinctively someone they've known as someone they've lived before with in another realm, another life. Connections bound and knitted ever so strong and tightly, seemingly unexplainable and yet it is there discovered as that which was discovered in awakening in which brought me to this gifted place. This assigned revelation that came upon through something impressive, liberating, revealing, and free. That which came about whence the moment of knowing that opportunity was always planned and existing as is the understanding and knowing of one's own existence, and all it required to fulfil this arrangement was allowing preparedness to co-align and meet to complete and unlocking the door to walk outside and beyond to being free beyond freedom, to tread the path beyond knowing love that exists below, amidst the maddening world with promise themselves to thus experience also. This was now that moment.

It came to understanding that God is having a large to play in this arrangement and embracing it comprises always of love. His love, to the One who has spanned 33 lifetimes before on this earth, His rightful acknowledgement that I was just one of the chosen twelve doing this work at this time upon which has cometh the era now to impart the teaching without alacrity and with His sanction and enduring blessings to the great work. In Paul's letter to the Corinthians of love, he explains precisely. "Love is patient; love is kind and envies no one. Love is never boastful, nor conceited, nor rude; never selfish, not quick to take offense. There is nothing love cannot face; there is no limit to its faith, its hope, and endurance. In a word, there are three things that last forever: faith, hope, and love; but the greatest of them all is love."

Pertinently more, that God does not give love, nevertheless, that God IS Love.

The link between these events from the past were mans intentions to forge a soulful path to remain always as loving pure souls, whose challenges are thwart with not men, but the mind. Someone who has goodwill in their heart with intentions of just and of righteousness, who themselves becomes the source of wisdom through which shares in the love of those who too desire of their true path to the awakened light. One who becomes weighed down not by the world, but by not holding willingly to their own love; remaining true and implicitly to peace and tolerance, the weight of suffering removed forever. To know love beyond what is known of it upon the Earth, yet knowing the depth and richness of Heavenly love, Janna love, love of the Shangri-Lah, the dimensions of the fourth, fifth and beyond exist eternally. That through your new embodiment of loves devotion, is drenched and entreated by your soulful unreservedness, tolerance, and forgiving. That the love in these dimensions, these realities are ever present, and it too will be realised one day on the Earth; when hate and mistrust, primitive greed and callous thoughts and malicious actions, are cast away forever, and because of you, the souls of this land will know that they too can receive the richness that love holds. Remember and believe that it first starts with you, and purist love is far greater than one can imagine for it can be rightfully experienced to know of its power, its strength, its offering, and it's all embracing source of all things, including abundance. It may not yet reside as yet upon your Earth, it is lagging at the rear however somebody has to lead and someone has to follow. Embracing and accepting this plan, Gods and the dimensions beyond the third realm, chart now to keep indeed, the arrangement of hope alive and more so embodying ones heart and living eternally with undying faith to see anything through, and know that surrounding it all is the Oneness of the everlasting.

"Ko te whakapono te mauri e whakatinanahia nei i te kaumingomingotanga o te ao." "Belief is the force that manifests unlimited possibilities of being into reality." (Te Ngako-o-te-rangi).

The Agreement

As we sat, blessed and bathed in loves' radiance, of serenity and peace. With a feeling of harmony and pureness that all the troubles and toils of life beyond now light on my shoulders were just memories. Papa's words, his wisdom flowed, through God, yet nonetheless his inspiration, his source of testimony and love, exuded patience as if time was of no consequence.

As I dipped my fingers into the pool of water, the ripples formed circles spiralling outward as each drop of water from my hand echoed as it hit the pool below. My tears falling, eyes cast outward and up. And afar in the distance was the mist beneath the sun, weaving itself through the foothills of the reaching peaks. The plains were fields of emerald and gold, yellows and blues, blossoming hues of reds and pink, as they swayed in the warmth of love that filled the air.

There was the moment, when our eyes met. Papa smiled, his skin glistened as did his light. As I looked down at the ground, I knew this was the invitation to let go my pain as his heart cradled mine as he sat waiting patiently for my heart to pour from my lips.

'I don't know what to say Papa. Caught between two loves and yet bewildered and confused to imagine that you are gifting me a choice? I feel this is my home now, and yet my heart yearns still, and my mouth is too frozen to speak.'

To my knees, the weight of this burden brings me down, to his feet, bowing and searching for strength to force out the words.

'Kia kaha, be strong. Spill from your soul, your heart, faithful son' as my eyes searching across the soil as if the answers lay there through welling tears bearing pain on this heavy trodden heart to be given the most difficult decision I ever had to make.

Yet he speaks as still as stillness resides upon the traces of timelessness, and his patience unfolding.

'Papa, I'm cherished by this peace, this love of heavens love. And nothing comes near to what love holds in this heavenly garden. If a choice tis I am given, makes it difficult and complicated though I am blessed, this tray of your love before me, being offered by you. In return, I will do whatever is wanted in exchange to see my children and that of the work for the new Earth God seeks.'

With that, undeserving and forgiving, of any suffering for breaking their hearts, Papa raised me up, his eyes into mine, his smile of approval lay in agreeance of this task before me. His words drew a device, and a warning to bear. For going back to your life will offer light and of truth, of wisdom you'll share. But remember tis not your words, but that of God's love within, as his hand placed upon my heart. To always remember whose power you have, for you are merely the messenger, the envoy, the bringer of this love, His love. Your message will be all about the Love. To bring heaven to their Earth thoust you are not of it anymore. You will share in the purist love you now know exists and will be for those who find their own truth, their love, their radiance in their heart courageous to find.

Religion is of the Earth not of God, and like my brother Jesus knows too of this, that finding unblemished and unreserved love means finding the path that leads to the pureness of their soul, and no religion, government, despised cult, dictator, king or queen, will have the means to serving the purpose unto Gods love and rule but through the spirit of accepting Gods love in all things to the new Earth. And too, not ever to feel afraid, but always keeping faith close to your heart, for you will suffer, and remember it will be that you shall see suffering pronounced to whence you go forth to the new Earth to bring forth renounced love.

You will be rejected, hated, despised, and deposers will seek out to nullify you out of their worldly mouths they seek. They will try to own you; and some, they will try to kill you, unknowing that only God who holds that authority, and the suffering you will endure will cease for a time if you hold his love as your guide and your strength. For they will share in their contempt by evading Gods order to bear by holding unjust and ravaged pride of unforsaken lust for things and of money. And they will carry the scars of shame unbeknownst to them for the fruit from their lineage and from their own greed they did eat, and their actions of their own minds, not knowing of their own heart, nor knowing God's gift of love within, as his hand pressed lightly to my aching and crumpled chest. And not until then will their own suffering cease, though love them all the same as you are loved here my son.

With that, it dawned to pause, as my eyes cast across this demur heavenly realm for the last time to the faces of my tipuna, this seeking son benevolent in his grace and receptive approval, and to this paradise, this heavenly paradise land we call home, accepting forth-willing, and with tears of love I chose and bade farewell.

To this Papas arms stretched high, and from around, and with this, his strong white wings appeared and embraced my soul as he bid me farewell, held close in his arms, the arms of an angel.

Transcending the Vortex to Earth

The minutes click by seconds, electric shocks shook the floor as adrenaline lines into the heart, still no sign, no nothing. Pressing on, with urgency in their voices, the heat builds up as the sun starts going down. Pounding chest, ribs cracking like sticks on a fire, and shock after shock, bouncing body off the floor, still no sound of a beating heart they plead to hear. The communication, the teamwork, so precise yet tense and clear, as one paramedic takes over another, like clockwork, sweat pouring from their brows as fading bewilderment overcomes the angel, her heart and faith filling with love.

Oblivious to Gods hand and numb of this inclusion, perpetuated fear of horror unfolding, yet strangely, entranced by the sight of the peaceful body laying there among the calamity and disorder. The waves of electric shocks fill the air. Fifteen minutes pass by and fast approaching twenty, two exhausted medics pass over to another waiting crew. Discussions intense, is it time to call it a day or push on? Then, the angel called Jason takes the lead as shaking heads fall away to exhaustion. Another statistic to the list for no-one lasts more than this.

Still, the jolts in its body, the needles into the chest, the crunching of bones, the guardian angel's endurance is put to the test, as the helpless face of the other caught up in a nightmare, summoned as a witness of innocence as distress and dire consequence unfolds.

It's time to switch it all off, call it quits, it's beyond any surmountable hope though loyal to the cause he digs deeper and deeper as the clock hits twenty five.

On time of declaration, a stroke of luck or something else perhaps, nonetheless they get a shock of their own, a beep, though faint, a sound like music to their ears. Eight shocks, so violent, and a handful, a cocktail of drugs it took. 'Talk about skip a beat, this guy has come back after skipping two thousand or two,' one shattered and relieved disbelief the medic gestures to the other with a deep sigh, his own heart calms with patient relief and reprieve. Like a miracle delivered from God. As the angel of life, her emotions reinstated with joy, her fingers through her face revealing a tear, and unknowing that it was not over yet.

'One of greatest questions to man that has yet to reach a point of critical mass theory of acceptance. This surrounds the disposition of immortality. Does it exist, or does it not? ~ JahAnanda

'Farewell' ~ Martha's Song

In the silence of entrapment,
The solitude of this place,
The eerie void between heaven and earth,
Paralysed from thine feet to thy face

Voices out there,
Deciphering every word,

Explaining the fate,
Not thinking they'd be heard

My God! I think solemnly,
It cannot and will not be all that bad,
Yet the reality kicks in,
Do they know I can hear them?
My mother, my babies,
I can, it's your son, your dad,

The day my eyes opened,
Sleepily gazing from the left and to right,
Unable to blink or respond,
But shed a tear,
To say I'm alright.

The hours crawled by like days,
Dull to the pain and the fear.
Observing and listening in peace,
Just one word is all they wanted to hear.

Alone in the comatose solace,
Chained to deafening silence,
Day in day out paralysed.
Hey dad, I'm here, how you doing,
It's me and Rata,
Please dad, open your eyes.

The urge to try harder,
With venomous fight,
Just one word is all I need right now,
To say, 'boys I'm doing alright.'

He touches my hand and gives it a squeeze,
'Tis' his will that brings some strength
And some joy.
With throat so dry, to take a short breath,
His ears, he hears a rasp quiet whisper,

'I love you, my boy.'

Unconditional love holds no boundaries, no judgement or fear. It seeks out, knocks on your door, no matter how many times it slams in its face, it faithfully knocks until opportunity and preparedness lets it in with eyes open and arms outstretched. It is the doorway to the heart, the soul, the unsullied spirit of forgiveness, the richness of what always was, from the time you were born. It is Gods most purist gift.' ~ JahAnanda

CHAPTER 6

Spiritual Attunement ~ Song of the Piwaiwakawaka

Spirit connecting initially, and for some months after coming out of the coma was harrowing, confusing, odd, and extremely frustrating to understand, cope, and deal with. Deciphering whether it was the drugs and/or medications prescribed or a psychological disorder or such being discussed by doctors at that time as being the cause yet the chatter and visions averting my attention, deployed my mind to mesmerised disarray. Nevertheless, there wasn't an urge to feel afraid, confident in newly acquired faith that the answers would soon come in time, once the dust and puzzlement had settled. All that composed this reformed conscious body of light was God, JahAnanda, my guide, love, and offering light, my gifted spiritual esoteric force, bestowed, given, graced and touched. After all these years I had finally found Him, not in a church or under a tree, or at the top of a mountain. Perhaps other people may have found Him in these places yet for me; we are all singular souls connected.

The month in a hospital, unable to open the window, given the world below seemed undeniably foreign. It was like being a visitor in a very strange and copious world. Gazing through the haze from the 7th floor window from my bed, people outside were going about their business below, and from my strange and peculiar bubble of a distant familiarity, of a world I once knew, observing and immune, and strangely comfortable that no longer was I feeling part of it anymore other than a visitor, a servant from another more familiar world. A world peaceful, light filled, and enveloped with unblemished love. Yearning home-sick and at the same time this dizzying and beeping world was too was but a temporary one for the agreements and retribution that I was given.

The adamant point of flickering consciousness arrived several days earlier. What happened in between that time was like catching a quick glimpse of a sign from a fast moving bus or train as it speeds through a station not assigned to that route, and then watching the rest of the world going by like a movie screen on fast forward again before it sped off into a tunnel. Feeling spiralling nauseous in the dark, hospital voices echoing in and out, my mind swaying like I was in the bows of a ship at night on a stormy sea, swaying to and fro and taking big breaths in and out to smooth the waves from outside. But it was inside, not that I knew exactly what it was, perhaps it was the drugs, or the sedatives slowly wearing off, or maybe it was my aliveness quietly returning. Mind you, all I felt like doing was sleep and peer exhaustingly through my heavy eyes at the wires and drips attached to my body and rib-bones poking through my chest, the gaunt consequence of coma days and nights, a venous tube feeding liquid nourishment, a seemingly emaciated body of losing so much weight, and yet, the familiarity was pulling me out for a time to gaze and piece together the scattered pieces of a jig-saw puzzle. My eyes were still heavy to open, just listening to the chatter of voices out there and feeling too exhausted to move, not even my mouth. Recalling what Riki asked when my eyes first opened, Dad, are you ok? Faintly through a dry and parched mouth and exhausted body, he heard faintly just one raspy whispering word, *h-u-n-g-r-y*. To his shock and surprise he whispers, hungry for what dad?

Again, the slow parched reply ushers the faint word.
K-i-n-a, to the mirth and hilarity of friends and family, He's back!

And for a moment, recognising some voices, and even though, feeling too dazed and drugged up to mutter even a word, the urge to force open my eyes, as heavy as they were, was the only available option. There they were my sister Pania and brother Marty. It was their voices, and there they were sitting at the foot of the bed. Thinking that seeing them there, like a young couple seeking permission to be married and then realising that they were saying goodbye. I hadn't recalled them ever saying hello, but that was another problem. It was like seeing a flash of a picture appear and disappear as fast as it appeared, and it was black again, as though the sway of the boat and the sea rocked me gently back to sleep. They had been at my side for almost two weeks, taking shifts between mum, Den, Daryl and the children. During those weeks, they had been taking calls, meeting with doctors and nurses, telling stories, informing the visitors who came to see me but were denied access because of the nature of my condition, and organising food and sleeping arrangements at the Wharenui which was connected to the hospital. All this time my chest and ribs were wracked in throbbing pain.

There were times where I had tried to escape, apparently fearing that doctors and nurses were taking too much blood from me. Once in the middle of the night, the boys in the midst of a situation too complex for them to manage without summoning Den to come quick, and after pulling the needles and drips from my arms, being held in a bear hug so the doctor and nurses could sedate me back to another dream. That wasn't it, for days after, the vacant mindless body was found another day sitting in the hospital car-park, in a gutter with urine drip trailing and leaking between my legs, and nonchalantly feeling the sun, and the breeze on my face, listening to the birds, and enjoying a very short-lived freedom.

'Showing love is recognising a part of you in someone else.' ~ JahAnanda

Den and Daryl reminded me, of which I had no memory of that I'd escaped from hospital three times. The furthest I had gotten in my hospital gown, still dragging bloodied and urine leaking drip cords still attached to me, was into Newtown. Again, apparently slipping through the hospital cafeteria without being noticed, I was found sitting in a gutter smoking a cigarette that I had bludged from some street kids. After that, I had a minder sitting at my bed 24/7 watching every move I made. I remember waking and as my memory was innocently non-existent, wondering who this person who reminded me of muscle bound version of Pewee Herman sitting there smiling non-stop and studying for an exam reading books, not saying a word, just smiling every time I studied him wondering if he himself was a patient also or that he was my new friend and just wanted to keep me company. Nevertheless, I was too tired and drugged to talk to him, and as pleasant as a mime, he became a new addition to the hospital room furniture.

Such was the world I had come back to, vague as it seemed, and as homesick I was, the lure to pick up one of the steel chairs in my room and throw it through the window and jump out played in my mind. Whether I had the will, or the legs to stand, let alone lift anything, from the sedatives to keep me in bed. Whatever it was the urge to be home or in nature, than being aware of the minds of everyone around me was losing the allure to that of being with the irreverent peace and love that was back in heaven.

It was an immensely confusing and harrowing time. I had lost my last five years of my memory. Not knowing that I had a house, wondering what I did for work, where I lived, even questioning Riki one day when he came to visit how he travelled to the hospital. He apparently saying that he had driven, and immediately I asked, in whose car? I drove your car dad. To this I again quizzed him, how could you drive Riki, you're only twelve years old.

Wanting to feel and hear the sound of the wind, the birds, trees, even the cars below, the only sounds that became familiar was inside the hospital room. The monitors attached to my body, twenty four hours, each day, constantly and rhythmically, they beeped, screeched, buzzed and whirred, feeling like a robot, monitored by robots, yet aware and reluctantly accepting that they were just doing a job.

When going to visit a friend in hospital now, or to have a check up, or to talk or offer counselling with a patient when the hospital has asked me to come in to speak to one who is unwilling to have an ICD device fitted, the sounds of the machines become all too familiar again and the memories fill my heart and emotions just for a moment.

New Friends

The first conscious experience of seeing spirit was in hospital whilst still ill and shaky on my legs, and for a long while, the hapless mind of a two year old. This improved over time but it was over many months which felt more like years. Each day felt like living a dream, as though the world was outside my consciousness and I was inside this plastic bubble and for some even weirder reason, thinking that I was in a hospital in either Auckland or Siberia. The ability to make rational decisions was crazy but nevertheless, the mind too, not having a care in the world.

Early one morning and using a walking aid to go to the bathroom, there were the usual handful of orderlies, nurses, patients, and doctors in the ward. Walking down the corridor, in the distance, I could make out someone in a light turquoise blue gown sitting on the floor, legs tucked under them self, their face buried in their folded arms. For a second I didn't give it too much thought but then realised what on the earth is this person doing on the floor and more importantly, why wasn't anyone else stopping to help her? She had long jet black hair, her arms and her exposed feet were pale white. My eyes were transfixed and intrigued in this figure. Directing my vision fully on her and then scanning each person walking along the corridor who I thought were just ignoring her sitting there. As I got closer, I forgot about everyone else in the corridor, my eyes fixed to this sad sullen creature.

As I slowly walked past her, she looked up over her arms and down the corridor and behind. She spied me staring intently at her, whilst she in turn did the same. Her dark eyes looked hollow and vacant and wide as if she was lost and crying out for help, her seemingly painful body of arrogance and anger was like a trap in her conscious state, and an illusion in both of ours. They were bloodshot yet they looked like deep dark pools of emptiness, of fear and hurt. I noticed in the crease of one of her elbows something that looked like puncture holes. They were red dots and immediately, not sure why or how, but I could see that she had passed away some time earlier in the hospital, perhaps from some kind of drug overdose. I saw her several times in various parts of the ward. One time I saw her sitting in the television lounge on a recliner chair with her legs still tucked up under her as though she was cold, lonely, or frightened.

Even though it was sad and strange, seeing her trapped in her pain, I didn't feel scared or afraid but I also didn't know how to help her and remember feeling heartbroken for her. That was the beginning of what was to be, daily encounters with a gift Id not brought back with me, but revealed something that was already there.

Once I was asked, 'Have you brought back any gifts with you from the other side'? Thinking to myself, I replied. 'I have exactly what you always had, what you still have now. I just removed everything that didn't matter, and there they were.'

Bathing in the River

My sister Irene had given me a small video player to watch some dvd movies she had given me to pass the time. There were two movies in particular I watched over and over again. They were called No.2 and Siones Wedding.

No.2 was about, in this haze, an old Fijian woman who had observed the need for the family to rekindle their tie's back to their homeland culture of Fiji. She was in her last days and she wanted her family to plan a big gathering followed by a feast for her before she passed on. Her objective was to make it a day of family togetherness or whanaungatanga, having fun and more importantly, she would choose a new young leader for the city residing tribe. The hilarious and sometimes sombre antics of the younger members of the family who had stories of their own, their family dynamics and punctuations reminded me of my own family and bathing in the river back home at Huramua.

It wasn't until some months after coming out of hospital being told how many times I must have watched these two movies over and over again. I began to think and became more convinced that I was in Auckland Hospital. Even through the long nights under my sheets so the nurses wouldn't see, I was captivated by the stories and the lyrics of the songs, like a child with a new toy.

I started to realise that I was recalling my own childhood memories as though they had just happened the day before. Recalling flash backs of milking our cows and more unusual was how I could remember the dogs and horses we had, and seemingly almost every single cow by colour, breed and by their ear tag number they wore. Not knowing exactly who I was, what I did for work, what my house looked liked, and where I lived, yet these visions stretched far back into the past. So very strange it was yet not knowing my most recent memories and strangely seeing my childhood past like it was yesterday. The days of being a child again, yet strangely they were as clear as yesterday. Oddly and bizarre as it were, there seemed to be subtle messages in them, of the flashbacks, and how they were linked in some fashion to the present and going forward into the future. The compulsion to close my eyes or watch these movies began to trigger more and more frame like pictures that I'd seen in the Nirvana dimension from where I had been. The heavenly dimension, Jannah, Shangri-Lah, but I didn't or couldn't equate any of these beautiful places ever having a name, just a new but resonantly familiar occurrence. An experience of the past, the present, and the future, yet intricately they were linked to an open vortex of stirred sequenced events like pieces of a jig-saw puzzle, some falling into clarity whilst others remained puzzling.

For some reason I could visualise before the new cowshed was built, the days when we milked the cows in the old cowshed which was down by the river and how primitive it was milking compared to the new cowshed. It was so mysterious reliving and recalling with such clarity the multitude of events whilst growing up on the farm and the memories yet not knowing what I had for breakfast. It was like a time forgotten but for some acquainted and eccentric reason they came flooding back like watching an old movie from long ago.

Even the aroma of stagnant mud from the farm, the large milk vat stirring the chilled fresh milk ready for the milk truck to collect, the freshly bailed hay, and aroma of baked Maori bread from the oven, the calf milk powder, the rows of corn fields, the river, the sounds of the silver poplars in the wind, even the crunching of walnut shells in the old whare down below the homestead where we used to play and rummage through the old newspapers dating back to the 1920s which were stuck to the walls like wall paper. They told of old planes back then which were new, and news from a bygone era.

How, all of a sudden, could I remember almost every single cow we milked, my grandfathers tangi with such clarity, scrub cutting, and the burst blisters on my hands, spraying and burning the dried and wilted blackberry which covered the hills we worked. Even the lambs and farm animals we lost up there and finding them dead where the baby lambs had fallen in under runners caused by underground springs. The list went on and on, even as a child when we would hold our breath for as long as we could in the bath and opening my eyes looking around and being entranced by the silence, stillness, its tranquillity, and then coming back to the 'world' again.

The more I watched these *movies* the more the memories came flooding back. Whether it was seeing the similarities of their Polynesian lives or the haunting lyrics of 'Bathe in the River', I don't know what it was but I do know that I hardly slept and when I was awake, I'd quickly play the movies again and again and sometimes with tears and emotion just pouring out of me from under the sheets.

It was as though the brain was connecting to music and emotions from another life and inadvertently and subconsciously those sounds and emotive feelings were triggering and linking senses to familiar memories from the past. The brain had created a vacuum and like one wave after another from birth to the NDE memories came flooding as though it had rediscovered a lost fountain of youth. Through the music and emotions which had vanished, as if dopamine in the brain began to flourish and formalise again even the simplest sensory perceptions of this new life commencing. It was like a child experiencing the wonders of the natural world for the first time or a vague recognition more significant than one month and one decade ago and feeling newborn all over again.

Both the contrastingly horrific and enchanting memories of this childhood kept rolling in the consciousness like a slide show of constant sensory sights, sounds, aromas, and emotive feelings. Day and night I was being fed through this vacuum and having to deal with the media and the steady surge of questioning and probing from all quarters only helped to hinder and confuse this child more, on top of the rigorous daily rehabilitation and therapy to readjust back into the world.

There was no time for what was going on out in the world, or what was going with the news and on television. It all seemed too arid, low dimensional, uninviting, uninvolving and unwarranted. They were just moving mouths, hearing nothing but blah-blah-blah. I wasn't and didn't feel part of the world anymore. It all bore no interest and all the while observing other people talking, discussing, laughing, perhaps gossiping and complaining about other people in the distance, this place seemed dubiously foreign. Hearing someone say how happy they were going to be next week as it was their birthday and puzzled why they needed at all to wait until next week to feel happy, why can't they just be happy right now and why does it take a birthday, or Christmas, or any day for that matter to gift them happiness? Can't people be happy every minute of this life and realise the liberated feeling of being so blessed and joyful that they have woken to a new day whether it is raining or not, that they can walk outside and feel the breeze or the sun on their face and realise that they are breathing, grateful, and alive?

Others were glued to the television sets watching a soap, advertisements and the news and I couldn't help be reminded how, time and time again, that I was a visitor in a vaguely familiar but very peculiar and strange world.

I'm Watching You

One time whilst being wheeled off in my bed to have tests done in another part of the hospital, I remember going past an old closed down part of the old hospital. Through the large windows I could see my reflection and the orderly who was pushing my bed.

Inside the old ward I could make out an old reception area. The lights were out so the room was dark other than the natural sunlight which shone inside but clearly I could make out three spirits wearing hospital gowns gathered around the reception desk. Two were standing and the other was sitting on the desk talking to each other. One of them was staring straight at me intently and the other who was standing was just watching me in the corner of their eye. The other spirit who was sitting on the reception desk had his back to me and to me it looked as though they had the whole ward to themselves. It was their home.

Hospitals have a lot of spirit. They are those who haven't passed on beyond their earth based spirit world. They have become trapped and lost on this earth plain and though they have physically 'died', they as yet haven't passed over for various reasons. They could have unfinished business or they just haven't been formally acknowledged or called to continuing their next journey. Back then I had no idea of how to help them so like an untrained apprentice, I guilt-fully, just left them to it.

Be Gone!

There were other beautiful and sometimes mystifying experiences when I came out of hospital. Rather than thinking that it was the drugs and medications playing tricks, I began to continually realise and remind myself that I was not the same person. It still felt like a dream. A dream where the consciousness had been so far backwards and then forward so far in time beyond this period, and then back again. It was like living day in, day out; night in, night out; each minute it seemed, like a cautious step upon another, on a surface made of ice, in a strange yet vaguely familiar world. I felt I had no control whatsoever to making 'them' go away and leaving me alone so I could live, albeit find, my life, and at least get some sleep.

First Steps Outside

My final day after a month, the first official steps out of the bounds and safety of the hospital ward, which had become my temporary home, resembled a mere paucity of a distant memory. As ugly as it felt stepping out from pureness into oblivion, my senses aroused and awoke to the sounds, smells, and feelings of nature on my face, my feet all of a sudden feeling this fantastical reborn renewed connection of the earth as much as the earth's own heart itself touched mine.

Den held out the door, my hand takes grasp, managed each step up and into his car. And as quickly as my butt touched the seat, outstretched hands reached out to unwind the car window for the breeze of the wind to feather my dangling feet waiting. Not believing that any of this is real, still. Like my present catching up to the past, acquainting myself again like I'd been away on a journey of journeys, with tears flowing across my face, speeding along the motorway like I'd been away on an adventure like no other. The pain and confusion of wondering what I did in my old life and what my house looked like began to play over in my mind and meet again with no answer to my questioning mind no matter how hard I tried. Like a new born baby into a new world. Alive, amazed, intrigued, profoundly, yet innocently confused.

Having spent many weeks in the hospital I was first admitted at Masterton, in rehabilitation, visiting counsellors, a trauma therapist, for therapy doing memory exercises, unscrambling simple puzzles, constructing things using pictures as a guide, learning to read and write again, performing exercises from stories being read to me, and co-ordination drills. People would acknowledge me in the corridors after reading the newspapers or seeing the television program feeling like a cross between a zombie and a newborn yet knowing it more precious to only a dream.

The intrusion of news media, television cameras being poked in my face and being asked questions by people I didn't know or trust. To simply say no thank you, but really I wanted them to just go away and leave me alone. Being asked if I lived healthily and whether I had taken vitamins or supplements and worked out often to determine how I could have survived so long without oxygen nevertheless I couldn't even remember what I had for breakfast. My family answering them saying yes that I did exercise regularly though what it was I didn't know and telling them that he had taken for some years a stem cell supplement and a sea plant and organic Aloe Vera wholefood (1) but not any vitamin tablets. Asking me what was in the supplement wholefoods, I just shook my head confused. Perhaps these too played a large part in my survival like an insurance policy in a bottle.

What seemed more embarrassing was that people would say my name and but even though there was a vague recollection of who they might have been I couldn't for the life of me remember them or their name and how and where I was supposed to know them. It was like seeing pieces of a jig-saw puzzle and not knowing how it all came together. That in itself was daunting, frustrating, and awfully confusing. I gathered that people understood even though at times I felt and looked almost retarded with my wobbling shaking legs and body. Even though I felt embarrassed and extremely discouraged and confused sometimes, all the same I was happy to at least be alive albeit in a strange familiar world.

Mental age assessments coming out of the coma was that of a two year old. Although progress was improving slowly, but to me it wasn't improving fast enough and life was a constant struggle. Becoming intrigued and amazed at small things, small things that mattered, like watching children playing, flowers and bees, hearing birds sing, the sounds of the ocean, and seeing the sunrise and beautiful sunsets.

God Slapped Me

It was February 2009 and almost three months since coming out of hospital and still having intensive therapy and getting my balance, memory and thoughts processes functioning better. Driving was an issue as my reflexes and reaction movements were still quite slow and slow enough to have three accidents, two were reversing and the other thankfully was a driver who ran up behind my car which already had a fresh dent from another reversing accident two weeks earlier. The driving instructor found that judging mirror distances was a factor so it was easier not to drive at all and still now I choose not to drive anymore.

It was still summer and we needed to organise firewood for the winter so Den and I went to visit Priscilla and Julio who had a small farm with trees that they had recently cut down which was perfect for our fire. They had recently moved which I assumed I knew exactly where they lived attempting to hide my lack of memory and confidence with lots of veiled confidence which probably didn't hide it all that well. As we drove up to Lansdowne I pointed out to Den that was Priscilla and Julio's house so we parked and I walked up the driveway to their front door which was wide open.

As I looked down the hallway I knocked on the door calling out Priscilla's name with a 'Yohoo, Priscilla are you home, it's me were here!'

Faintly I could make out a distant voice saying that she was in the kitchen and to come in so I stumbled inside taking my gumboots off and leaving them at the door and walked nonchalantly down the hallway to the kitchen. It was then that I realised that we had arrived at completely the wrong house. As I turned left into the large wide open kitchen from where the voice was emanating, my eyes searched the large kitchen and dining area for who I was looking to find.

In the distance instead was this figure of a woman though not Priscilla, busy working at the kitchen sink saying 'hello, come on in, sorry I'm just doing some baking and I've got guests coming over for afternoon tea, how can I help you?'

My mouth froze as I looked at this amazing woman. For months I had come from this coma, being bed bound and struggling to breath from still healing rib injuries, trying to think and walk in a straight line feeling pathetic self pity and depressed about whether I was going to get well or become a 'vegetable' for the rest of my life. What a combination what being a sook and perspective does to truth, one person had said, to even contemplating jumping from the seventh floor of the hospital. This woman had me in shock and total disbelief, she was an angel before she spoke, even her gentle yet kind independent words and light shone all around her like she was protected by something quite powerful and that her radiance began piercing a part of me that was totally wrapped around my own self pity and ungrateful sombre which literally threw the bandages of repentance to the floor.

She only turned her head to me momentarily and continued busily in the kitchen as I explained who I was and that I'd just knocked on the wrong door and how sorry I was for interrupting her day. This petite woman was encased in some kind of frame with wheels which held her body suspended from the floor as her legs just dangled as though she was standing upright. With her mouth she was operating her arms which too were strapped to what appeared like a robot apparatus and she was working and chatting and smiling as though she was fit, healthy and living life to the fullest, to which she was.

The miraculous vision of light and beauty, her nature and charm and inconceivable liberty and freedom hit the pits of my sorrowful suffering out of the ballpark as she explained that six years earlier she had broken her neck in a car accident and how lucky and grateful she was for being alive. Immediately I realised that she had lifted a weight of my shoulders not with her body and strength of her arms but she did with her perception and her spirit, and how she appreciated the blessings she still held close to her heart.

We talked for what seemed like twenty minutes sharing each other's stories and Den beeping the horn outside wondering what on earth was I doing. We thanked each other for our unacquainted and unexpected meeting as she smiled and waved and walking away down her hallway to the front door and towards Dens car. I then began to realise that her mind and will was no different to mine except that she chose to be a winner, and she chose to be independent, and she chose to be happy, and the angel of light after all these months was the happiest person I had ever met other than my children, friends and family, but I don't ever remember seeing them happy because I was not completely conscious other than hearing their voices.

It was an apparition, a self serving measurement of righteousness taught to me from the hands of someone who had known suffering far greater than me and I thanked and love that adoring soul for aligning my suffering to a place of reflective peace and privileged gratuity.

It was some months later after that memorable encounter which played over and over again and each day I became more determined to try harder and manifest stronger my blessings and instilling my purpose that too was looking like an enormous mountain, that of the promise I had made to my Papa and God. But God wasn't finished with me yet.

Being excited about getting my first Kayak brought back memories growing up. We spent many years rowing and training on the Wairoa River back home and going to Regattas in the summer and later years Waka-ama on Out-Rigger canoes which too was much fun and a great way to stay in shape, being on and in the water always felt refreshing and exhilarating.

Whilst crossing the main road to the beach at Oriental Bay with my kayak over my shoulder in the corner of my eye I caught a glimpse of a blind man with a white stick, tapping the wide footpath from left to right as he walked towards me. My paddles were rubbing alongside the kayak and he called out 'kayak?' to which I replied 'yes it is!' and we began chatting and again how he had become blind and how long he had been blind, all the kinds of questions I was sure he's been asked a thousand times before and he replied as though he had replied to them a thousands more also. He asked if I was going out in the harbour and he began telling me what the conditions were like for kayaking even though he was blind and that he was going for his daily walk around the waterfront and over the roads around the Oriental Bay and Mount Victoria. I was again hit for another six. Here was a completely blind man, independent, strong, active and extremely fit and confident. He was doing exactly the same things a sighted person would do where sighted people in some cases perhaps choose not to out of lethargy, but not this new angel. It felt as though Id not ever recalled ever seeing angels and since returning there they were almost every day in different forms, different natures, seemingly and completely obsessed with making conscious beings see the light of just on with life; they are shining down at that minute just for me, feeling that maybe God wanted me to snap out of it. How all those years gone by seeing a quadriplegic person or a blind person without actually imagining and holding inside my own heart their reality of their own perspective of their suffering and their journey and seeing nothing but blessings and total independence, and a vitality for living.

Realising that they no longer had time to complain nor time to suffer or feel sorry for themselves because they had found their true outlook and their true perspective of their life, and they were taking their blessings and their opportunities with both hands and running the race of freedom and joy and succulent bliss like every day was another new and exhilarating day.

It was about that time that I then felt that God had slapped me enough.

Witness to Bliss

Another time, it was one early morning. I had just woken around five. It was very quiet and still, the sun hadn't yet risen and as I began to wake, I lay in my bed as the coolness of the morning air waved around my shiny hairless head. After hearing for all those weeks in hospital the electronic burring, whizzing and rhythmic beeping like clockwork, day and night, night and day, constantly doing their job, continuously, melodiously, and at times, disturbingly frustrating. Even hearing them in my sleep, like the cash register on Pink Floyds, Money track; it never ceased, dizzyingly, swirlingly, hypnotic.

During that time Id not heard complete silence before in my new life, and yet on this cool misty dark dawn, the seeming symphonic stillness reminded and took me back again, to the farm at Huramua again. Before the dogs woke, before any boat came racing up the river below, before the warble of the magpies, it was just me and God, it seemed.

Then suddenly, out from the silence, came a solitary chirp in the olive tree outside my window and then a moment, a long sullen period of empty anticipated peacefulness again. Then came another, and then another. After what seemed like only a minute or two, the whole silence of sullen dawn was quite suddenly a chorus of birdsong beyond the first rays of sunlight that reached across the sky. Remembering the enthrallment filling yet again, my heart and body, that here I was, witnessing the very first birdsong of the new day whilst what seemed like the rest of the world slept.

It was like everything that I had once took for granted, from the madness of being unconsciously busy, suddenly had a whole new meaning, a symbolic radiance, of feeling fortunate, of blessedness, of wonder, a gift of gratitude from a time I'd let slip away. It was like being born over and over again, as though God, through Papa, I had built a newfound relationship with, and through this transitional wakening, my eyes were opened to the creations that had never left. Knowing that we can be born again, ridding all that had no meaning from life, and just starting over again and remaining and simply being. Imagining Papa all those years ago saddling his horse and in the early morning air riding up into the hills to check his stock, to take for a moment to giving credence and offering to having his gifts in his life, in love, and for God and nature, as his eyes searched along the river far down the valley below as it snaked its way and out to the sea. Like him this soul had rediscovered presence and holy peace, a familiarity from many years, past lives and wondrous moments. Never again would the worries of defections and concerns, fears and worries that had afflicted this life all those years would now become something of consequence. Never again would this mind be permitted to lure itself beyond the reality of the present moment, and with each savouring minute, the enthralling and captivating snapshot of each passing period of this new life and the multitudes of past lives, affirming to vow that these would under no circumstance evade this grasp no more.

Spring flowers awaken, expelling from the midst of its bud. Its fragrant beauty graced and gifted from heaven and the stars.

As clear deep, spring waters flow, to the song of the waves of the oceans rushing swiftly across the clusters of sand grains below, spells the coming. You too are consciousness, alive, resplendent, beauty divine, and free.' ~ JahAnanda

Life is so very brief, that had come to the ultimate realisation that it can happen to anyone, anytime, and anywhere. To have the courage to live life like there was six months left, as what happens in other people who are broken the news of a terminal illness by their doctor. That is how every living soul should and could live, who cherishes their own life like it is the most precious treasured jewel ever handed on a silver and gold platter. Imagine if that really was the case, how would their life thereafter un-fold. Would there be fear of what other people might think, would there be any concern to watching the television set again, worrying about a pimple or hating someone because they called them a name or stole their car? Or would they make plans to live life care free with God's love discovered in this moment, beyond their wildest dreams; to help another person, to shine a light for someone tormented by poverty or illness or their own misconstrued and clouded beliefs and fears?

And as the sun rose handsomely across the dawning sky for that person and those people, and all because you as that someone showed them Love. That bird sung their first song just for you, that little baby smiled and shone its own light solely for you; their love, the love of the earth, the same love you too can share with another and the world. Over and over again, I began to think about the haste I had made to do the same, as though I had a train to catch. And the sooner I work to getting this confusing balance on my legs happening again, and my memory sharper, no matter how long it was going to take, all it took was manifesting this intensity to live life right this moment with this new found gust and passion for living and life to keep my promise to my grandfather, God and the agreements.

Hello, friend

Remembering people in the street who I knew in my past life was a difficult time. As years went by before the NDE, understanding why I never felt comfortable in crowds. Becoming innately aware soon after, what kind of crowds brought anxiety and bewilderment. Without giving it a name yet it became apparent it was the unconscious that harboured ego or had unrealised enlightenment in their lives. Sensing how uncomfortable these souls would feel in a silent domain and if they couldn't talk about another person, boast or complain about anything but could spend their day sharing dreams, what lifts their heart and makes them feel appreciative about life. In spite of the challenge, nevertheless to still love them and when they need light in their lives for enlightenment, afford them the time to letting them try. After a while I didn't enjoy going into town out of embarrassment of not knowing who people were and how I knew them mainly and having to answer the same questions people would ask over and over again.

Den, my brother could see the frustration I was having so I went to stay with him in Raglan, to a place where I wasn't recognised and could rest. After the television program on my story aired no matter what town or city I was in I could see people pointing me out and whispering to their friends, 'Oh there's that guy who 'died', and so and so . . .', cringing at the word 'died' thinking to myself brashly, we don't die, we live, just this shell of a body dies, what is more important, my shell or my soul, you stupid humans just don't get it!

Each night lying under the stars feeling safe and home again, searching across the wide landscape, the vastness and feeling the divineness to wairua, and of Gods mighty sovereign rule. And to my ancestors, my tupuna, embracing this soul from the expanse of the heavenly world I had travelled.

The longer I lay out on the grass with my arms outstretched, the night sky came closer to my face and I was then for that moment, home. Neither was home defined as a place, a town, a city, a church, a mosque, nor where I grew up. Home was now where my heart lay and for a time, to being a teacher to do this work. The constellations of the stars looking familiar from this earth, like gazing down on Tokyo or Jerusalem from the night sky miles and miles away, seeing clearly the people going about their lives below. And casting an eye across this earth, and into their hearts, their lives, their pains, their loves, their desires, their sufferings, their strengths, their passions they have for life and for the earth.

Bringing and bearing the assurance forth to let them know, that there is nothing at all to fear but live in this moment of presence. By living totally in peace embraced and shrouded in the utmost purity of Love, and instilling in them to dream passionately in concordance with the co-aligned free souls, purely and in peace, through unabated freedom, and strength. Nurturing the dream safely, guided through Gods light into the reality of blessedness not of suffering, but through unconditional love.

The surreal knowing of the many past lives flashing before this life and on beyond another horizon into a new present and futuristic light and further. The memories present in the total serenity of peace, and the silence of simply being.

Somehow I confusingly wanted my old insignificant life back but really, I didn't, just purely the memories. Being a dad again, going to my Rotary meetings and Cycling Club rides with Phil, taking the children tramping with Phil and Di to the Tararuas, but trying to remember any of it was a nightmare, yet strangely I felt serenely like the child back on the farm missing that and my life back with my tupuna, Papa, Aunty Mako, Aunty Kui, my kuia, and Tane. How was it that I couldn't remember what I had for breakfast or my own house, yet like it was yesterday, I could recall every waking inch of the farm again all those years ago, every sheep and cattle dog we owned, every cow, every horse, every menial aspect of my childhood, yet I couldn't work out for the life of me this town called Masterton and trying to fake the whole debacle so faultily. This life was to be the awakened transition to the great work, the one of being part of the collective alignment in bringing love and meaning to manifesting, creating, knowing, and peace. Actioning somehow to bringing heaven to the new earth, but what an enormous mountain to climb if I cannot serve this purpose properly to do it, I had to hold faith closer.

'You are to someone, to them, who uplifts their spirits with laughter. Who shows you your strengths: feels your concerns, your fears, your joy, and your pain. They know your weaknesses and differences, they see into your heart. They see that your difference gladly refutes to imply deviance, but your soul expression. They testify your faith and fortify your soul. They emphasise the greatness within you. To them, you are one in a million, to them, you are their true friend. You are blessed.' ~ JahAnanda

Home-coming

On one of the first trips back to Wairoa, and to Huramua, I showed Daryl our local beach, Whakamahi. In the centre of the Hawkes Bay coast where Whakamahi lies is a long and wild windswept black sand beach with large pieces of driftwood and pumice tossed up by the deep unforgiving waves and tide. We as kids, used to spend many memorable times fishing, making a driftwood fire and cooking sausages and fish, and at times wed camp out on the sand. At night we used to look across the bay towards Napier among the stars was all we wished for as the moons light shone over the ocean.

The rivers mouth sits at the northern end of the beach where large trees are carried out to sea by the winter floods and then washed up onto the shore. Whakamahi had a magical essence, a deeply spiritual place. Even on quiet still nights after a storm you could hear the thundering waves from Wairoa town-ship where many boaties had lost their lives trying to cross the bar at its entrance.

We parked the car and walked along the beach. Across the bay, I pointed out to her Napier city in the distance, the southern entrance of Hawkes Bay, and to the left, the tip of Mahia Peninsula, the northern entrance to the bay. It was a beautiful calm and clear day, a peaceful late afternoon sky with the sun close to going down behind us. We found a large blue gum tree that had been washed up onto the beach, its long stretched slender branches smoothed clean by the sand and from its long journey down the river. We clambered up along the trunk and found a crevice near the top to sit between the trunk and its extended branch and opened and can of gin and tonic dangling our legs over the side towards the sand below. I shared the times as kids we used to have on the beach when we would light a driftwood fire and cook sausages and surf cast with our rods that Gerry had made for us out of Rangoon cane. I shared with her about the time where we had Guy Fawkes with mum and a few of her friends, I had sneaked a sky rocket from the bag of fireworks whilst they were down the beach. Little did I know how to light a sky rocket, and thinking it was much like an aeroplane taking off and it would just rise up into the air, I then laid it down and carefully lit it. The tip gently glowed red, and with an almighty hiss it roared like a space ship out of control and whooshed off in a straight line towards mum and all her friends and children. Chuckling to Daryl and recalling this figure of mum marching angrily in my direction and if my heart wasn't racing when I lit the sky rocket, it certainly was seeing mum seething and fuming in my direction trying to set a whole group of her guests on fire.

We laughed and whiled away the afternoon sharing stories and looking over the calm ocean when, as Daryl was talking I looked up into the sky and noticed this enormous rainbow above our heads and over the ocean. It was unlike any normal rainbow, its width filled almost a third of the sky and its colours were thick and incredibly bright. I looked across at Daryl expecting her to have been taken by the phenomenon but she just continued talking, her mind was elsewhere. Mine wasn't on her conversation at all, but at what appeared to look like an eccentric rainbow UFO just hovering above our heads.

Some colours were much brighter than others particularly red, indigo, and blue hues of it which made it look even more unusual. I immediately interrupted her asking her if she could see what I was seeing and confused by my question she shook her head and frowned at me as if I were crazy. I pointed it out to her and still, she couldn't see a thing. Perplexed and a little dumbfounded I quickly put the sequence of events aside yet the phenomenon played in my mind for the rest of the evening.

It was almost getting dark, the sun was setting and we decided to head back into town still reeling at what I had seen.

The following day mum and a few of the family decided to go to our family Urupa out on the farm at Huramua. My son Tane is buried there along with my family, grandparents, aunts, uncles, cousins, and their families. It too was a beautiful blue sky day, no wind but as it was mid morning, it was going to be another hot summer's day.

The women were tending to the graves weeding around the flower gardens and straightening ornaments and enjoying spending time with our loved ones whilst I walked around paying my respects to Tane, Papa, and other tipuna. Then unbeknownst to me again I was met by the same rainbow and exactly the same bold three colours again with other four colours less dominant. It was just as big as the one I had seen yesterday right above us and filling almost the whole sky. This time I wondered and puzzled by the fact that certain colours appeared much larger and brighter than other colours and again I looked towards the family to see if they had noticed what was in the sky. They hadn't, and I realised that it was a sign but what the sign was and meant I couldn't quite compute its meaning.

Some weeks later, back in Masterton, I slowly learnt again how to use a computer. Astonished I was to find my inbox full of emails from people, well wishers from around the world who I didn't know, telling me they had read about my story. Finding it all too hard to comprehend, walking away from it all, to be alone, alone under the stars, with nature, the earth, in silence again.

Among them however, were several emails from attuned spiritual people who somehow knew what I was going through as though they were with me and knew me well. Astonished by the accuracy of some of them, some meekly confusing but nevertheless, I was touched. I had been through something big, life changing, but I was not taking this new life at all well and it was like I was still in a dream.

Enter, an Angel

She knocked at my door that night in Oriental Bay. Sue Nicholson from television, a program called 'Sensing Murder.' In it were three internationally renowned psychics, Deb Webber from Australia, and Kelvin Cruickshank and Sue from Aotearoa, New Zealand. Their work on the program was to investigate cold case murders by connecting with the victims of these cases in an attempt to finding who the possible murderers were and in my previous life Id be amazed at how well they accurately pin pointed most, if not all, of these cases in minute detail without any prior knowledge of any of the cases that were featured.

It was as though two lights met again after an hiatus period of lifetimes before, and like a sheet of data rolling from a computers printer there was a resonant knowing of who and where each other had been and were going, and that this space of connection was completely enveloped among a radiant glow of love and immense light. Strange as it seemed, it was a though there was no need for talk, just presence, and it was as if we were communicating non-verbally through our hearts, that there was no need for questions or any substance whatsoever of the physical dimension. We were in fact already in communion, a dimension of understanding and trust that we were brought together for a reason, to a place of revelation; of another page unfolding and revealing.

She told me of the rainbows and asked of those colours I had seen, were there some that were more prominent than the others. I spelled out to her what they were and that yes that there were and she began to disclose why this was so and the fact that those specific colours meant certain duties on my new journey and what strengths and weaknesses other spiritually gifted souls possessed and mine being no different.

That, for me, was a night of clarity and relief. And even though the richness of this new gifted life was embodied and appreciated, and that all the skills and God given gifts I was bestowed was coming together slowly, day by day, what this blessed angel of light and love had done to make clearer my path. More and more reckoning of 'knowing' became realised more expressing, and how faith is having a greater part to play in this journey, and being meaningfully reminded that the course of any existence must always comprise of the most imperative and essential elements that love and faith is far greater than what souls on this Earth perceive them both to be. That every ambition, every thought, every molecule of connection, alignment and re-alignment must come always from setting free any evidence of ego from the body and always being a disciple to the vastness and finer quality that pure faith and purist love holds dearly and supremely to all other things that forms as a manifestation. I felt that night, that meeting Sue was a reaffirmation time, a time for clearness and a time for acknowledgement. That the invisible forces which have more authority over anything materialistic in this world, held true, and that the more we as workers of light can bring together more and more people, more souls, more disciples of living through and learning love beyond what they perceived to be all that they needed to know, until they came not to a place, but to a process of growing and being totally present, and at peace. This is what this angel reaffirmed yet again, in my heart.

Mama

Not long after, one evening, it was a full moon night. It had been a long day and decided to go to bed. The moonlight and street lights outside was inviting. Leaving the curtains slightly open to let the ray filter in, it was time to sleep. Lying on my back, eyes tracing the steel blueness of the light as it shone down and through the curtains and onto the foot of the bed. There at my feet, pushed into the covers, lay a tiny set of arms and legs and feet. They were so small and moving, as if were a baby about to be changed and frolicking in the warmth of the bed. But it was much smaller than a new born baby as it resembled an embryo, but alive and happy. Its tiny body, arms, and legs, were transparent, and through its see through skin, making out the lines of what looked like red veins. My eyes began to be drawn up along this light, and mama appeared.

Mama was Linda's mother, her real name was Meile. She gracefully floated down the light, her eyes and face beaming with love, her smile warmly at peace. She spoke and in the same way Papa had spoken to me on the other side. That she was at peace and home, and how she is always with Linda and her grandchildren. She wanted this to be passed onto them, and how much she loved them, and if any of them wanted to draw her near, all they needed to do was to light a candle, and she would come. She then smiled warmly as she touched my face and bent over to care for this little infant child we knew. She kissed him, wrapped him up, and together drifted back up into the light.

Mama was much like Linda, a very beautiful woman who along with her husband Tom raised their children in Aotearoa. She along with members of her family including her brother Vytas and Meiles own mother Ona arrived as refugees after the invasion of their homeland of Lithuania during World War 2. She was an extremely humble person and we became very close perhaps her spiritual connection from what she always referred to in her broad Lithuanian accent as 'old country'. She seemed to enjoy and revel, and relate much too Maori customs, waiata and spiritual beliefs. She had a deep fondness to the Bolshoi Ballet and classical music and no-one could cook borscht, cakes, and biscuits like her however it was her love for her family, children and grandchildren that she treasured the most. Mama was a big part of our lives and to have her make a connection meant so much to us.

Remembering mama and her family, and their struggle through the war, began to play in my mind, the fight we fight when our lives depend on it. Thinking of the faces of childish adults angry at their partners, their wives, their children, their husbands, or a friend, but unaware of their own thoughts and actions, and those who seek revenge on another just because they cut out in front of them on the road, and those who feel the pain of someone who has lost their 'true' love from a soap opera on television. Thinking of what perspective does to another and understanding that it isn't really what happens to our lives that matters as much as how we deal with them on a simple conscious level without taking anything personally. And how we have the choice to remaining internally blessed for all the other many blessings we sometimes let drift past in one's own lives. Do we really stop to play with a child, to kick a ball, to laugh, to stop and smell a rose, or to tell someone close that you love them.

It was stopping to pause, to think what someone else has gone through and understanding them for who they are right now and imagining someone like mama and her family being torn from their home, their farm and their business, and their homeland. Being sent in different directions by the Russians, some to Siberia to perish working in the salt mines, some to camps and prisons, some to work in other lands, against their will, and some simply shot. 'Suffer quietly' was one of her quiet natured ways of soothing the children when they were babies. Perhaps it was her way of telling them about the law of truth, and perspective and when anything attempts to erode our own peace and harmony to remember also to 'Suffer quietly' for there is someone truly suffering right at this moment.

The 3-Tiered Cake Stand

Another time, about six months after leaving hospital, I was staying at a friend Simone's house with her and her flatmate Ryan, in Wellington. I decided to head off to bed and read a little whilst she stayed up to watch television. It would have been about 1030pm. The bedroom door was slightly ajar and over the top of the book I could see the hall light on in the distance.

Hearing a noise I thought that it was perhaps Simone going to bed or to the bathroom which was next to my room. My eyesight wasn't the best since the NDE but vaguely I could make out the shape of a dark figure walking towards my bedroom door and it seemed too short to be Simone or Ryan. The small bedroom lamp was on beside my bed and next minute through the small gap in the door this little old woman came into the room moving toward the lamp light and near where I was reading in bed. She had dark brown old fashion trousers or slacks on and a cute little cardigan that she had buttoned all the way to the top and this beautiful warm smile that illuminated in the light. Her hair was tied up and couldn't believe how little she was and in her hand was this beautiful silver three tiered cake stand. On it was this incredibly striking array of slices and petite cup cakes with lavish icing on them, and another that looked like a banana cake with an assortment of biscuits on the top tier. She looked very proud of them and she offered them to me saying how she spent the day baking and it was something she loved doing and they were for me as a token from the angels for their love, never restless and present through my struggles and pain.

As I was scanning over at the amazing array of delicious treats, she began stroking my head saying that she was feeling sorry for the betrayers and arrogant few who milled over their greed and jealous torment for what had happened. I thought for a while what exactly was it that she had meant.

Then it came clearer as she spoke and I knew what she meant. My heart sank, pained, having to relive that horrible event again. There had been the media and a woman lost who had lived her life on welfare, abandoned father and mother, had lost custody of her children, with minds compassionless and intent to riding the tail of this meek survivor. With the mind of an unbenevolent child nevertheless this charlatan and like a vulture cloaked as a Samarian, a wolf in sheep's clothing from Babylon, her depleting self respect with eyes searching for scatterings of coins from the innocent mind of the 'infant', the angel continued as she offered her tray to me. She continued, saying that her eyes gleaned circling its prey before it vehemently pounced with green-eyed desperation, and so too the notary succumbed, too indolent and insincere, fixed exclusively on currency offerings and onwards to pursue the next case of bickering and justifications convincing their diminutive minds upon futile lies. They, unperturbed not knowing that before them lay the untainted soul offended though their minds too entrapped and blind to see that in their company was one of the awakened. How then could a serpent know of their own truth as much as a leader, a teacher, a politician, a lawyer, a judge, a dictator, or a friend, until they found their own truth, their own revelation to the pureness of its meaning and their own love? The enveloping chaste essence of the soul, and of love, until they themselves walked upon the light and the light of the blessedness of heavens truth, of Gods truth, and that of their own. How horrible and unecessarily repugnant can humans live with so much enraged malice and hatred. Whether fuelled by jealousy, envy or greed, or the need of imposing their demonstrative will and control upon another. This was what God had made me aware of through Papa, that there would be more insurgences to come and it is up to me and those 144,000 teachers to seeing the new Earth, that is and shall be my will.

The healing through her offering was ample and appreciated, accepted to go forth and justly serve the promise, unto the grace of God and to never to forget this path and to keep faith close and that forgiving a most heinous act and upholding the will to always remaining unconditionally loving and unopposed. The strength to push forward with love undying, filling my heart to the offering made by this angel, this compassionate old woman, this kind and benevolent soul.

The angel smiled warmly, her eyes speckled like diamonds in the mist she pointed out her family and said that she was Simones' grandmother. She asked to pass on some messages to her and I nodded and said that I would. She then smiled and disappeared up into the light and faded away with my blessings.

'What that is not seen does not mean that it does not exist' ~ JahAnanda

The following morning, I described her grandmother to Simone and asked if she was a good baker telling her that she had a beautiful three tiered silver cake tray. She was shocked and surprised at what I told her, saying that she was a wonderful baker and that she remembered the tray. I passed on the messages to her feeling happy she got a visit by her grandma and it was then it dawned on me that perhaps this gift was something Id brought back since the NDE and somehow it was a treasure that needed acknowledging and giving credit and respect towards obtaining yet all along the warning bore to be awake and keep faith on this journey.

Who's behind you?

David my producer lives in Kandahlah, a suburb on the western side of Wellington harbour. Once in a while we meet up over a coffee in Oriental Bay or go for a stroll around the beachfront. One particular evening we were Skyping which is like a video calling programme where we can talk and see one another. Late one evening, it was the middle of winter, and we had arranged to talk. I remember seeing to the right of him that he must of had a bright heater or fire burning to warm his lounge room. As he was talking to me I couldn't help but notice a sharply dressed man in a dark suit standing in the door leading into his lounge just behind him. David was talking away and I was replying back to him thinking that perhaps he had a visitor and maybe he had forgotten to introduce him to me so being distracted by this man, David was having to keep repeating himself as my mind was elsewhere. I then thought I better remind him about his guest so I asked David who the guy behind him was. David's face froze for a second as he turned around rather puzzled and looking even more bamboozled as he couldn't see anyone. I said, pointing in his direction, he's right in the door way.

As soon as I said that, the man then nonchalantly walked out of sight what looked like to go down the hall. As David started talking to me again he appeared again and walked towards where the fire was burning. David said that it was a fire he had going as it was a cold night as the man's face glowed over the reflection of the fire as if he was either admiring its warmth or he himself was trying to get warm. He then turned around and then just walked away. David's interest was piqued. He said that he didn't feel scared after reassuring him that everything was ok, and then added that I better go and get back to work again. It was then, he realised that I was about to hang up leaving him alone in the house. That was hilarious for me more than him and never thought of his own feelings and sensed fear, so I told him that it would be fine and just to let him know that you know he's there and telling him firmly and politely that when you want him to go away, he will listen.

Fred Fisher

Some months later whilst in Sydney, I had some friends to visit and my brother Brett and his family. Bron and I had spent the day walking around Sydney town then around Darling Harbour to the Opera House and then we caught the train to the Central Station. I noticed there was a lot of history in and around that part of Sydney. I felt and saw much spirit near and under the Harbour Bridge near an area called The Rocks. There were many very old historic buildings there and there were three or so properties that were teaming with something that kept drawing me to this particular place. As we left the harbour and made our way through the subway again there was plenty of spirit seemingly lurking the area around Central Station. Bron asked if I was seeing much spirit in and around this particular precinct of the subway and I said that there sure was as I pointed out three or four small groups of spirit. Some were sitting or standing against the subway walls but then I pointed out to an older gentleman who was standing at the entrance leading up to the west onto George St. She asked if we could talk to him so I approached him and introduced ourselves to him. He was very coy to begin with, he had a long coat, quite an old coat and very old with worn out shoes. He was a tall man with a slight stoop and he introduced himself to me as what I thought his name to be Derrick but preferred me to refer to him as Fisher. So I called him Fisher even though it was an odd Christian name, but he was happy to be called Fisher.

Under his coat it looked to me like he was trying to hide something and as my inquisitiveness got the better of me he told me how he lived far away to the south west of the city, a place called Campbell Town. Id only been to Sydney a few times and that I'd never heard of it but he explained that someone had done something to him which had hurt him for many years. When I asked, he said that he had been murdered by a so called friend of his a long time ago. I could tell that this must have happened well over a hundred years ago and that it was more like 150-170 years ago, by the way he was dressed. He explained that it was about a large block of land he owned and that he had been murdered and his body dumped so the murderer could take ownership of the land as they were close friends as this man Fisher had no close relatives in Australia other than those back in England and the murderer would take the land over himself. I didn't continue the subject much as it was becoming quite late as it was after midnight, when he started talking about a railway line proposal which was to go through his land at the time. He then looked at me and said, 'so I see we have two things to celebrate tonight don't we?' pulling out a bottle of spirits which he had hidden under his coat.' Feeling puzzled I just nodded. He said that he knew it was my birthday that day, the 17th of June. I smiled very surprisingly and nodded again at him and said thank you very much and bid him farewell off into the light, and we went on our way.

Two days later I came back to Wellington. Bron had done some research on Fisher as certainly being a Sydney local, she herself had heard of a man called Fisher who lived on the outskirts of Sydney who had become some kind of mysterious icon. I had not heard of him before we met in the subway entrance and was astonished when Bron had sent me a link of the same man we had met only a few days earlier. It was incredible. It was like hearing the same story again but by reading it in a news website dating back all those years ago. I couldn't believe it, Frederick Fisher. But as he disliked Frederick and preferred to be called either Derek or Fisher, was Fishers Ghost.

And every year in Campbell Town the townsfolk celebrate this apparently folklore gentleman every year with a festival of markets, music, and a fireworks display, and we had met the man of the moment who lived almost 200 years ago. It was quite bizarre and on the other hand quite remarkable. More amazing was the other date he forgot to mention that coincided with my birthday. It was his anniversary, and that the June 17th was the day he was murdered. And the strong spirit under Sydney Harbour Bridge? That apparently is where the murderer is buried. George Worrall.

Coffee? Newspaper? Ghost?

Beach Babylon is favourite cafe not far from where I live in Oriental Bay. Sometimes I go down to the cafe and buy a coffee and flick through the newspaper or just say Kia ora to the locals and it's close to the beach and the staff are always welcoming and convivial.

One morning whilst waiting for a coffee at a table just inside the cafe, a lovely woman was sitting by herself at the table next to me. I noticed a newspaper on her table and as she wasn't reading it, I asked her if she didn't mind me taking it to my table to read. She obligingly said of course and as I took the paper there was a man probably in his mid 60s standing in spirit behind her. As spirit can be like people and appear almost anywhere and anytime, I just ignored him and started to read through the newspaper.

All of a sudden, I couldn't help but notice that he was looking at this woman and then looking at me and pointing at his legs. He wanted me to observe him walking around the table that this woman was sitting at, and for some strange reason to see his legs. Without disturbing the woman next door, I asked him what he wanted and what was he doing. He explained that the woman was his wife and that he passed away two years ago of a stroke and that he had encountered his first stroke when he was in his mid 50s, becoming partially paralysed, where at the time he couldn't walk without assistance. He said his name was David and that he had passed away at around sixty two years of age. He asked me if he could tell the woman that he was there, and that he can walk, and that he loves her very much and he is always with her.

My head began to spin. Here I was out for a coffee, hurting no-one, annoying not a soul, and a spirit wants me to tap on a strangers shoulder to tell her that he loves her? Give me a minute I said to David. Thinking long and hard and trying not to let on to anyone, let alone this woman that something really weird and embarrassing was going on. Whilst I'm trying to build up the courage, he's still walking around the table and around her pointing at his legs saying 'I love you', with a big wide smile on his face!

With a slightly nervous look on my face, I leaned across to the woman and asked her if she knew someone called David. With a deeply paranoid and suspiciously cautious look on her face, she nodded and said, yes 'I do.' He smiled as his eyes lit up, and threw his arms up like he had heard his lottery numbers being read out. I explained to what had occurred and how I accidently fell into it, and that I generally don't approach strangers in the street with the kinds of offers her husband wanted me to pass on. The more I began explaining, the more I wanted to tell David that's it I'm going, but, it was too late, I had a resolution to finish this predicament amicably and without too much of a fuss.

Still unwearyingly nervous, I asked her whether he had a stroke in his early 50s and that he couldn't walk and that she took care of him until he passed away in his sixties. And immediately tears started flowing from her eyes and I pulled my chair closer to her and put my hand on her comfortingly, explaining that he is right here with her and that he had been trying to get her attention and mine to connect with her since I had sat down.

By this time it was beginning to get too much for all of us, but not David. I continued to tell her how much that he loves her and that he is always with her and on it went. She bought another coffee and we talked some more. Then she pulled out her wallet and proceeded to give me some money as I politely refused and said that I didn't seek for any payment and I certainly didn't ask for her husband to interrupt my quiet coffee at the beach. But I was happy to see the pain of sadness and sorrow drain from a complete stranger's face and the happiness on her husband's and to see them reunite again.

The spirit of loved ones can, at times, appear at the most inopportune moments. They too like those of physical beings, hold dearly to them also, their undying and untarnished love close, and we as spirit beings contain the sixth sense and the God given ability to connect, yet sadly through mostly by religious connotation and conditioning and the throes of failing to trust in the gifted source diminishes as the squeeze of what is right and wrong is considered and taught as illogical, and at times demonic and needless, by so-called ideological and theological beliefs. And those, as a result, who suffer in their grief, feel a sense of loss and despair as they struggle to find for a long time after the answers to their pain, consciously knowing in their heart that there is something out there and within. The innate inclusion and conscious realisation which tells them that even their loved ones spirit lives on always despite the belief that through what they are taught that the soul and spirit dies with the physical body, ashes to ashes and dust to dust couldn't be more further from the truth.

Mantra

God,
I offer and give praise, my superior, my guide, my light, source of divine power and wisdom. Appreciation to you JahAnanda, Yaweh, Atua, Io, Allah, God, for all eternal blessings, grateful

for all the wonders and beauty of all your creations, bestowed
unto and to give, share, and receiving of your love.
For the magic and splendour you bring, for the gift to share with
all things and creatures, and above all, your sanctuary of wisdom.
For the silver linings and contrasts you bring,
To accept your solemn peace, courage, gratitude,
trust, knowing, and your undying faith,
And those which we stand yet to experience, knowing
that these facets of your creation are there in helping
souls who realise your power and love.
To discover and savour the resolve of pureness, eternal inner
peace and unreserved love and the strength of one's own soul on
their journey to living with unblemished faith and wisdom of the
highest. That to find everlasting love, joy and offering comes from
knowing first your power, authority and acceptance into our heart.
To grow, to understand clearer, the path and
journey to enriching ones destiny,
To touch, to enlighten, and to enhance the lives of
those who seek your divine inspiration.
God, I humbly ask for your redemption and forgiveness for our sins
and misgivings knowing that we are imperfect and ask for the strength
to be able to walk in the path of light and perfection set by you.

We give solemn thanks for the gift of unreserved love
and holy praise through you, in Your Holy Name.
Namaskar and Eternal love.

Connecting with Spirit and the Soul ~ Yours

It has been shared, bestowed, and imparted to those enlightened, loving and blessed souls who seek wisdom and understand the power of universal devotion. Precious and unique, though not exclusive, this gift known for many tens of thousands of years, the power of source through God, Allah, Atua, Yaweh, present and eternal. Whatever name brings forth, you will know or not towards attaching any name at all. The fact that time is of no consequence in spiritual source reality, as in physical reality, it is through connection that spiritual source resides. Where time present, future, and the past can be activated singularly and simultaneously. This is the substance of accepting the wisdom of Godliness within and through the totality of the collective alignment of Oneness that transcends the pure conscious state dimensionally forward, towards the knowing and experiencing beyond physical reality.

It is through which amongst the madness and suffering upon this world that spirit is holding forth its light, the effervescent light of connection, wisdom, and direction. Oh how horrid life is without practising stillness, without discerning and radiating all that one wishes and desires and seeks for this world and beyond. By practising enduring love, gratitude for breathing and life, for just acknowledging one's own existence and trusting in faith, even for the lay soul disciple who is just starting to walk their new path, believing and knowing and trusting the seed of this once unrealised wisdom which always lay within and like a flower bud. And, in time the bud of connecting will flow like a super highway unfolding and revealing to the esteemed wonder of radiance and beauty, your hands opening like the petals to receive and through the blessed peace of one's own stillness you will have arrived to this place. It is from this domain of presence and sourced stream wisdom that is the directed path to Godliness, from God, from Source, and from the crystal clear shining light of love that always lies present, beaming, and waiting for this moment of arrival, emanating the fullness of its strength, its power and its grace. Through your persistence to knowing who you truly are has come and revealed itself, conquered by nothing but the fullness and passion of this desire. You too are finding deep connection to the love, the spiritual joy of your heart, and handing over all that was once thought of as important meant absolutely nothing at all. No longer will suffering dwell here, nor the need to watching the lies of world on an electronic screen, or keeping up with the Jones', or one's own lure to living unconsciously ever again for what is discovered, for now in your hands and heart is more powerful, more worthy of trusting and revering from this moment forward that you have the power and commitment now to touch the lives and hearts of another who is crying out to know love which was, to them, assumed unconquerable.

Thus, is the examples seen on this planet that what is termed as extraordinary feats of the unconquerable, conquered by those who used their connection, to giving credence, to having a relationship with Godliness and God through knowing, trusting, accepting, embracing, and acknowledging the power of love and presence through Gods love embedded in their blissful presence of consciousness.

Courage flows from trusting, and patience and that knowing comes from faith. All things from these elements of experience through an evolutionary point in time by which ensuring sustainability of higher ascended dimensions of *Being-ness* flows primarily from the paradigm world of unreserved love and peace for all.

We can think of just some of the world's great minds such as Michelangelo, Job, Gandhi, Martin Luther King, Einstein, Beethoven, Bach, Monet, Mother Theresa, Jesus, Muhammad, the Buddha, Daisaku Ikeda, Rembrandt, Solomon, David, Apostle Paul, and John Lennon. These souls who were born of this age, who fought for their God given autonomy and acknowledging their own freedom of expression by understanding the importance of love to all through spiritual source. They dreamed bringing rightfully, heavenly peace to this Earth. God and source to which all things are created in precision, in accuracy, and effortlessly, including the individual and soulful expression of inspiration to create and expand. These people all knew that the foundation to every thought and action was indelibly seeded first from love.

That living a life of unconditional and irreverent love is the pathway to spiritual connection and the mirror of beliefs has little truth and is futile to the mirror that reflects the one who lives entirely from the soul.

Sacredness of Life from Blessed Water

Water is among the holiest, and since mans existence has always been considered a source of life and spiritual connection. Reason being that a greater proportion of the world chooses to live by the sea, a lake, a desert oasis, river, or stream. The conscious soul finds connection, source, and resonance with water as it too holds its own conscious power and source unto itself. Connecting to water gives the mind time to unwind, relax, reflect, become at peace and at one with nature and to the soul. When a soul connection is made to a source such as water, an explicit and alignment of this distinction begins to take place and through meditation or prayer, allowing an unobstructed and natural vortex of aligning, acceptance, and connection to occur with all things esoteric including spirit and the soul. This alignment is recognised by spirit hence why it is used in spiritual ceremonies for thousands of years as well as the knowledge that spirit themselves are drawn to elements such as light, prayer, offerings, the soul, and to water.

We, as physical beings find peace and resonance with water as we ourselves are comprised of 97% water so it is a reminder that we are all with the one, the second law of creation, and the reconnecting soul becomes at peace with its own consciousness which in turn enables the conscious soul to vibrate in a pure unimpeded state to reconnecting with inner love of its purest form.

Water is a conscious substance made up of molecules which form crystals. These crystals change its charge positively or negatively of its resonance by how it is affected. Pollution changes its molecular structure negatively in an opposing way purification changes it to another. Whatever vibration it gives off, manmade or naturally occurring (that is, by environmental forces such as decomposition, or volcanic or geo-thermal toxicity) the vibration it reflects thus is a result of its effect to it and its crystal and molecular structure.

Hence is the reason waters divinity and position is recognised as an important and innately integral role in blessings, baptism, spiritual cleansing, as too in purifying the organs and cells within our own bodies. Mankind has an obligation to ensuring its purity is addressed and sustained for it is the holiest anointment to all life and the plants and creatures who too treasure the sacredness this precious source gives to this planet.

'Water is Life, deserving of supreme respect.' ~ JahAnanda

Everything we eat comes from source, through source, by source. Understand too that we as physical beings are that very same matter, consciousness. Trees are no different, they too are consciousness. We give off carbon dioxide of which trees require and they give to mankind and life, oxygen in return. They participate in the intricate balance of life, like the Torus which vibrates and energises all within and beyond this Earth, and thus both relying in the symbiotic cycle of life through nurturing, growth, and sustainability. Trees are like aerials to source and the universe. Like transmitter's, they require the suns energy for growth and in return it gives to the universe its coding and acceptance as being One with all things earthly and in the stellar dimensions of which they too are an integral part thereof.

Being Maori, the care, conservation, and preservation of both wildlife and the forests in which we live in is esteemed and treasured and valued spiritually as equally as our own, to which is a vital thread of the identity to our identity in our tribe of Ngai Tuhoe, as 'Children of the Mist.'

This is the understanding too that abounds indigenous civilisations such as the Mayans, the Indigenous tribes of the Americas, the Aboriginal, Egyptian, and Polynesian cultures to name a few, all innately knowing of the fine balance of life and nature.

Those who tread the earth gently, when the ignorant speak to them, they only utter peace. In the privacy of the night they meditate.' ~ Quran (25:63-66)

CHAPTER 7

Unscripted, Trusting and Unlearning

Being grateful beyond measure even though losing full functioning and ability to simple tasks such as walking, balance, co-ordination, seeing, and thinking was an exhausting challenge beyond anything I could ever imagine. As though this body was in a plastic bubble and out there was the world going about their business, me in my world and them in their foreign land that thought they knew well. They were challenges and some remain still today however each new day brings a new exciting opportunity to grow and develop as life's journeying is an ongoing process of *being* rather an objective. Having lost certain physical albeit minor capabilities, being blessed with a devout connection to source, intuition, insight, and the internal use of instinct has simplified life and trusting my new bestowed authority though new and adjusting ever so slowly to this new stream of life again.

Not even knowing what an awakened soul was other than being who I was awakened or not, instinctively aware that I possessed something, call it divine source, wisdom, power, or nothing at all, but I felt certainly alien to this vaguely familiar yet curious world. Saying this, having very few like minded people who understood me meant that I was immersed among people who reflected from a past life yet relating or connecting to any of it anymore became a distraction to my new journey. Finding and meeting other like minded souls who had an understanding was very rare and as time went on, I began to meet others who themselves had a collective share in making full use of the 6th sense. They could assimilate, understand, equate, and solve problems, yet remain close to their own source of understanding of their form from a soul perspective and remain admissibly reverent to their humble Being-ness within their conscious state of self.

'Forget everything, forget troubles, forget fear, forget worry, or any notion of despair. Forget any interpreting, forget it all . . . even the worlds troubles. Embrace self belief and trusting. The world is not destructive or degraded, it is merely correcting and always realigning. So too is your own body and mind. Be still, be quiet. Fulfil your entirety with all which embodies pureness of love and offer as your mantra your blessedness in giving thanks to all that lays at your feet.' - JahAnanda

Wise Men

Jeremy and Karl were two friends whom I knew in my previous life. I always had a lot of respect for who they were, how they lived their lives by the simple fact that they knew who they were both spiritually, physically, and emotionally. After returning, it was like a big piece of a jig-saw falling into place. I began to see them in a light of clarity, that their form resonated with mine yet the only difference was that while I looked upon myself as an apprentice to this new realm of inner bliss and love, they were, in my mind, masters. They had struggles in their lives of which everyone does in varying degrees, yet in their individual journeys they continued to ask questions, never being satisfied with what others said even if their own hearts and minds told them otherwise. For them it was the commencement many years earlier to their following their own truth and renouncing their resplendent liberation to their own freedom and path to knowing the quintessential meaning to life, love, presence, existence, and beyond.

For these angels of peace and undying love who I knew from my past life and felt aligned to all those years ago yet whilst not having the conscious conviction to follow, this unshackled force to walk beside them was alluring and a revelation to their chosen paths of truth began to form and impress upon my own. Through their association and presence, like laying out all the cards upon a table to see, be they Christianity, be they love, be they religion of any kind, be they spiritual understanding, be they presence, be they faith, prayer, meditation, or determined will. That we all constantly have the opportunity to walk on the path to truth, that there was no judgement of but purely acceptance, and like disciples to the knowing, they walked beside me too and in which their love I too felt the connection of our souls come together after all these years.

I am the way, the truth, and the life - Christ Jesus

How this can be, to an Angel?

It was a day in all my years, one I wasn't expecting to meet. He wore slim dark trousers and a radiant blue shirt and dark square glasses. He reminded me immediately of a young Rick Ocasek from The Cars and through a friend of a friend we were planning on going for lunch with his wife to Pravda Cafe in town yet something drew us together as we sat down at our table. I couldn't help but notice that they both had American accents and began to wonder why on Earth they would be visiting Wellington.

As we talked we began to share one another's stories. His unravelling commencement made my heart sink as he explained that he had recently been released from prison after spending almost twenty years in a high maximum security facility with drug dealers, murders, gangsters and robbers and as he spoke I was muted and dumbfounded how this could have happened to someone still so very young.

Damien was on death row for the alleged murder of two little boys along with two other accomplices when they were teenagers in Memphis. Over the corresponding years the mounting evidence was beginning to point that all three of these young men were obviously innocent of this heinous and violent crime yet the Police and court were hard pressed to accept that these highly vulnerable and naive young souls were blameless and not culpable for the scandalous misdeed.

As Damien spoke, I couldn't help but notice that here was this obviously adolescent and innocent soul willingly sharing this deeply tragic tale and although he was in his late thirties, he talked and acted like those eighteen or nineteen years in jail had done little to advance his maturing body. He carried an air of childish wonder about his new world, he had no experience of the world outside and like I was when I woke from the coma, I too had harboured a similarly childish and juvenile appreciation too for the simple things that I had missed during those obliterating decades of unconscious survival and together we began to revel in sharing our new lives. Without too long, the minutes began to turn into hours and over in my mind I started to wonder how it felt to be locked away and for over half of those years he was in solitary confinement. This poor soul being subjected to abuse so cruel, being beaten, harassed and threatened by other hardened inmates and yet here he was speaking so frank and so delicately meek and polite with such a forgiving and humble persona as though he was more than grateful to now have this opportunity to resume his life and be undeniably appreciative and accepting for what he had been subjected to. My heart sunk and felt more and more that sitting next to me was this young and extraordinarily naive and evidently innocent soul. How any person could have ever survived such a horrific ordeal let alone the torment of fearing that his life could have been removed so callously either by a noose or an electric chair. To now blatantly observe that, instead of fear, he was now free, alive and totally contented.

'Live a life of humble appreciation, for if life feels like sometimes that you've been hit by a train . . . . just remember that perhaps your version of a train could very well be more attractive than the one who actually did.' ~ JahAnanda

Doggedness of the Will

The memory of fighting for this life, the vision of the fight, the challenge to meet, set before me. The figure of this vicarious figure of a man climbing this vast trembling mountain wall, at first it seemed initially easy, and looking down below, there was no ground. Amongst the blood curdling calamity were rocks tumbling down, smaller ones and larger ones, finger tips agonisingly bruised, bloodied, and grazed, feet searching to gain hold to the cliff, dodging with my head the rocks as they began to fall like raging sledgehammers.

Across the face of the wall there were others climbing also, ramped with fear, their faces pained, sodden with dread and terror as they too were trying in vain to reach the summit. As I made another foot hold, sinewed and pained arms exhausted, people were falling into the dark forsaken abyss below screaming as their voices melted into the silence of impending. I knew that to give up was not an option though the thought to let go seemed so very easy and so many more had chosen to let free their pain, yet onwards, with fingers bleeding, knees grazed and body bruised, my heart filling with fear of the unknown as more and more despairing souls let go.
I kept thinking and yelling to them 'now's not the time to give up, you're nearly there!' But didn't they hear me or did they just give up?

And questioning my own strength and will to let go and be done
with it, into the unknown sought to overpower this will.

I saw those people as a symbol,
Who if they tried that little bit harder they too can come back.
And remembering the child in the bath holding their breath,
Seeing how long we could go to beat the clock,
To beat Den and Marty perhaps, but really it was
a test against my own will to survive, staring at the
watch under the water as the seconds ticked by.
Thinking, that any test, comes down to finding the peace within,
the breath, and to just relax, be still, and have faith.
But why were these souls falling, why were they letting go?
Damn it, damn everything, don't fear or give up, even I don't know
what's there, don't give up, just have faith and you will know!
At the end, it is their lives not mine,
And one can only give so much encouragement.
Life's like that.
So too is 'Death.'

The last remaining ounce of strength,
Carrying this torn body up and to the top,
Exhausted, and alone, and then the flicker of light
seeing my sister Pania and brother Marty,
I've come home, I've made it, and I've arrived!
So exhausted I felt, and it seemed I could sleep for days on end.
Not even knowing that this brain was not what it was.
Amongst the flickers of darkness and light, confusion and
love, that mind was that of a child, of which nevertheless
brought a tear to the vigilant and the loved.
Nevertheless,
I had returned.

Faith

Faith is like breathing, incomparable than hope. The body consciousness is aware to the blessedness of life by each breath it takes to physical life. The consciousness embodies faith because without it, like love, it does not exist. Faith does not rest once adversity has passed or until any storm has subsided. Faith continues on accepting and revealing all things it bears through patience, in attracting abundance, to giving, sharing, loving. To live and breathe faith in all things, especially you, and forbid anyone who seeks to question faith for they know not it or their own true power through which faith lies dormant, until it is placed on the throne of love.'

'Nevertheless, there is a job to do, no matter the circumstances,
No excuse to not set sail,
A task to relish,
To place faith in Gods light, Gods love, protection and grace.
Even to die gives strength and fortitude with
willing and promise in justly deserve.

Faith, from what is observed, of its extraordinary power, is misunderstood. People know of it, talk about it, believe in it, yet when the going gets tough and they don't see any improvement, they turn their backs and the power of their faith is lost. They're back to square one. Some complain, despise, some turn to drugs, or alcohol, or take it out on loved ones or themselves unruly. They may feel dejected, upset, silly, a fool that they believed in faith too much when in actual fact they didn't believe in it enough. They gave up when the going got tough and as a consequence, their life ceases to develop, grow, and learn positively from the experience that might have advanced their learning, their power, knowledge, and wisdom. Faith is nothing but that through which life exists beyond existence itself. It is the gateway to freedom, transformation, and ascended revelation.'

Faith does not desert the summoned mind, wretched with fear. Though the penchant nature of stubborn desire fuels their determined truth like a manic driver heading down a road, yet on and on they fight their dogged blind will. And strange as it seems, tearing their hair and fearing their fear, wishing that the malaria carrying mosquito and the savage terrier bites and nips day and night at their feet, oblivious that life is waiting to gift a bouquet of spiritual ecstasy and delight, yet blindly believing that the road will eventually bring reward for their hope. Faith says face the savageness, face the fear! If you find yourself in a room with a malaria laden mosquito or in a cage with a lion, pray that you choose the lion and then you will know that your fear meant nothing, nothing at all and so did the sleepless nights and tossing and turning, when you find that you live forever more.

Guided by Spirit

Life can be a flagrant and sometimes painful journey. As pure souls, the intentions of wanting the best and highest good and choosing the rightful and easiest path towards fulfilment is mankind's instinctive human nature to seek. Rather than what the world expects of you, whether it is to abide by its rules, its control, its indoctrinated beliefs, and the expectations and rituals spelt to the consciousness by reckless physical minds to control the weak to conforming to their means, and their world.

The life and existence of pure soul seeks to fulfil a simple set of paths inherently absent of subjection, guilt, loss, and confusion. The pure soul follows only its instinctive heart by love as its sole source and means to which all things are accomplished for their own good and that of the world towards peace, harmony, abundance, and prosperity. And, what becomes of its revealing form by knowing the power of its innate acknowledgement of its heart source, it allows pure source to flow from it in a natural and unbinding way, to radiate and embellish its self and its form, in its unblemished pureness of being.

The pure soul understands God and source, and as importantly and equally, to share love with all that is part of its consciousness and its world.

The consciousness is also aware of not only its connection with its physical world but more so its existence and connection both spiritually and universally to the cosmos and its acknowledgement that it too is a rightful and integral member of the divine universal consciousness.

Being blessed with life renewed, graced a new set of paths to follow, as a trusting awakened intuitive soul. The body indeed is not immune to challenges and pitfalls along this journey, no different to anyone else. The only difference is the filter, the ability to arrange, gather, and embrace, if the consciousness is drawn, and similarly, devoid and let pass non-relevant, encroaching, and unnecessary streams to simply pass by. Any stream that enters the consciousness can liken to a frog on a lily-pad. It chooses and instinctively follows its highest excitement. If it seeks to maintain its vibration of fulfilment, it simply chooses to follow a path or jump onto another lily-pad. Pure souls similarly choose to play, read, meditate, listen to music or pray whatever it is by following its instinct to seek joy and matching it to its desires.

The key to allowing forethought in the awareness in which choice and direction one seeks to follow. By which the predominately unconscious past life, unashamedly the filter was less discriminate and jumping to the next lily-pad was met with illusionary 'walls' in the middle and finding the self hurling again into the water.

Believing now, by following and trusting the light of one's higher mind and allowing spirit to guiding ones path thus gives to anyone who understands its strength and power to make better instinctive choices.

To doing this involves some 'housework' by clearing out any past conditionings, habits, and beliefs, which were thought of as important but were really dragging us down. The ego or what is referred to as Evading Gods Order, is one major impediment to overcome to regaining personal power. Having the strength, the will, and the courage to releasing all in our lives that has consequence, no real importance, justified solely by pleasing others is the greatest illusionary mountain to accomplishing. The world is riddled with abstract unimportance. The lure to buy a gossip magazine and watching the lives of others self importance and drama like a soap opera in which the obliging soul feels warmth and self assurance in relating their own drama to another's. There seemed an unknowing unconsciousness in one's life to which everything had a reminiscent importance to it, yet to the awakened soul it all resembles a mishmash of 'blah-blah-blah' outside the new state of knowing, of awareness, of peace, and ultimately, wisdom. Old beliefs in the past may have been such that 'if it looks like a duck, flaps its wings like a duck, and quacks like a duck, then it must be a duck.' What goes on outside the gem, in which we hold sacred within, is the safety and presence of harmony, irreverent peace and discovery, and what doesn't resonate to the consciousness becomes purely, 'what is.'

Inner peace is not something that is attained in the future because the future remains always the future. It is an illusion. That the pure state of the consciousness, of being, of awareness to its surroundings and itself, without attaching any thought or emotion to what goes on 'outside' that doesn't align to our joy. Through understanding, learning, and nurturing the power of self love and internal peace, no matter what, the heartfelt contentedness that we can deservingly attain this state right in the present moment.

Suffering Souls

This past life, like many souls, was as a suffering soul. While not born a suffering soul, physical beings are born into their new world as pure souls to some large or greater degree. Within that scale, it establishes how a soul is conditioned by their life experiences. Parents, foster parents and care givers play an intrinsic and vital role in how and what carves and creates their density fulfilment journey. Understanding that mistakes and wrongdoings were merely paths of corrective strengthening are important and integral aspects towards learning independence, wisdom, and intuitive knowing, all part of the journeying soul. Too often children, whilst given love, can later in their lives harbour resentment towards their parents as parents realise that as now young adults that their nurturers cannot be there to answer each beckoning call as they would when their children were younger. By not allowing them to make mistakes to propagating their own independence in the first five and most critical years of their developmental lives, these skills are lost and teaching them later in life becomes a battle to instil at this age thus resentment can therefore perpetuate anti-social behaviour.

Nurturing and fulfilling their path accordingly to their current dimension or density wisdom determines how constructive or destructive in nature their thoughts and their actions are perceived. How a self-less and loving spiritual being pre-determines or manifests a rightful path in making certain decisions are made as a result of the perceptions to new beliefs through experiences they encounter in their lives using the wisdom brought into the world as pure souls.

As a victim of sexual violation as a child was a definitive period to my life path. It was inexplicably horrific for an innocent seven year old child to go through as would any child. Thereafter, other contrasts and consequential decisions occurred directly and indirectly as a result by the experience, as horrible it may be to bear as an innocent child and without the skills to deal with it, I was too afraid to tell anyone for many years. The ego too became an over powering and controlling mechanism which became an unconscious and debilitating master. One that helped realise after the NDE was less of a noose as a result of the myriads of detrimental decisions that had been made thereafter for four decades. As a result, there were other discourses that occurred also which made my unconscious self a poor controller of its destiny by having an insecure nature and puffed up ego as a child, mainly to hide my immense fear and shame which where I wore as a mask to the outside world, albeit poorly. Things such as following the 'in' crowd, watching endless hours of television that nurtured my suffering soul, getting high on drugs and alcohol, stealing even if it was just the neighbours fruit trees, or from our mothers purse. As a result, making poor decisions nevertheless, in hindsight, it was still viewed in the mind all those years as anti-social behaviour. These behaviours gave the perception of being bullet proof and unstoppable in the wounded belief and sometimes reckless demeanour and from then on unknowingly, my childhood was destroyed and taken from me. Closure was through acceptance and forgiveness to the feelings harboured deep within the hurt and pain, and too the perpetrator also, to whom forgiveness was fundamental towards healing.

School work suffered and even though becoming a prefect, academically I failed miserably and sport was the only saviour as it was a means to release the pent up hurt, anger, and self imposed remorse by myself in attempting to heal the suffering. I wasn't or didn't think I wasn't a bright kid, nor did I have an unhappy childhood but by comparison having such a demented contrasting experience only tarnished what could have been. Other than that experience I certainly wouldn't have changed the rest of my childhood for the world and even now I feel so blessed to be part of such a loving family nucleus however by highlighting my childhood of such experiences, I hope will help other people, or suffering souls, who have come from a similar background whether worse or not, may be able to know that there is hope and love, and it never dies provided faith is held closer to the heart.

CHAPTER 8

Light, God and Darkness

'I te wātea te hinegaro, me te kaha o te rere o te wairua. Ka taea ngā mea katoa. Free the mind, be strong of spirit and you can achieve anything' - Maori Proverb

The world beyond being a child was and is, just is. It often never composes many children's thoughts at all what the world is doing whether it is five miles beyond or in another part of the world. Like what it sees, like a flower, cradled in their hand, or the intricate and radiate beauty of a sparkle of sunlight through a dew drop. They know that it is the pure essence of life. Their world is just what is within its immediate space and in its own knowing beyond. There is nothing else except, their friends and family, school, playing games, the river to swim in, and the animals. Their lives are purely on exploring, learning, sharing, wonder, expressing, and fulfilment. Later in my life I used to think about other kids sometimes. Like those who didn't have wide open spaces, who lived in big over crowded cities and ghettos, and had never been out in the country or even saw the ocean, but the world itself was too far away and being happy in my small corner of it was all that mattered.

After coming out of hospital the world still seemed to be contrived, composed in achieving something, and in a lot of cases, I could understand, gaining something without actually caring for the other persons well being or the ramifications of their actions. Nevertheless, nothing had really changed in all those years and something continued to burn inside that being given this second chance again of life, my legacy was to uphold the promise I had made to God and my Papa.

Having brain damage as a result, I couldn't remember for a time a lot of my friends and acquaintances. I couldn't remember what our house looked like or what my job was and initially it didn't bother me but over the corresponding weeks and months it frustrating trying to remember who I was from my previous life. Imagining being a pilot and coming back from this horror, to sit in the cockpit and trying to make sense of the dials and buttons, let alone fumbling with the seatbelt.

Those first few days back at work in the clinic were no different. Clients looking at me for guidance and direction, whilst I still staring at the simple calculator it seemed, not sure exactly where the on button lay and over and over in my mind, this role was not why I had returned. Realisation of this in which I had accepted of this task, as formidable as it seemed, knowing innately that Gods plan was for me to doing the great work. And with His love, guidance and faith, that His will and grace will be done like those before, to see heaven on this earth. No longer am I be part of it bar a descended messenger who will return.

Looking out my window down on the street as familiar as it seemed this role of serving was not being behind this desk, nor was it to make idle conversations or to encourage the entrapping minds fixed to the television screen in the next room. People looking at my old shell thinking that he's back, alive and simply slide into the old me. But, I wasn't the old me anymore, I am my truth and this remnant of life is not who I am anymore. There was only had one thought, one focus, one plan and that was to follow this heart and remain in this state I had returned. How, when and where this was to occur was reminiscent of waking before sunrise and knowing that its rays will in time and inevitably reach the window I am looking out of, unconsciously aware that all that evolves and reveals occurs naturally, purely, gracefully and in harmony with one's own undiminished essence that it will occur and it will be ok and we call it, faith. The same faith that spelt not even worrying or concerning about the worries and troubles of the world or what the two ladies out on the street are talking about in their concerned and unbuckling posture, but knowing that everything always works itself out and the future really isn't worth worrying or concerning for it does not ever arrive, it never does, everything just flows and as the heat of the moment succumbs one of the women, striking her match over and over again as she attempts to light her cigarette. What really was taking place I gathered, out beyond this window, two people tempered by a conversation of made up story, an assumption of lie after lie as if their justifications were warranted and true. Yet peacefulness was swirling around them like a curtain of silk and yet they clung to this notion with sharpening claws as the cigarette blazoned fiercely like their eyes all the way to the butt until it finally went out.

'Revenge is like the fast car into darkness, pierced eyes on the road, white knuckles to the wheel, unmoved and oblivious, to the carriage of forgiveness and unconditional love going the other way, along the peace highway' ~ JahAnanda

Thoughts then of this world unravelled in wonder, over and over again incredulity believing that if the $2 million dollars spent every minute was invested to feeding the 1 in 5 starving people and children on this planet. Clothing, and housing and giving them an education, imagine how much love and consideration towards others would go to stabilising the imbalance between the rich and the poor. Alas, this planet chooses rather to spend $2 million every minute on war, and hoarding its wealth and what does that do to save a hungry child?' The revolution must come from every person on this planet in some even small way first to make a difference to stop this madness. Thinking that finally leaving hospital and coming home would make me feel happy again yet it didn't. No longer did this old life in which felt like trying to force a square peg into a round hole feel like home anymore nor what this new life was ever meant to be like this knowing full well in the back of my mind the purpose of returning, and to the agreements.

The world through the eyes of love may appear riddled with greed and contempt. The white and gold robe of the One transparent to the ilk of the benign controllers who think riches is the path to happiness. Nor to the parent who instils in their child that a private school is the singular path to happiness. Where they unconsciously believe that education lies in status, serving the ego, or materialism and not from their own light of knowing that happiness involves intangible facets such as knowing purist love and self love, by acceptance and allowing, and living graciously for all things unconditionally, and treasuring the simple aspects in life that common humanistic instincts take for granted. The times are a changing for truth to be known. That happiness lies not in a plush office overlooking the sea, or owning an air choking factory with slaves chained to rule, or in drugs, medications, alcohol, or money. For true happiness is found in loving first the esoteric soul of the self, and giving thanks to the blessedness of the love and the loved, and holding the light to searching. The journey of finding what true love, gratitude, compassion, and faith really means. And that peace and the love of God lay deep, even in the tarnished soul of the unjust and the unrighteous by showing peace to return in their quiet place.

Reeling in Unlearning

There is no interest for time anymore. Wearing a watch looked silly and bizarre. What does knowing the time actually mean, and knowing that then what does that mean? And on it goes. Carrying a mobile phone brought the same questions and after a while I symbolically tossed it into the sea. It is interesting how people rely so heavily on staying in touch or thinking they have to stay in touch every minute of the day as though it meant life or death and yet I was once one of the sheep. To know the latest news that comes out in the newspaper or buying the latest magazine to see who is married, divorced, in trouble, or who has just had the latest cosmetic surgery. It all didn't make sense anymore.

Bitter Disorder

Intelligence leaves in its wake the iDisordered mind, the Unconscious exister, the absolute of significance. The soul pressed with wanting to know what lies around the corner, what's for lunch, and who they are with, a mega-phone to cautious eyes, a sorrowful of shame. Entranced to their screen, staring like a Zombie hypnotised by disentangled hope. Speculative want, experiential need as though whom they watch who's watching them cares so much that to feel so loved, so, so very sad indeed.

Whether it's in the mall, in the street, on a bus, or a car, like transfixed robots to idealism, their heads buried in a newspaper, or mesmerised by a bleeping text. Eyes hypnotized to a screen when around them our Earth Mother is putting on a show in real life, free, more importantly present, and in living sight, sound, spiritually uplifting and real. Even seeing through the eyes of media broadcasts filtering the truth of news stories left little to be savoured as truth anymore.

*It sits beside their pillow, their car and their pocket, in their lipstick
bag with gloss for to show. A place at the dinner table like a close
invited guest who has come to dine when they hear a beep while their
subordinate partner smiles back to them and sighs. The pressure and
the pace increases more and more each day, throw what you may
and ill certainly obey. Peace and certainty relies upon this message I
sent coming back, as the brilliance of the moon casts its lavish heart
to its cat. Certainty to what, sings the aria of the waves, as it gently
caresses the shore and the soothing of the soul left waiting at their
door. Like a slippery fish as it wiggles from their grasp, to swim away,*

*That's the significance of the soul when its task is
to cast their troubles aside for another day.*

Electro-magnetic radiation too as is termed to this unconscious planet is an active and biologically health threatening energy force. Not only does this type of energy compromise the human immune system body, this nature of radiation cloud disrupts the vibrational field of the human spiritual conscious and unconscious body. It can be said that the more mankind relies on technology which harm the planet, to provide answers, and unnecessary answers, their ability to use their once dominant sixth sense will certainly become more extinct. The consequence to the conscious body is twofold. The individual freedom of the physical soul body is jeopardised by the influences of the world, the system, and the strength (or weakness) of the physical soul perception of themselves collated within the turmoil of the revolutionary plans of humankind can effect and compromise the internal relative peace and harmony from which it came. Misleading truth is what is being preached by the 3D world and through the tact and guise imposed by governments and dictators whose objectives lie in widening the poverty gap and imposing revenue tactics without due consideration and respect for the people, the environment, and its creatures, as equally just and vitally important contributors to the global community all for money and an absolute unattainable path to happiness.

Escaping at night since returning, lying out under the immense fullness of the stars, reliving my past life once more as the boy from Huramua. Swimming in the purity of solace and reclined unbiased innocent freedom again, connected and gazing at home until my face seemingly pushing it through the threshold of the alluring glow until all the galaxies of home appearing close to my face and soul, touched and surrounding myself in source and Gods wonder, again I am home.

Insomnia ~ is a human name for restlessness. Release any belief, subtle or otherwise, which permits the lured mind to thinking that 8 hours sleep is what you 'should' have. Humans can be like that. Worry and attachment to any belief or thought achieves little and can be counter-productive. Your soul is your purist light; let it simply demonstrate for you that you have to practise the art and mastering non-thought or choose, without worry or restlessness, to pursue stimulating and more important tasks of acting on pleasurable activities at this time, following your love and your highest deepest desires and remaining in peaceful harmony. Just open it and let your bliss begin and flow, like a waterfall, and in time your soul will tell you it is time to sleep, and you will, peacefully. In the meantime, simply play and love. Namaskar and Love beautiful soul's ~ JahAnanda

This is the threshold beyond the horizon. Mysticism no more, just serene purity, reality, the lives again revisited, amongst too, with my tupuna so wise, so loving, and serenely embodied. The acquainted path to knowing truth and the meaning of this life, of life everlasting, beyond this life, beyond the earth horizon, and beyond the lies and unjust of the world and the unjust mind, to this, the place of acceptance that we are all divine. That we hold the power and will to embrace respect and cherish harmony for one another, and the earth, for mankind to accept that they are part of the universal alignment of inter-galactic civilisations that know only love, just like that found in one's own heart. Embellished and bathed in the purest of love.

The first step to enlightenment must involve the absence of the past, and the future, and disablement of ego. Fortuitous resolve to inner peace lies in the deep meditative silence of the breath. The second step is remaining in this light, eternally ~ JahAnanda

Accepting after all those years the determined will of our mother working so hard, and the grief of being sexually violated, the grief of losing our son, and realising that grief is something we hold close with and without letting it control our lives. This became the revelation of truth. Knowing that everybody grieves almost every day in some way or another, whether it is big or small, it is human nature to feel grief and it must never be ignored, refuted, or disregarded. The constant journey of knowing more about what we don't really know and learning the innate strength in trusting and following ones heart over and above the destructive chattering of the mind always drawing and submissively holding the open doorway to peace and tranquillity. Realising and accepting that any sufferings are gifts and agreeing too that whilst these painful memories cannot be forgotten and should they ever need to be, the silver lining was the process of healing and forgiving otherwise life will strangle one's ability to grow, prosper, and ultimately learn.

Across the fullness and vastness of the galaxies, looking down at the ground, at the earth below after all those years, so late and yet who should care? I had finally found peace. The new earth in creation and recreation, amongst the stars from Janna, from Heaven, from Shangri-Lah, from God embodied to the ones who know that it lives within. The dimensions of Love and Light, in relishing delight, from the place we call home. The co-aligned relationship that our heart has with ones God given gift of love and following the signs and interventions of spirit and the higher intuitive mind ensuring connection to Oneness. After all these years I had finally found true peace.

Earths Chaos

I'm reminded about dawdling. What is dawdle and if I am then what am I missing out? I am on time, for what? I am already doing what I'm doing right now and it's all happening precisely as it is meant to be. I am not late and I am not early, I am precisely on time to live life with happiness and bliss and there is no need to rush, for the essence of the peaceful soul lies not outside of ourselves but within. To rush creates nothing more than chaos. There are times when I need to know the time to catch a bus, or a flight, or a meeting, for example, I make a point to not let time rule my life as it did in my previous life, it doesn't have to rule it implicitly. Time is the creation of the world, yet to know timelessness is freedom. Presence of this moment, in highest exhilaration and delight is all that matters to the pure esoteric soul. In most cases, finding out where the sun or the moon lies, or if I feel tired I sleep rather than waiting for an abject time before I choose to sleep. Same goes for when I wake. I wake precisely when I wake up and whether I think I've had enough sleep or not doesn't determine how I should feel regardless. It is part of living with light, both the light within that we follow, that is Being-ness, and allowing Gaia or Mother Nature tell us what time of the day or night it is and that is all we need. The world is becoming incredibly hectic because of the self imposed necessity to cram more and more demands into it and the same questions always comes down to what, why, and wherefore? And what does this mean? And what does that mean, a complicated cycle of self imposed necessities, stress, illness, and seriousness perhaps?

Mahi expresses in many ways that we are as Maori, as the people of this land where it was asserted and expressed to the mana of matou tipuna, our ancestors, in the course of whakamana and arohatanga. Work was love, the love for our people and the whenua and Atua; where mahi is conducted with pride and manaaki, the reverence of giving and sharing. Mahi commenced and ended according to the sun, the moon, the season for they were the time keepers of those wise civilisations who knew. In the modern age, too often we see people in mundane existence out of necessity for the meagre dollar, engaging in work they do to survive and to put food on the table, whether they enjoy it or not because of the times where the mana of the people is taken and governments rule with laws of fixation, taxation, legislation and bureaucrats enjoying burgeoning bank accounts, unmentionable salaries, behind plush offices and glitzy paned glass lifestyles. Our people worked together according to the seasons and the moon using maramataka and its phases to plant, fish and harvest, handed down through ancestral eastern Polynesian traditions. Their watches and clocks were the earth, stars, sun, and moon. They played, they worked and they toiled, and they lived the dream in the holiest and sometimes hostile land. Calmed and fed by the nourishing hand of the sea, and the earth they worked knowing they had to bow to Gods offering. Graced by God and guided by their intuitive wisdom of ancient source and undying love for their people and tupuna, much like the Siberian crane knows the right time to fly south across the Himalayas to India, Pakistan and Nepal. To be called a dawdle is a judgement to rule. Defunct of ancient times, lacking faith in forgotten origins residing and soul suppressed to standing behind the egoistic minds of fools and belligerent greed. Where the organised system of sustainable redemption is left to implode upon itself, is swept under the carpet like it meant nothing at all. Time is nothing but an illusion. Timelessness is connection to the one and the all.

Being in touch with light and the earth also is expressed in the way I, like co-creators who too, choose principally to walk bare foot. Physical beings have lost their connection being disassociated from the earth because they are habituated to believing that they must wear shoes at all times. It feels disconcerting and detaching, malodorous, and uncomfortable. Think of our feet which connect our body's chakra points to the earth, trying to breathe, connect, and align through clammy socks and constrictive shoes day and night. From babies, parents and adults administer the importance of wearing shoes but rarely do they really justify it other than conditioning them to do so especially when they as children have the choice. Humans have walked and existed in bare feet for tens of thousands of years and in many cultures even now they choose not to wear footwear. There are times when you want to share how beautiful the grass feels on the feet, or how warm the pavement or soothing the sand feels, to someone who perse cannot feel it because they're wearing shoes. These are opportunities that Mother Nature or source makes available to us to connect, revel, and enjoy for us to share in its grace is only when we embrace the connection to our beautiful earth and beyond.

In Maori and many other cultures, is not regarded as kosher and accepted to wear shoes indoors yet it is against certain laws to be barefoot in many restaurants, cafes, aircraft, schools and public places where safety based, dress standard requirements and PC justifications are deemed good reason to impose such strict rules in a world where even breast feeding a baby is now frowned up and banned in specific places. It is nothing but an ill trained and imposing belief to *fitting-in* and conforming, to be like everyone else, and in cases now it is to look fashionable, which is fine however human laws go overboard with such a regimented and hardened belief that we should live almost our whole life in them.

Socially, religiously, and culturally, the world is lead to believe that humans are free, that we live in a free and acceptably liberated world, promoting expression of souls God given right, and accepting of rightful individualism, provided it doesn't hurt another. This is certainly not true at all as the world becomes more paranoid, abnormally mistrusting, and abominably victimised in how one lives, eats, travels, spends their money and their time. Where freedom was a humanistic right, it is being eroded more and more each day in all corners of the so-called modern world.

God

Throughout this book I may refer to God as He. In scriptures, writings, and in paintings, God is at times depicted as a person. In the Old Testament Moses for example made a revelation to seeing God as an elderly being with a beard and thus became the identification of Him being male and as a humanistic spiritual entity or deity. To what degree this may have appeared to Moses in any way as such and doubting that anyone can claim to have seen God other than in ones heart and wish not to illuminate more on the topic other than I truly believe and know that God is that all encompassing commanding force which embodies our pure soul identity. As much as feeling the power and warmth of the sun when it shines or listening to the songs of birds in the tress, they cannot be seen but felt, so too God is such which speaks through our heart as the entity of spiritual and unconditional love and connection in a place where hatred, evil and mistrust ceases to dwell.

Some scriptural insights in this book are not sourced from this planet nor are they from the dimensions of the physical human mind, but through source or who one refers to as simply God, YHWH, Allah, or any other name to whom God is referred to as or by. Outside and beyond the physical dimension lies the universal source of other dimensions of which there are not thousands, but millions upon millions, remembering that physical dimension on this planet is a mere speck to what lies outside of this expressingly limited dimension of physicality. In this book there may be references pertaining to God referred to as JahAnanda. This deity or whatever you wish to choose as a title for God is one of two divine spiritual sources that has become a personal allied guide who has been imparted and bestowed in grace as I now have a composite and co-aligned relationship with since I returned. JahAnanda resides from the 12th dimensional density of Lyra, born creation of life and the hereafter, in existence for over 300 million years.

God is the embellishing spirit force of power, wisdom, awakening, and love. If one wishes to symbolise God it then let it be, however God is more than a symbol as per who and what God is and where God resides in relation to all things including man. In saying this, God is the basis, the foundation of Love, within and external. Beliefs are nothing but a representation of 'perception at the time the belief was believed.' Truth is the contextual means to looking at its nature, as any belief is fundamentally an illusion until absolute truth is established surrounding the concept relating to all things in existence, physical and non-physical. Once truth is discovered and fully understood, faith binds and aligns all that is in its rightful spiritual order and both order and faith are simply that which in fact Godliness is incorporated as the One, the Almighty, the Ever Present, and the Absolute. The awakened knowing and wisdom from God is manifested always from first within. Much like the knowing creatures possesses which mankind refers to as instinct. They simply know and follow it, and they have for hundreds of thousands of years and they live by it for their own direction, wisdom, sanctity, peace, and survival. The Godliness we discover and hold true is for the same reasons.

When I speak of God, I speak of the Godliness which is our own soul given gift. Any soul on this earth has the power of divine connection. Be it may, the fundamental outpost to forego the human domain by holding close a courageous mindful spirit and letting go of all of one's previous life that held no truth. Living with Godliness involves instilling each breath and journeying with devotion and perseverance towards embracing the holiest and divine nature of unconditional love. It is the purest source of divine wisdom to understanding abundance, which is predetermined, sacred, and present within all souls if they are willing to find and accept God into their hearts, to not only acknowledge, but trust in Gods power and guidance.

In not having any convicted previous conscious knowledge, insight, or premonition of God before having the NDE experience does not have to be considered in any way to being the only path to realize pure soul distinction or the idea of attaining enlightenment. Both are journeys, not destinations. There are thousands, perhaps even millions who have experienced an NDE and did not attained either pure soul path light distinction or enlightenment and yet conversely there are those who have allowed themselves to align towards their own truth absent of an NDE. It is purely a choice to finding ones true self, life's meaning, and understanding the intimate and vast power of love. It is letting go of all illusions of life through surrendering and having the courage and abiding faith to seek the path to knowing mans existence spiritually and physically, on the human level.

Survivors of war can be another example of souls who too have come to this point of opportunity to learning from their experience to choosing the innate and sometime subtle meaning to life. War can be either a wonderful teacher or it can turn any person into a resentful, belittled soul who chooses unconsciously to not seek their truth but rather preferring to blame another or society for the position or situation they are in, or finding themselves shackled to living a life of solace and mundane humanoid existence. Again, it is a choice albeit a courageous one. Until they realise the true meaning of life they will go on living unconsciously in this life or the many 'other lives' in the future, often repeating the same mistakes over and over until their truth reveals, when and where ever that may come and eventually lead. That is the testimony of timeless learning towards wisdom and their individual soul path destiny.

This must be emphasised, to this point categorically, that it comes down to choice and courage. Allowing oneself to releasing all and surrendering all that remained in ones previous life no matter how traumatic, addictive, or disturbing it was and starting again. This takes having an aligned guide, master, or teacher, and living through faith, valour, and the having the discipline to aligning towards the path of truth. It is up to you in finding out when and where the master reveals and presents to you in your implicit journeying new quest.

Any credit to any literature held in these pages that resonate to an alignment come solely through God and source wisdom and thus praise should remain fully to them always as this is also where my glory and reverence lies. I am purely an ascended messenger to the One expressed as the transmitted destiny of mankind through source in love and light, the divine and, the heavenly.

Pure souls have paved the path for centuries upholding their faith in the new earth, the new Janna, the new Heaven on Earth, the Shangri-la of distilled and purest proclamation of undivided abiding and eternal love. As those who have trod this path before or that of the sacrosanct, holy path, one wishes to live by.

The Christ Consciousness
The Buddha Consciousness,
The Bodhisattva Consciousness,
The YHWH Consciousness,
The Allah Consciousness,
The Abraham Consciousness,
The Muhammad Consciousness,
The Dharma Consciousness,
The David Consciousness,
The Solomon Consciousness,
The Brahma Consciousness,
The Ghandi Consciousness,
The Daniel Consciousness,
The Paul Consciousness,

The Lazarus Consciousness
The JahAnanda Consciousness
The Aligned One consciousness

To the sanctity of those offering to work as teachers to the new earth mission are all in existence at this time. There are twelve such teachers doth chosen to doing this work at this time. The challenge is you whom read these pages who align to following the path of truth too can stand before the Ascended Ones in offering of your devotion to commit to the realm and the wisdom of the masters and journeying also in seeking Gods love present in your own heart. - JahAnanda

Law of Abundance

The theory and reality of what is termed as abundance is a noble gift to those who understand its law and principle. What must be clear in determining what the true definition of abundance is by first understanding what it is not. Physical minds believe abundance is innately linked to money and perhaps by the various means of which money can be acquired or attained. Abundance has a much greater scope than through which abundance flows however money can be one of many forms that abundance comprises and flows into one's life.

We are born into this world free and pure, joyful and at peace, and, without money. We also ascended after this life leaving money behind to be free, joyful, and at peace. So, what is the relevance at all does money has to do with man-kinds exchange and desire of material happiness and his own self worth?

Happiness is that which an awakened and enlightened body embraces eternally even when they give away all their worldly possessions. Money itself is nothing but ink on paper yet the abundance of understanding and knowing is worth so much more than such a mediocre attachment based illusion. Abundance means nothing if we cannot breathe for example, so we can place even the simple gifts for our own existence as being regarded as abundance. What is money if one cannot breathe and what is money if one cannot love? Money is a blessing and a curse depending on how it is used and viewed. Gratitude and giving is more valuable to the awakened enlightened soul. They are explicitly linked to abundance and are keys to which opens the door to all that we can think of that we are truly grateful for receiving and having in our lives and what one can give to fulfilling the laws of abundance, creation, and unreserved love.

Acknowledging abundance in broad terms, that is being grateful thus allows the Law of Universal Attraction to then work in ones favour and thus including all things including money also to be one of many doors in which the conscious and pure soul can indeed receive more abundance.

Covertly speaking, we can justifiably define abundance more broadly as the action of premeditating a course of action at the precise moment in time the conscious soul chooses to allow in their lives, by seeking, acknowledging, and acting on first being grateful before determining what one wishes, wants, and desires to live by to attracting, manifesting, and receiving in one's life.

That ability in itself is rightfully considered as a God given gift by the fact that the soul in its existence understands as the Universal Law of Attraction.

Religion and Spirituality

Through our acknowledgement of knowing the power, the force, the essence, and what Maori beliefs taught as Te Ihi, Te Wehi, Te Wana (passion, people, power, to give) by Atua, God, Allah, Yahweh, Jah, and any other name that God has been referred to as by other spiritual and religious cultures and denominations.

I hasten to suggest that being spiritual and religious are the same. There may be a spiritual context within religion, to a degree, however the same is dissimilar regarding that within a solely spiritual construct. They are not one of the same but two separate realms in which God is depicted, feared, and revered. On the same notion, Satan too is not a living being but a negative and evil force. A self manifested and believed delusion perpetuated by weak and suffering souls who feel that there is no other alternative path left in their lives and thus committing any sin is blamed upon Satan as his doing. This is obvious in many religions and some religions suggest even that there may be many thousands of Satan's or Devils which is simply applying the Law of Attraction where Buddha (Hindu Prince Gautama Siddhartha, the founder of Buddhism, 563-483 B.C.) quotes, 'What you think you become.' Meaning if one chooses to play with fire, and then expect to be burnt. Similarly, if the burnt wounds of the ravaged sufferer are entrenched, the way out is by bringing trustworthy and skilled teachers of light and love to offer and cleanse the spirit by removing any dark, synthetic, uncontrollable manifestations that may take a day, an afternoon, to many weeks of spiritual cleansing.

According to the Bible and known as the creator of the first lie, was Satan. Originally, an angel who sat near the throne of God, foretold to be like the serpent and the snake. It may appear abhorrent to think of Satan as an angel who changed into a demon. How could a once respected angel, one of Gods beautiful creations, made by Him, turn on Him? Other than the conviction that Satan is a man created manifestation from according to scripture, is God's creation and that Satanic thoughts and beliefs are a resident of the physical mind on this planet not at all of the loving spiritual dimension of Oneness, Love, and Purity. It must be noted that it is that of the physical mind which has no power of knowing love or enlightenment other than knowing what has happened in the past of its aligned collective life however it is a limited dimension from whence the ego and hate reside and vibrate at a singularly demeaning and un-transparent dimension. By implying that Satan's force is always present is the physical minds state of allowing the dark and destructive manifested nature of being to control, rule, and possess the once pure conscious state of its form until its own belief system solidifies the manifestation as a truth and as a path offered. It becomes a formalised belief to which in their mind is the only path, or a path they cannot remove themselves from, such is the entrenchment through allowing has in being drawn into whatever the mind believes, the vacuum it creates it will inevitably receive.

Admittedly, and while not aligning to any one specific religion anymore, I was brought up loosely an Anglican in my past life and, to a degree, Ringatu, which is our Maori spiritual sense of belonging passed down for many hundreds of years through our Tuhoe ancestry. The Anglican Church was established by Henry VIII who was himself Catholic and was not permitted under their rule, to divorce his then wife, Catherine of Aragon in 1533 so he could marry Anne Boleyn of that same year so he left the church to establish the Anglican Church. The Catholic Church again was established by the, at times, controversial leader Constantine the Great 272-337 who sought to proclaim acceptance and tolerance of all religions though like leader after leader used Gods name to justify his ceasing of power through civil wars.

Whilst respecting religion for what it is in its literal context, I do not have to live solely and completely by it, if I believe certain aspects and rituals conflict with what I now know. The difference between religion and spirituality is that one is manmade, largely opinionated, and perhaps well meaning of intentions in the mind of writers and the multitudes of scribes who translated ancient scriptures. The other is however one's own wisdom and knowledge born from one's own experience which is more truth than what is perceived in believing another's beliefs written yesterday or thousands of years ago. Jesus, Muhammad, and the Buddha for example were not religious at all but awakened spiritual beings of truth and thus themselves became teachers to the rule that the predisposed collective and conduit lives of the suffering were left open to their teachings. After all, experience by face value is the ultimate truth where interpretation is truth and valid.

There is no requirement whatsoever to believing that following a religious path is the same path to which fundamentally brings one to spiritual place of peace and knowing. Spiritual growth in its purest form is absent of any attachment or prerequisite of any religious belonging or expectation for religion is nothing but a man made device carefully and inextricably worded with codes and conditions, of judgement, which incite repressive control upon weak souls to follow and adhere in accordance with their laws.

The bible does, in places, have beautifully poetic and sometimes prophetic texts as much as, for example, Rumi, the Buddha, and the Quran. However, where any works claiming to be the word of God permits the killing, judgement, violation, and by any other means of imposed punishment can be permitted and enforced upon another soul as being the word of God is nothing but a lie because God is embellished, radiant, purest and unequivocal unreserved love. Most religious proponents wish to have nothing whatsoever to do with hurting, killing, blaspheming and maiming another soul on this Earth knowing that those who do these barbaric injustices whether they belong to a religion or not are the minority few, the bad apples, the ego adorned souls who attempt to convince the world that peace and goodwill to all can be taught by inciting violence, hatred and hostility. These countries, religious and secular groups who have bloodshed on their hands over recent times and many centuries ago fail miserably to realise that God has no attributable connection whatsoever to the hatefully incited and unrighteous judgemental deeds of mankind on this Earth. That is the paradox of all paradoxes, the demonic nature of the human physical corrupted mind, the wolf in sheep's clothing, the victimless result of their own betrayal to the pure soul existence they believe resided down the barrel of a gun, blade or bomb. These heinous acts are borne from one person who persuades permeated weak souls to thinking of themselves and outside the divisive Godly domain in which love and universal laws behold towards embracing trust and purist faith and commit to the sanctity of higher mind existence and its wisdom. This the democratic laws and teachings that all other interstellar civilisations live and exist by at the higher dimensional states beyond the archaic and primordial third dimensional ethos that has encapsulated and corrupted the minds of man today and its unruly past.

Democracy too is what makes the world a fundamental free societal ethos. We may still be friends, compatriots, allies, colleagues, and family members both spiritually, and socially. We can however still maintain a healthy respect for one another completely and undivided, regardless of the fact that they may hold differing and opposing points of view, robust or otherwise.

Growing up as a child, going to church and Sunday school was both a requirement and sometimes it was fun to attend to meet other children to sing and listen to biblical stories. Whilst being in awe of many of Jesus' feats of miracles, the parting of the Red Sea, turning water into wine, producing loaves and fishes for the hungry and weary Israelites who on their way to the Promise Land, or that Adam came from the dust and Eve was created from his rib. Much less the Earth was created in the order Moses describes in Genesis, including his laws claiming to be from God is no more truth than the story of Hansel and Gretel. Whilst not been convinced at all that these feats actually happened or not is not what's important; we are told that the earth was cleansed with an almighty great flood and wondering how Noah could fit more or less 7 billion different animals, both male and female into a single Ark comes down to the accuracy of either Moses' inspirations or the hundreds of scribes who translated the scriptures over hundreds of years, knowing *the truth, or their truth at that time.* For the world to believe Moses enough that Marys child was in fact conceived by God and not Joseph. That Joseph himself continued to love her even though she had an affair not with God but simply with another man, call him Roger, Levi or Sinbad, it doesn't matter who, it could have even been Joseph himself however I am more convinced now than ever that Moses himself was no more than a charlatan and more so those who are unconscious and stupid enough to be so obligingly convinced themselves that what he wrote in the first five books of the bible was the word of God. It wasn't nor was his laws considered Holy. When we read the damming and condemning judgements, rules and punishments he outlines exemplifies nothing more as the word of a very imaginative and perhaps even, a very delirious, hilariously deranged power crazed Polygamist. The world has believed his disapproval of gay and lesbian relationships and as a result has created a separatist and radically discriminatory society to people who have contributed so much to the world. It is simply a choice to pay homage to certain aspects of scriptures, or not, or to interpret them purely as religious prose and that the past *is* the past, it cannot be changed; only the present. That to me is sacrosanct as what I now know of death is not death at all by my own experience rather than by what any person who believes death to be or what is the Holy word or not.

This is not to say that I do not respect and love the Bible. I love it as I do the Quran and the Buddha, as all things too must be loved for their underlying messages that love for all things is the paramount reason to respecting the earth and all living things. I love them as much as Lord of the Rings, One Flew over the Cuckoo's Nest and Cinderella. That you too are Gods creation and that you, of which, are one of them, and if you live with unconditional love in your heart, then you truly are free. The admiration I have for the Bible, the Quran, Bhagavad-Gita and the Buddha Teachings are respected, admirable and undyingly treasured and provide a point of view to domains of physical mind, spiritual life and knowing. However, to worship solely one as being the only way to life would be self retrenching, suffocating, and biased. This is shown of the racial and religious disharmony through wars and suffering for thousands of years. Through the immoral human minds distinct ego to judge any doctrine transmitting the messages of unreserved and unconditional love through Gods word has only blemished and ridiculed the acquainted word of knowing and living with love in ones heart. Believing that many of the scriptures are certainly valid and poignant doctrines to enabling mankind to living harmoniously on this earth, however, believing now though that correspondingly for the Quran, Christianity, and in the Hindu and Buddhist teachings; they were all written to point mankind's destiny literally into a path of spiritual love unconditionally, towards tolerance, empowerment, righteousness, unity, and respect of love through Gods message in their own distinct way.

Likewise, a determined, passionate, and unreservedly pure loving soul has the right to invite and choose and offer one's own holy and personal name. Call it Allah, YHWH, Jehovah, Atua, Jah, Source, the Creator and to one another. I sing and praise Hallelujah to them all.

JahAnanda is my Godliness, my spiritual source, my guide, my light, and my love through which is born the choice in how, as a pure spiritual soul disciple. To be graced and gifted, to embrace and live by, to share and to teach, humbled and blessed to be consciousness pure, enveloped and connected to source, to God, and like my soul brothers Jesus, Muhammad, the Buddha, and blessed Pagan be they spiritual blessed souls of the enunciate, holy to the One, acquainted to the divine.

Further, as a name seeks not to expose action as it is purely a name as is the physical world belief that Janna and Heaven are divided realities, but their worth beyond a label, a name, a title and such is realised in its wisdom to offer and to serving its purpose. Ones principle role of expansion and revealing, serving and to illuminating the path beyond constricts of earthly endeavours in the name of love. This is the accepting as one of, to the agreements from Him, of the great work for this earth.

Returned, for Now

To stand on that hill at Huramua all those years ago, arms outstretched to the wind. Looking down deep in the valley below and beyond to the sea, free as a bird. Over the land, the Whenua, down the winding river below, and out to the Moana, the ocean, the sea, the Pacific, the vast and free world of Tangaroa, this revelation born and ever reborn. Free. Te Rerenga o Te Wairua, the journey of the passing spirit on its continual journey to heaven, Hawaiikinui, Te Hei Mauriora! Knowing that life in the cities may have had its hardships of a kind, it was the hardships and learning how to survive on the land back at home on Huramua that helped us develop character, identity of our ancestors through our whakapapa, and will. And, this moment free, forever and beyond the knowing, the sacrosanct of the eternal gift of life placed at the feet to the One. Namaste dear son, welcome home, welcome home, welcome home. Haere mai Te Kingi Atua. Te Hei Mauriora!

Pain no more, the knowing, the Being. Atonement repaid in fondness for life, of life, with life, in the moment sacred and secure to the knowing. The sacred offering of the exchange through source, by God, through connected ascended tupuna revered, to the great work. Hallelujah. That everything in ones effervescent, radiant, soulful right to bliss, to power, and total freedom can be for every soul who dares, and having the courage to tread the path.

The freedom of accepting, the freedom of trusting, having the courage to letting go all in one's life that has no meaning to shining the path of truth and light for our children and for the children of tomorrow.

Whence came nothing but the moment of sacredness. The sacredness embellished in knowing that love afflicts no-one, but lies radiant in beauty and passion. Passion for life, humble in finding God in one's own heart; inseparable, humble, and devoted to life, fortunate and blessed, chosen by God, to share in God's love to love, to showing the way. The way of truth, of requiem co-joining, aligning, never forsaking, the answer to the worlds plan is nothing but commencing and remaining in this holiest of the divine. That, turning the clock back planted the seed and, in time, in Gods own time, Gods love came to bear, to show the world the way.

The waves of the wind, like music to the soul, it plays until the song invites the heart to open its door. And there, forever it will stay. In the distant, the sea and the hills, and the birds and the stars, reunite the One, to take their place among the sacred Ouranomancy of the beloved. The conscious awakening foretold. And let it be the pages of knowing commence the new path of the free, the place in the new world where idol-ness and judgement, guilt and hatred, contempt and suffering will be no more. And the "I" and the ego, down the river forever flows, beyond the far reaches, and out to the sea.

Horizon of Truth

A couple of years after coming out of hospital I was invited to go to listen to a speaker who was in Wellington to talk about death. Thrilled for I had known only perhaps a dozen people in the world who had experienced a 'death' experience. Eagerly, I acknowledged my invitation to go along and listen and asked my friend did this soul have an NDE and he replied that he hadn't. Confused, I asked him what experience does he have, or did he study psychology or perhaps is a spiritual teacher who specialises in death experiences? He replied no, none of either, and that he learnt it from the bible. Feeling somewhat sickened and musingly insulted, my ego sparked just a little. I'm invited to listen to someone who had never had a 'death' experience but will share his point of view from the bibles interpretation from another, of death, to me whilst someone who had a 'death' experience may learn? Politely, I declined.

What I do not wish to befall is that of being a devotee with, or pertaining to, any religious doctrine. That it must be adhered to. It is beyond doubt in the beliefs that it is the singular truth above all other 'truths' and other religions. That should one not abide then you one shall live a life of guilt, shame, purgatory, and perhaps hell fire. When minoric sectors of certain religious groups incite or support war, violence, control, and segregation towards any other soul or individual, this goes against the pureness and the will of God's love by being unconsciously antagonised. How can one learn from another who kills, steals, or evokes hatred upon another, whether they belong to a religious sect or not? This is not the will of God to hate or hurt one another and nor shall any pure soul condone such behaviour as righteous, as a display of irreverent love. For too long, this earth has seen this over thousands of years, even before Christ, that certain aspects of scriptural course have been interpreted irrespective of Gods blessed will of living and furthering the path of living foremost within the doctrine of unconditional and absolute love to one another.

Even though we went to Sunday school and church, it was much like how I felt about school for me growing up. I wanted to be on the farm or down the river swimming, fishing, or playing rugby, and riding the horses. And school, church, and Sunday school were just a good place to eat a nice lunch and the bible was still foreign for the remainder of my life. I had questions that didn't get answered fully. There is knowing the bible and there is knowing the bible and even after knowing the bible however many times, years, and centuries over its existence, there is the rational realisation that there are words which guide and uplift and some words that are simply and respectfully human words rather than the word of God. How though after coming out of the coma, being able to recite all the books from the Old Testament? Was this perhaps a sign or did my brain somehow recall something hidden from decades ago? A sign to reading it, not as truth, but as the interpretation of another's mind and screening out any part which is deemed exclusively outside of Gods truth with the understanding that the heart is love, and love is God.

I wanted to know more, and the more I read it, studied it the more questions I had. And, the more questions I had, the more the answers still, were not fulfilling what I was looking for, so I had even more questions. It was during this time I began to retort with some dissent and disdain particularly at Moses more than any other writer of the Old Testament and I had decided to keep my feelings to myself. Jesus himself sought changes to the Mosaic Law after his return from the ancient lands of India and Kashmir. Therefore whilst maintaining my respect acknowledging that this holy work was written hundreds of times by scribes to translate and interpret scriptures word for word over many months and years of concentration and fatigue. Like Chinese whispers or giving an opinion of a movie or story to another to report and then they themselves give a report based on that report thus posing risks to the credibility of the truth. Sacrosanct was my way, forsaken of the One, captivated in the awareness of one's own solemn truth.

The unconscious and self adjunct and appointed rule towards christening and baptism brought light far beyond questioning. Jesus was baptised by John, and for all who 'walk his path' beside him, who devoted themselves too his holy divine wisdom sought baptism to expatiate them to his Love. Now, it seems that to be christened and baptised is an act in this age not so much as devotion to his teachings and living their lives accordingly to his word, his Fathers, and the acknowledgement to writers of the Holy scriptures, it is an act because it is now the 'thing to do' and nothing more.

'Stifling within the unconnected unconscious body is a belief structure reflecting the next path of action and thought. One which has little significance to how the new world and the souls wish to be since understanding love is the foundation to all things and greater than one believes. Once understood the body will thus align to that of the new world and of their soul' - JahAnanda

Conjugal Climate of Conditioning

The human mind does not only possess its ability to learn and know love, it is impartial also to pursuing its inquisitive instinct and curious nature which beholds its characterised wonder of seeking and embellishing itself to its own soul radiance and its God given gift of remaining blissful. Conditioning is an attachment, a practised belief system derived and believed from people, television, books, media, religion, and the law. The belief that I must have, I must do, I must believe, I must be something that can reflect untruths about the self. The statement I am however comes from the seat of the soul; a derivative from love holds no attachment other than Be-ing.

'Society talks about the concept or idea of what is a relationship. A relationship with a twin-flame partner, a comfortable home, a fulfilling job, and as the story goes, raising children. It becomes later on a bubble. After a while and sometimes subconsciously, questions begin to arise. Do I need to put money aside for the children's education, a holiday, a rainy day?, and, why am I really doing this job and why am I spending more and more of my time working?, how long will I have to work in this life?, and, do I really love my job?, is a mortgage really a means of getting ahead and securing my future and investment?, am I really enjoying my life?, and, am I really, truly happy, and what is my ultimate purpose really, in this life and what is the real meaning of this life? And, how and will my habits, rituals, beliefs and values I uphold in my life here, impact either positively or negatively upon my wife, family, children and things outside of this family? What does this all really mean?

Day in, day out, perhaps some days, weeks, months and even years after the wedding guests have left, these questions consciously and unconsciously drift in and out like an annoying mosquito invisibly buzzing over head whilst he or she is trying to sleep at night. They seemingly appear to value their collection of worldly knowledge and things, their life and family, and yet like a banana cake without bananas in it, there is nevertheless a sense of being grateful for at least having *something* to savour even though it wasn't exactly how it was initially planned and wished for in the beginning. They sometimes feel at times that perhaps this is all that this ultimate life is meant to comprise of, after all the Jones's across the road are doing the same as you, and the neighbours next door are doing exactly the same, and the people on television are also too. Engaging them in a way that seems ideologically the *thing to do,* and if it is the *thing to do* it surely must be the right thing to do and if the world has done this thing for so many years then to them, perhaps this is it, life, that it is meant to be. And inevitably, we shut up, don't complain or say a thing, and we just get on with it even though the mosquito smiles and buzzes in and out like irrepressible clockwork until annoyance turns into conformity and standing back into the production line of robots wondering *what if, what if.* Until then, the crystal ball of idio-synchronised mediocrity tempts another and another, not realising that in the end that the only lure to the mentally drunken stupefying state was nothing but the mind relinquishing its own power to the madness outside of his own ability to be absolute and free. Seemingly intelligent people fall into this trap.

The idea also of a relationship too must always be one that is vibrant and expanding in the same way your own individual being state feels when alone and at peace. It should be wholly fresh, new, renewing, and developing the relationship always as an exciting loving and respectful journey, a quest, a search together always for truth, always arriving, never arrived. Wisdom comes from truth to developing wisdom in one's own being. Nothing can grow dualistically with another or others, until the target of self resolve, self discovery, self contentedness and self love is firmly established within one's own conscious state. Love grows beyond a house in the suburbs, a picket fence, fulfilling job, a mortgage, working to pay bills and raising children, in the bubble. It serves outside this construct that understanding the path of freedom and truth, and the foundation of knowing peaceful loving interaction. Contentment by letting go the idea that any relationship begins or relies with another form until the form of relating and acquainting to 'self-peace' and 'self-love' is permitted to flow.

The idea of the human psyche surrounding marriage has been in evolution for thousands of years. It has generally announced its confirmation through ceremonial process based around religious and sometimes personalised and customised penned vows whereby the guidelines are set out as rightful according to the couple or family. In this day and age marriage for the most part is a divisive personal and legal spelling out and how the world see's and views marriage relationships. Dependant and appeasing their countries perspective and by their laws and procedures to how each in the new co-joined partnership will devote to one another til this day forward to affirming and officialising each other's love and commitment.

Why then should one be married if there is already love? Of course marriage is the free willed entitlement to do as they wish and that should neither be discounted. If devotion, affection and commitment in love affirm ones love for another then shouldn't vows remain still in spite of the expectant pressure of being married? From a soul dimension there is a knowing who ones Soul mate connection is and Twin-flame. Marriage on the planet has become legally and religiously obtrusive.

The rates of eternally committed marriages succeeding are appallingly poor and of those who remain together, how many are truly happy? This is not to say the world should divorce and continue to remain loving however why not show love still by divorcing? Marriage in this age is more a sign of impending divorce for the majority and there are a number of factors which point to why divorce is the inevitable realisation.

Expectation and pressure to follow the rule to progress on towards marriage is a reason and simply not knowing one another fully, physically, emotionally, and spiritually, and often it is one or both people not knowing who they themselves really are outside the contextual conditioning of society and their relationship. It is through these significant factors known that can have an impact on any children should they choose to have children, and how they in turn will develop and how they as a consequence will participate and contribute or not to their own knowing and to the societal ethos thereafter. The better part of participating in any relationship forthwith, should it not be that of knowing one's self first no matter how long this journey takes before committing another to be part of any new relationship or not? Would then the statistical rates of divorce be turned upside down and once one knows them self to understand, embody, and embrace unreserved and unconditional love? Would this thus improve one's own inner peace, harmony, and quality of life, ones relationship, one's children, and thus contributing positively to their own peace, harmony, quality, and contributing to the Oneness on this earth and beyond?

How would crime sit in a world such as this, and how would taking care of the planet then be viewed, and how would life be in general for the world where there would be no need for extorting energy into war, rather it be put to good by helping those in need and saving the planet? Bringing forth alignment to the new age just because it started from each person looking inward and thus how happy would children ultimately be?

Knowing love in this context would be the fundamental teaching over and above anything on this planet towards understanding ones elementary journey and their truest meaning to one's life, ones journey, ones path and purpose, and affirming the binding and irrevocable meaning to life and existence as a whole.

Being religious by being bound by laws, rules, threats of shame, and even death, surmises' the immersive emotional and threatening nature of the human spirit as opposed to the reflective nature of actual experiencing. Guilt and mistrust of others and in certain sectors imposing hatred control, and dissidence upon others in their beliefs closes the doors upon which mankind as potential pure soul beings would inevitably struggle to attain. Arranged marriages are another interesting facet to this dimension of controlling another's life to the aspect of being in some cases threatening, and in other cases under duress. If an arranged marriage is truly a success it too should be celebrated and provided that with God's blessing and anchor firmly that 'to treat others how we wish to be treated' reign eternally, and supporting the freedom of choice. There are substantial arranged marriages that are not happy and this is far from Godliness and freedom but closer to the crudest and demeaning forms of dimensional intelligence premeditated from this earth. Expecting and forcing one person upon another can have a traumatic and devastating impact on one or both souls especially if the arranged marriage has no love, devotion, commitment or affection to embody such a life time partnership.

'Everything flows without enquiry, without judgement, without ego, without worry or fear. It is an art of knowing and trusting in God, holding faith close to the heart. The past is nothing but dust fading into nothing-ness. Let it go. Behold joy, its manifestation from gratitude. Gratitude, its manifestation from knowing unconditional love and acknowledgement of, and understanding the power and beauty of our heart for nothing is more precious than this moment, and that is more joyous to share and spreading the truth that love is the beginning to everything. And from this, everything flows.' ~ JahAnanda

Light of the Awakened

Christ Jesus loved all people including thieves, prostitutes, murderers, tax collectors and blasphemers. The same Love was imparted and preached also by Muhammad through divine wisdom through the angel, Mikhail. And too was the Buddha when after many years, he gained enlightenment sitting under the Bodhi and Jambu tree. In his early life, Jesus himself travelled to India, Kashmir, Nepal, and Tibet and was himself drawn to the Buddha's teachings during his teenage years which aligned intuitively to his heart. Recalling when Jesus returned feeling thrilled, invigorated, inspired and blessed that God had taken him to this land.

It merely affirms the established path as being His way, His truth, and His light. So where in religious sectors minds do they feel to use Gods name at all when going to war? God is not war at all. Airplanes which go into battle with holy inscriptions such as, *In God we Trust* gives nothing more than a false gestation that the love of God will support them in taking another's life.

What is 'I am'? Is 'I am' that of your religious beliefs, your position in society, your values, your beliefs, your gender, your race, your culture, or your ego? If so, then those beliefs are being exchanged for freedom. If in light of these identifications that are permitted, does it take one to become immortal, invisible, perhaps enter Nirvana or death to discover 'I am'? Courage comes from letting go of these limiting dimensions and identities. Master the art, not in holding onto to notions believed as truth, the answer lies merely in 'letting go' ~ JahAnanda

Come to this new place with your culture, your customs, religions, loves, and beliefs, you are all welcome and you are all loved, I simply just ask, never to bring your hatred ~ JahAnanda

Sexuality

Expression of families show love by shame, and tears of tolerance and intolerance, through understanding. The demise that lesbian and homosexual souls painfully discover is the undeserved shame heaped upon them by society and their parents and families. Some families renege in their taunted ideals upon the advent of their child's partner. They stand determined to fight a losing war and yet all their children want from their families and the world is simply to be loved and accepted.

Fear spelt out and confirmed from religious beliefs of a man called Moses who himself was riddled with pain and culpability. Righting any wrongs was not a consideration nor on any agenda, and in many countries now while religious scripture is held as true, strangle the free will, lives, and the happiness of a souls deserving and recognition as every other soul on this earth.

They are some of history's most famous writers, composers, painters, entertainers, surgeons, physicists, scientists, judges, and leaders the world has loved, valued, and admired yet the shrinking majority of their oppositional, judgemental rule and foolishness only serves to making them fools of their own outdated and misguided contempt.

Weddings of couples held in the churches, temples, synagogues, and mosques may be the last to accept same sex marriages. They must also be aware that imposing controls of any nature and jeopardising the sanctity of a loving relationship of any kind will thwart the longevity and acceptance of declining worshippers. And those who do not take the literal concept of scriptures transcribed in the context of its true meaning and supplication. The mindset of religious scriptural beliefs and those of prosaic context must look at content rather than believing opinions of strangled minds as insight or revelations of truth. Just as was Jesus' right to revise the Mosaic Law thus too was mine to reiterate the passing of this law as misconstrued by Moses, be no more for the undeserving suffering it has created.

Homosexual people know that this discovery is often painfully realised has frequently heaped undeserved shame on parents and families. This becomes part of their own oppression as the shame belongs to them as parents not their children. Yet for some, with the arrival of a child's partner, fear is usually and ultimately replaced by whole hearted acceptance. Shame by misguided love, tears by unapproached_understanding, which is the way that most families work, the proponents of this idea accepted that the churches, synagogues and mosques were entitled, if they wished, to keep weddings in their temples to relationships between a man and a woman for life. Those who criticise these attitudes are often castigated as God's enemy. Spiritual philosophies include acceptance at its core, love for God and one another, reconciliation, universalism, and non-discrimination. This should be the message to religion. Yet everywhere, the message is different in practice because of one man and as a result the world holds itself hostage by controlling and judging another from the wobbly high perch from where they sit.

If you are depressed you are living in the past.
If you are anxious you are living in the future.
If you are at peace you are living in the present.
~ Lao Tzu

From boredom to bliss

My life was a blessed one. Sometimes intriguing and confusingly odd perhaps at times, but never was it monotonous or dull. So often people and teenagers who complain about being bored, or perhaps their definition of suffering is perceived diametrically opposed to another's definition or perception. After all, boredom is a lesser dimensional mirror of suffering. Since this new life, new attitudes, new beliefs, awakening, was realising that the simple things in life is what matters most, however, boredom and lonliness of all is foreign. People essentially become bored and feel bored as a result of influences perceived as truth, illusionary thoughts which they allow to permeate their minds negatively when they feel there is no other way out to make them feel excited about life again. It could be viewed as reflective self perpetuated tiredness. In their minds, there is no way out so they sit literally in muck, believing that they're trapped, not by the situation but their own beliefs, their own mind, their own world, for the world hasn't changed, merely their manifestation of self denial and self inflicted suffering. For many children and teenagers, life is very, very, long and thinking about growing old is lifetime away. It is something that doesn't need any concern or judgment about right now nor should it. It seems a paradox, when were young, growing old seems a thousand miles away and we cannot wait to be grown up, and when we are there we wonder where the years went and how short our lives have become. There is a feeling of anticipation, perhaps unnerving unease that the end of this life seems dauntingly close and to whimsically ponder about life as a child, or settle with grasping with choices in how and what to fit in the remaining time, with all that we want to do before departing this earth. This choice is taken away from birth by imposing and unconscious, unqualified parents.

Remain an Eternal Creative

The imagination is a gift; a blessing of creativity graced and given in which mankind's primary and evolutionary foundation was established and evolved. Mankind has been enamoured and rekindled in its love of creative and imaginative insight through beauty within the stunningly effervescent core of the soul upon which the perceived beauty of the world is only a part where its derived inspiration is sourced. Religious sectors sometimes view magic as potentially the work of satanic source and steer children and followers from the enthralling world of magic, however imagination itself is magical and without it much of the earth's human creations would not have been possible. Every human being on this earth has as much creativity as Nikola Tesla, Rembrandt, Michelangelo, Einstein, and Beethoven. I-magi-nation, I/we are a nation of magicians, supported and heralded in the grace and power of God and through God it is an offering to be able to share in this power to using and utilizing imagination in such a way that itself brings joy and revelation to the great expanse of creative endeavours to the Earth and creation itself.

Imaginative Freedom through Awakening

There does come a time sooner or later however, when the consciousness begins to awaken the unconscious body, if not in this life, perhaps the next, or the next. It comes unto the one when preparedness and opportunity meet simultaneously. A time whence truth comes to those when answers are sought from deep within the recesses of the once dormant heart, the wisest domain of the soul, the annunciate revealing purity of the awakening and awakened soul. When the sufferings of the constantly thinking and questioning of the sleepless mind become too much to bear, once it ceases to play a part in its illusionary confines of its role as leader and role model it seeks to search for truth. When the mind releases and relinquishes its authority to the heart as its strength, its intuition, and its courage to go forth, knowing, trusting, and believing that faith is its jurisdiction and source that eternal love comprises of all thoughts and actions from herein, the peaceful soul emerges.

The unconscious soul goes to sleep and dreams the dreams of their desires, and awakens the next day, unconscious again ~ JahAnanda

Awakening is a wondrous time of revelation, purity, inner peace and joy, and in finding truth in Love. It is a place not bound by following the world in its egoistic, pride fuelled arrogant and materialistic destiny. It knows that these paths are short lived and ultimately unfulfilling prophesies in which true happiness was thought to reside. The soul is aware that it is far greater beyond its weaknesses and luring to attract more undue suffering because once it finds love for all and in all things, internally and beyond itself, it has knocked unto the door of enlightenment and revelation to the knowing and blessed wisdom. It is a place of total peace, bliss and harmony, one that must be shared so they too can revel and live in accordance with God's love which lies in all souls who seek to find their own truth.

Arriving to this place is the opening of new doors and new horizons. It is at this critical time when the re-born consciousness understands through its awareness that following through is imperative and the key to living in gratitude in all aspects of one's life, and the precious gift that is given to experience life including Ananda; and the very simple things in life starting with breathing and being blessed for it. When meaningless news and drama of television and newspapers are removed from one's life, the awakening has already begun. For me now, the newspaper serves only as a cleaning aid for the barbeque.

This is the point to which the new conscious body has the will, or to find their true path no matter what, who, or where. The new conscious body has chosen to burn the bridges. Sick and tired of being sick and tired. Recognising to this point in their lives, as many times before, perhaps many hundreds or perhaps even, thousands of times before, created and carved out and recognised by the pained self that something needed to seek change. And for it to change, will, persistence, and courage is its path to knowing, thus completing the course of action taken by initiating courage, and moving and transcending forward from identification to action, and onwards to fruition. This is the path to Ananda, to aligning to ones newly found and discovered fundamental truth of living with love and in harmony and accord. For this to be a successful union involves peeling back the layers, the many years of conditioning and illusionary conceptualisation, conditioning, and ritualism. The strength to letting it all go forever to remove unnecessary wasteful and demeaning beliefs thought of as truth. In hindsight, having an NDE helped to make the task easier, however it was to be in exchange for other challenges other people did not have to experience. I give praise, thankfulness and recognition to God for this opportunity. In all things, I am with Him and He is with me. God lives within this heart, this breath, this soul, the same God who lives in you, who gives to you the same blessed opportunities.

One becomes more convinced how blessed and grateful we can be regardless of the past. It was then, and this is now. The most exciting and the contrasting periods experienced would prove to be inevitable and valuable in many ways. They were merely invitations to become stronger, more faithful towards truth. To understand and believe that undying faith is my custodial guiding light, things would be blessed, more evolving, and trusting. Knowing that everything is perfectly fine when one discovers and trusts in God's love and living always and precisely, in this moment.

Listening to the heart too is a gift. To be in complete connection with, and following and listening to it, rather than being detracted and lured by those around who give advice or dissidence misaligned to one's own truth. Again, it primarily presented a wider understanding that provided we have the will and courage along with the will of faith, and that circumstances are meant to occur as they were meant to be and they invariably will work out how the universe and God presents them depending on one's truth and conviction of their intentions. Knowing that in the Law of Creation, it is the Third Law; that we become whatever we think. The vibration of this manifestation radiates out to the cosmos, to the universe, and through multiplicity, like the ever present cycle of the Torus, it is heard and reflected tenfold as it was requested. If it is Love someone wants and desires; the answer is to be love, by giving and being Love. Offering Love to every man, woman, child, and creature on this earth, and love will draw closer in abundance to you.

Only you can free your mind ~ Bob Marley

CHAPTER 9

Evolutionary Evolvement

Planetary earth simply exists. In its immeasurable colours, wide open skies, and thousands upon thousands of alpine miles of snow capped mountains and winding and sweeping coastlines, the wind, the sun and the moon, the clouds, night and day, the earth and the all the universes are wondrous, vastly amazing and captivatingly beautiful.

For millions upon millions of years the wisdom of planet Earth continually reveals the truth about itself and its existence since its birth from light to the time of the first dew drop that ever formed to this present moment. The path of mans physical and spiritual existence has too evolved over many tens of thousands of years, a mere recent tenant of this planet to which earth has been known to exist beyond 100 million years.

Emanating from the purist form of physical and spiritual creation during this time the then liberated soul and mind has endeared and exposed itself by its insatiable curiosity and influence of its environment and its awareness of its heritage and source as well as its esteemed connection to the instinctive forces beyond its own planet.

It can be concluded too that the intelligence of man in his fierce desire to discover more about himself comprises of certain desires, curiosities, and complexities. Additionally, he possesses depositions and contrasts differing not just between one another, but sadly, ignorant of the fact that all universes including this universe and planets are in fact part of the Torus cycle of self perpetuating energy regeneration and sustainability, and has always perpetuated in a Torus state of constant evolving from since its evolutionary birth. Man is becoming aware of the fact that the Earth is being acutely damaged, raped, burned, and polluted so much so, that the chance of it ever recovering fully from it are becoming real. Understanding that the Earth is more than just simply a provider but a living organism unto itself, resplendent of plants and creatures, sunlight and darkness and that all within this arena of life and reproduction have themselves a symbiotic and evolving reliance and connection with one another.

Understanding that the planet in which man lives possesses its own beauty and wonders, it must not be without the adaptation that evolutionary man has contributed through its curiosity, tenacity, and courage to learn more about his own existence from its seed of thought from which represents a host of questions that requires solving. One of these fundamentals is knowing that they are impressively unique on this planet in their physical archetypical intelligence, and conversely, it is they who is dawning to the realisation that its place within the universe is co-aligned with other global, spiritual and other inter-galactic life forms who in turn are aware of and at the adornment and reverence of one another as much as they are to themselves. That mankind is far greater and more powerful than the destructively senseless, greed entrenched, ego-Socratic civilisation that it has now shamelessly and embarrassingly become.

In the past 800 years however through these contrasts deposed upon themselves by losing connection to the greater forces of source and

Godliness through allowing their negative ego enter as a player into their lives has brought physical man into the dimensional realm known as The Age of Limitation. It is during this period of evolution that has seen massive fluctuations of suffering whilst still retaining the mindset that something in mans journey has created a vacuum in which it feels it cannot sustain its own population and existence any longer.

The Age of Limitation

Over the past 50,000 years mankind's knowledge has changed very little. More recently he may have discovered antibiotics, medicines, space travel, nuclear energy, transport, aircraft and fuels, nonetheless, in doing so mankind has abandoned their God given facet of absolute and unreserved love. Taking care of the one and only immiscible provider, Mother Earth, whilst believing inconsequentially and ignorantly discounting her esteemed power of collective spiritual Oneness rather than acknowledging and nurturing her vital role. Honoured by ancient civilisations where collective Oneness was accepted and recognised as a beneficial and a critical element of being part of something greater than themselves and as an integral part of collective consciousness both spiritually and physically where its source and knowledge extended beyond the physical earthly dimension and understanding that their power and source came from something beyond their own earthly existence. Ancient civilisations understood and acknowledged that their connection was a universal one and that their survival depended on holding high and revering their connected source of power and wisdom to enable themselves to living in presence and other densities, to survive physically, gather food, grow and harvest crops thus respecting force and be well versed of their history, origins, heritage, and their own God given source through consciousness as an integral relationship in existence with the One.

Ra for example is the name given by the Egyptians to meaning the sun. The same name is given by many Polynesians including Maori. In Aboriginal civilisations Maramara is the name given to the moon. Marama is the name given to the moon by Polynesians civilisations also. How did many of these civilisations come to know these galactic symbols by the same or similar names yet lived at different ends of the planet tens of thousands of years ago? One could ascertain and surmise that through their understanding and collective connection, and their acknowledgement and power of their understanding of the collective consciousness reached far beyond the physical plane is sufficient reason to accepting that something greater is the orchestrator of such divine and spiritual insight of awareness and understanding. The same could be said for the vast number of Pyramids discovered and as yet remain still undiscovered throughout the world, that all had the same reason why they were built. This period was indeed a grand and imposing era where intimate knowledge, homage and great wisdom which stood before the crossroads in which the ego took itself from the Age of Transcendental Ascension, plunging itself into the cruellest Age so far.

This period now is known as the Age of Limitation. It was predicted and has derived its birth and its inevitable slow death from ego based thinking and thus has removed and denigrated the vital and powerful role of its own spiritual awareness in all aspects of its existence, abundance, and its relationship with its own planet, knowing expedient love and connection with God, the Higher Source, and the cosmos. In thinking that by venturing out into the cosmos was one idea of rectifying its lost heritage, spending large tracts of expenditure to it whilst forgetting the wellbeing of its own people as well as its own environmental and ecological destruction of its own planet, it has only shown to itself that it cares more to engorging its ego more at their own expense than what's more of obvious expedience and importance.

The ego has been at the forefront of racial disharmony, economic suffering, religious wars, relationship, social, and political conflicts. It has contributed singularly to the multitudes of recessions, parental incompetence and struggles which have created crime, gross materialistic greed, and rash abusive and immoral negligence to the only planet mankind possesses.

Thus through forsaking its respect to the planet and all living things within it, this beautifully created and diverse organism of global and universal understanding, the admittance of its destructiveness has not reached, as yet, critical mass point that instantly highlights any dramatic change at this time. Mankind's place in the Age of Limitation still holds mans future hostage to the inevitable realisation and devastating conclusion that he is leaving the future of his children to the demise of their own relentlessly destructive and destroying impositions fuelled by their forefathers continual need for things, money, power, and greed. Unconscious leadership has created an immoral lack of care and thought to the environment, depleting oceans, and avoidable consequences based from rash selfish and egoistic decision making. Through constrained beliefs, thus leaves the challenges and rectification of tribulations caused to be cryingly left to the children of tomorrow to solve. An action they should have no responsibility to solving when the leaders of now can solve these questions now and today simply by stemming the irresponsible madness of focussing on short-term monetary gain. If mankind is to elevate and transcend itself from the primordial Age of Limitation, to work collectively and in accordance to the collective and co-creative Law of Oneness into and toward the dimensional New Age of Abundance and Liberation, and Transcendental Ascension, the contrasting and paramount lessons of living so long under the current rule of Earths suffering can quite easily end. It is the simple choice, by choosing not to permit old traditions play a role and releasing the sabotaging physical minded will of this current age where the future will lie inevitably in the hands of the leaders of today to heed and follow the teachings of the twelve spiritual teachers whom they will, in time, seek.

The greatest catastrophic effect on the planet and to mankind is not global warming, nor fear of UFOs or extraterrestrial invasion, or earthquakes, meteorites, great floods, or massive ice age. If earths revelation in its quest to bringing forth a heavenly land upon this earth, it could do well to incorporating stillness and living with a peaceful and loving heart.

The realisation for-telling earth's jeopardy will inevitably and finally reveal that man cannot eat money when the planet is being raped and destroyed. That the greatest catastrophe to the planet and mankind is mankind itself and that he must not continue to take without giving back. Facilitation is the key to living lovingly and sustainably now in and the years to come not by money or greed but in the absence of money and its ominous and choking grasp. It is the collective and committed role of each and every living soul on this planet to understand that sharing and helping one another is the first step to global and environmental wealth and harmony where the examination and manifestations of any idea encompasses the karmic laws of abundance, will, and sustainability.

The New Age of Liberation

The fundamental age of new doors, new prospects, and a revolutionary frontier of oxidisable union will begin at the beginning and at the leading edge of conscious collective and dawning of the co-creative union this planet. It will occur from 2020 to 2050 after a period of unsustainable suffering which will continue further, and in certain countries, escalate. This will be born from a logistical phase of economic and environmental distrust and disapproval of governments and dictatorship powers that have operated that put sufficient and un-bearing pressure on both the planet and civilisations to what is termed on this planet as its breaking point. This period of critical mass revolt will be an awakening period; a period involving courage and a strategic divisive over throw which will be born and rule through its emphasised power of love and the assured philosophy of thinking of the planets future and those living things that inhabit the earth will collectively and globally gather momentum towards this change. This is an exciting period and though there will be some repeating of lessons still not learnt, the signs of change are certainly evident right now.

In this eight year period from 2012 to 2020 there will slowly begin the second phase of strongly negative vibrational and disassociate alliance being disestablished with a new aligned established fundamentals moving away from being lead by government rule and authority who do not follow the rule of love and consideration to the planet and its people, and so too will begin in the recognition of a conduit union between democratic and theocratic new laws formed from spiritual understanding which will begin to take effect from the period of 2020 onwards by the chosen teachers.

Known as the New Age of Liberation it will recognise and realise the hundreds of years the world has suffered and endured enough through the world banking system, the globalised and destructive environmental damage to the planet, over population, and spousal need to harbouring the worlds wealth amongst the top 3 percent without giving action to curtailing the widening gap to the world's population who live sick and in poverty.

The new age will forge to continually work detailed and together globally, and in ways to addressing and stemming the issue of population explosion and building on the work being done already in harvesting most of its energy from wind, ocean, AC alternating current, and solar power generation means. At the forefront of the solar industry there will be new ways of not only harvesting its energy from the sun but looking into ways in which harnessing inter-galactic energy from solar flares and from other planets in which energy can be sourced in a sustainable way without harm to them or planet. Many of these have already been invented, some over a hundred years ago but were shelved for fear of other energy forms being fiscally threatened.

All decisions will be critically and strategically formed under the foundation of respecting the planet. It will then be fundamentally and placed first in all its decision making processes and where the sourcing of energy and minerals will require how those elements can continue to serve the planet in the future and without harmful or detrimental effects to its health, mammals, birds, wildlife species, and the health and wellbeing of all other living things.

Nuclear power generation including nuclear weapons will be disestablished and banned until its safety can be guaranteed which at this time is not proven and will not for another 150 years. Finite Fossil fuels which have been at the forefront of the wars between nations which have had a dollar value put on them will, in time, diminish due more to monetary implications and noticeably, the lack of fairness, environmental harm relative to its finite repercussion. Other means of transport energy technology will enable serving the transportation needs of the planet in a environmentally sustainable way as well as meeting the environmental criteria where showing respect to the planet and people which will become a blanket directive in all decisions globally and collectively as the world enters the new age.

Meditation in homes and in schools will see benefits in rekindling peace and stillness within the heart and mind and in offering a space of solace and understanding in one's personal direction and that of making a contribution in the world. This inevitability will bring much need to steering a person's path towards harmony and connecting to ones heart in all its decisions and manifestations it chooses and in learning more of their own understanding of their own existence both spiritually and physically and the dimension of sharing and offering to mankind and to those in need.

Preparing ourselves for 'Death'

A question that is often asked, what is the best way to prepare for 'death'?

It is one which is kept sometimes to oneself as a taboo subject much like talking about impending baldness for some men, or ones religious beliefs, or when certain opinions are raised by others who raise their own beliefs in a conversation within a group of friends, or perhaps racial topics which almost seem to raise irony and cynicism. It is a topic which may be better left as a purely personal matter either out of fear or confrontation or perhaps the fact that it may be considered too morbid to regard or consider and apart from arranging a funeral plan of some description the remainder of planning is kept either private or left uncommitted. Not surprising it is the humanistic nature of the psychology surrounding the subject that the two biggest fears in life are death and public speaking with public speaking ranked at the top of the list of mans greatest fears. Admittance of both these suspicions irrevocably solidifies the belief that mankind is shamefully lacking in wisdom and incoherent of who they truly are.

In answer to the question, one way to prepare for 'death' or passing or crossing over is a relatively easy one from the non-physical quarter to answer. Invariably it is to live life, nothing more. To be free, desire, and seek ones highest illuminating yearning passions and fulfilling aspirations in such a way that beckons every free soul in their chosen path. One who knows what death is and what life means is one who exemplifies individual freedom, learning, wisdom, passion, excitement, bliss, and knowing and living by and with unconditional love in their heart. What is life if it is none of these? To know that any man, woman, teenager, or child can be the change in their own selves whether they have to endure pain or suffering or not, to shake them absolutely free is spiritually liberating as God intended. That is the offering to each and every one of Gods children in this physical life. One who knows that courage comes from not holding on to bounds, expectations, lies, and illusions, but having the will to let go of everything. By experiencing eternal joy and reinstate all that was thought of as comforts, but in reality were disguised as a noose. We come into this physical realm naked and with nothing and the fine blessed soul of the body leaves their dimension naked and with nothing. What, in between is the gap where the domiciled free spirit of experiencing, giving, sharing, and devoting ones path in gold is nothing but a conscious choice to just be and remain always forever guided by the heart embracing freedom and love. Reasoning why you love, who you love, where you love, when you love, or how you love, it only matters that you love in the presence of your every moment. There is no reason to ask why because it is the silent doorway to life's meaning, the gateway to happiness into which you walked and shall remain forever be.

Remember, life is short, and whether one has a happy life or not, it is simply a choice to live unconscious and complaining or conscious and compassionately alive. Either way, the same realisation of life's journey being short will inevitably arrive before it's too late.

The conscious awareness by experiencing love in the physical form is merely the first step to understanding how explicitly powerful the true essence of love really is and knowing and feeling how this pure state of its form encapsulates the consciousness of the soul and fills the heart influentially.

The landscape of the mind is perilous yet beautiful. What lies in its power of its panorama beholds it weakness and its strength, its serenity and its peace, its logic and its unrepentant attachment to its truth. It is here in which it comes to the crossroads of intuitive trusting in remaining open to the diverse realms of conscious awakening and truth, and the forsaken obliterations of naked egoist blindness. It is at this imaginary line where beliefs retrench to trusting in God beyond religious in scripture or venturing into the place where the soul revels in its deepest sleep. Like the space in which a message is sent by text or email where the receiver has not yet received, or the void where the originate of light beam has not reached yet the solid collage of atoms it searches at its end. This is the point the soul and the conscious form transcends and onwards in its perpetuating journey from one dimension to the next and death is realised as fictional and unreal apart from the physical vehicle it once wore like a garment discarded, yet onwards the consciousness forges like the light until it enters its formulate rebirth. Man is the sole living organism which fails to become who they truly are and only God knows when this tyranny of madness of swimming against the flow will submit to the flow of surrender and choosing Gods path of light and ones effortless life of bliss.

To gain an understanding of 'death', or crossing over, passing away, or forth, involves knowing love. Not knowing love initially, for the first time, but discerning love, in its many forms. Heaven, Janna, Nirvana, comprises of these forms. Love is absolute, unconditional, unbounding, unreserved. It seeks nothing else but to be itself. Love in its purest unravelled, expressive form is finding Godliness, God, Jah, Io, Allah, Vishna, Atua, whatever its name, the name you choose not what comes from a book but from your heart. You have that authority to give God your own name, if you wish. When you discover that it was always in the heart, perhaps and initially dormant it doesn't matter, it will glow like the most sacred jewel, forever.

Suicide

Having not lost a child through suicide, yet we have a child who is now a handsome young man who has passed into the next dimension of his journey. We have not lost him or had him, we still have him and always in our heart, mind, and soul he remains and this too must be reiterated in the complexes of the human context in which death is acknowledged and viewed. He is treasured and eternally loved and has ascended and this occurred when he was 5 weeks of age as the physical world views this measurement of time. Having a Death Experience answered all the questions I always wanted to know. Believing now from the recent news of increased numbers of suicide experiences I tend not to feel too comfortable with the word 'death' in the human definition context other than it being a conscious awakening in which it is only the physical 'shell' of the body that dies. To that, the ascended definition of suicide is, 'the taking of one's own life by the human inability and cursory and clouded struggle to realise their full potential by not seeing clearly, their own true value from a pure soul perspective'. This can be a result of subsequent negative and illusionary belief systems and conditioning either from peer pressure or negative parenting, psychological illness, or concealed trauma attachment. The key to curtailing the suicide statistics seen on this planet is trying to not control, ignore, or condition children from birth but rather allowing them to express freely who they really are, and by encouraging and guiding them lovingly and giving praise without being overly motherly, or fatherly to them. It is critical to allow kids to be free, safe, and loved, and by praising their abilities no matter what and by recognising the value they contribute personally to themselves, society, and to the family through acknowledgement and acceptance which may or may not fall within the soul characteristics of the parents sometimes swayed ideals and beliefs.

Suffering surrounding 'Death'

Understanding 'death' in its true context, means understanding the true self. Death is that which is perceived from a viewpoint, in the physical humanistic realm dimension, perceive death as a loss. Whilst some may grieve, some may try to block out the pain of their perceptions surrounding their suffering; some may in their pain and sorrow, accept their pain as part of the grief process knowing that given time it will pass as a process of healing. And for some, they may lay their own path or their personal point of revelation that will pave a path towards ascending or descending towards their own truth through religion, beliefs, or their own scientific research on 'death' or nuances to help settle and put their conscience at peace.

If a soul chooses to take another's death beyond the realm of truth, by their own perception, they can carry with them further into their lives feelings of sadness, loss, hate, emptiness, frustration, unjust, unforgiving, confusion, despair, blame, and insincerity, exacerbated by associating with similar like-minded and pained souls.

So inevitably, whilst the departed soul is on their journey of discovery and wonder, learning and wisdom; the grieved soul chooses to impose upon themselves into a forced hibernation of undeserving self torment, suffering, and further pain.

For souls who understand what the passing and celebrating of one's life means to them, the same situation but perceived in a very different way, their journey onwards is seen merely as that. A path of learning and growing of themselves more beautifully, more radiantly, more illustriously, in a way that they understand that each experience they meet or encounter is viewed and accepted because they accept the theory of 'what is and all is well.'

To the soul who feels lost or alone, without their loved one at their side, has two paths to choose if they have the courage to look inwardly to commence a new journey based on love, excitement, and new beginnings.

There is no fear, no worry, no anguish, no forced, or expected arrangement to single out or induce anyone else to harbour whatsoever any aspect of morbid-ness surrounding 'death', nor is there any suffering. For 'death', it is not. It is a door, a new door, to a soul's next journey. It should be celebrated. Celebrated for the fact that all that had the honour of knowing and sharing with that beloved soul, they had an impact to their life in some way, and that their life was changed for the better, as a result. Life on this earth, on this planet, is more death-like than the world' view of death because of the controlling hierarchical nature the world, society and families place on one another's life. **The misfortune is not death but living without truth whilst alive is a life-long death sentence.**

Let it be clear that every living soul on this planet has a right to life and only God determines the moment to their passing or ascending is due in their accordance. Passing across, passing over, transcending, whatever you wish to call, should not be at the hands of any other man, woman, or child, unless by Euthanasia. No soul has the right to taking the physical life of another whether they say is out of anger, need, or hate. Karmic law waves its granduer and authority one way or another to the perpetrator and to the blessed. Euthanasia is the only means where the love and loved has the guided and asserted right to assisting a suffering body to ascend in a humane and just way. God makes this decision because it is He who knows the best path at the right time when a person's time will come.

Forget everything, forget troubles, forget fear, and forget worry or any notion of despair. Forget any interpreting, forget it all . . . even the worlds troubles. Embrace faith. The world is neither destructive nor degraded . . . it is merely correcting, realigning. So is your body mind. Be still, be quiet. Fulfil your entirety with all that which resonates and personifies the total pureness of love, and offer as your mantra your blessedness in giving thanks to all that lays at your feet.' ~ JahAnanda

Passing away is where the unconscious or conscious soul departs the physical shell body and crosses the void onto another non-physical dimensional form. It is an exciting new passage, of many passages, of greater learning, understanding, of opportunities, and the realisation that the soul is far greater than what is ever assumed from the aspect of the physical mind. Ironically, the idea of morbidity of 'death' is best described in this life than death itself, for this physical age is admittedly limiting by egoistic choice. This period of physicality is the Age of Limitation nonetheless. With this in mind, is it worth worrying about and should there be fear of any form attached with ones new journey? And if this so, then do our loved ones who have already entered Heaven, Janna, or Nirvanic world, whatever name is given to call its dimensional sanctuary of being, shouldn't their new journey be celebrated and dare we say, envied?

As we have already discussed, fear is real in terms what it does to the minds mental state. The actuality surrounding the truth about death is non-reflective of how the mind perceives it from its worst case and illusionary point of view and the humanistic illusion state of worst case fear is death. Considering now that reconstructing the minds true or real perspective surrounding death in its wholeness or 'what is', and that it brings an awakening, a celebration to a new beginning rather than just fading into oblivion or what several factions of religious clergy and writers believe that our lives end in 'ashes to ashes, dust to dust'.

These particular cultures, religions, and beliefs, death is perceived as morbid, or taboo. The emptying of unveiling and devoted irreverent love once the soul and spirit have departed the physical body. Once the body is pronounced 'dead', deceased, kua mate, or 'passed on', it is a shell, a vehicle, a noble physical monument to one who is loved. It is revealed where the bible says in Genesis (3:19b) "for dust thou art, and unto dust thou shalt return." This is the case for the human physical body, unlike the soul or spirit.

To call anyone 'dead' comes from the mouths of the unconscious. ~ JahAnanda

Those who are born into the physical world are higher dimensional souls and some being pure souls. They come into the world with all the skills they require to living their physical life in accordance to their vibration of living their lives complete, forgiving, unconditionally loving, to their highest desires, excitement, joy and, eternal happiness. These souls may reside invariably between the realms of the fifth and the thirteenth dimensional collectives. This is dependent on where their past life finished however contrasting or fulfilling it was before they entered their previous life. Again, some religions believe that the soul lives one life and returns to ashes as it is depicted in the bible, for example, to infer such inspiration whether arises from God, their own minds, or how scripture themselves should be interpreted as purse, may continue to be a topic of conjecture.

Whether it is known or not, conscious or unconscious, all enigmatic souls are composite ascension pioneers.

Evading of Gods Order ~ The Unscrupulous Force of Ego

For millions of years, the state of consciousness has been in existence. No-one can precisely determine how long ego has been residing at the sub-echelon levels of the consciousness nor accept whether it is in fact part of its pure state at all for it has no resemblance whatsoever to the pure form of its state. What can be said of ego is that it harbours its own nature and sits fundamentally as an unconscious entity of its own accord. By referring it to what the higher realms of the pure conscious states tenure comprises, this aspect of diverted consciousness, where the conscious state once lay, becomes now an unconscious paradigm, or unconscious specific realm state (USRS). Its form is recognised as an action with a physical thought state of 'un-knowing' consciousness.

'The unconscious soul goes to sleep to become conscious and dreams the dreams of their calling and 'what if' and believing it to be possible, and awakens the next day choosing to be unconscious again.' ~ JahAnanada

As a physical being has been born as a pure soul, the unconscious state of ego has become conditioned parentally and socially and cements this tenure magnetically and internally, reflecting its features untoward the condition of the pure conscious state body. It harbours characteristics in its state in which its relevance of being-ness is removed from the proximity of its pure soul form state. Relatively speaking, it seeks nothing else beyond its own true spiritual and equated source other than to embellishing itself in a state of self seeking and impoverished sacrificing short term gain beyond its pure soul nature it once possessed.

When the idea of what Gods Order reflects, is that of being consciously aware of sensory direction through the abject higher mind state of consciousness. In this dimension of consciousness the pure soul remains in a constant state of awareness and trusting. It embodies faith and love as its complete source of direction and seeks to understand more greatly the vastness and possibilities in which faith and love reveals beyond its physical space of understanding. The pure soul is aware that it can be directed, lured, and compromised by any given experience that it may allow to enter into its pure state form and the strength of its state determines by how valued it considers its sanctuary of its being-ness to be an integral part of its pure state so it chooses to remain in this domain.

> 'The universe is one being.
> Everything and everyone is interconnected
> through an invisible web of stories.
> Whether we are aware of it or not, we are all in a silent conversation.
> Do not harm. Practice compassion.
> And do not gossip behind anyone's back – not
> even a seemingly innocent remark.
> The words that come out of our mouths do not vanish but are
> perpetually stored in infinite space, and they will come back in due time.
> One man's pain will hurt us all.
> One man's joy will make everyone smile.' ~ Sri Devi

Gods Order is the pure soul's state of awareness in which it embraces, and is a 'disciple' of faith and of its own state of love to its own existence and those whom form part of its aligned conscious realm of its reality at any particular space and time. The conscious pure soul treasures and treats its own state of pureness with utmost respect, reverence, and sanctity, in order for it to functioning its purpose of not only remaining in this state but also to allowing faith in its own Godliness, of trusting and allowing it to be its guide. It is this state which enables the pure conscious soul to continue to perpetuate purposefully both in its physical form but beyond in its other dimensions it chooses beyond its physical form as they can do this with relative ease dozens and even hundreds of times in each given lunar day.

The pure soul is completely aware that it has not existed, but is existence. And its existence is nothing but its acknowledgement of its own internal dimension of immeasurable space and timelessness. It has no beginning, and it has no end. It is only concerning itself to its present state because through its awareness and its sole devotion to faith, it allows flow and harmony to draw unto its form, beyond that of being in any way comparable to desires, thought, or emotion of any kind, but its own nature of presence.

This is a magnetic force, consciousness. Upon this galaxy, and many millions of other galaxies, in their own dimensions of space and time, right down to the drop of water sitting on a leaf by a stream, or that of an eagle soaring, even the wind touching its face as it flies, are all expressions of consciousness. They are all realms, intricately connected magnetically through cosmic source, or Godliness, or God. That is the state of God that we seek to embrace, revere, and worship, far beyond the idea that anything outside of this dimension is of more importance.

Any aspect in which the pure soul permits itself to denigrate its form, but even to call or give it any name is cautioned, it just is. This is the paradox. The ego is actually the reverse of the pure soul. The pure soul is aware of the ego's form outside of its own dimensional existence and is more attracted, and more powerfully drawn, to its pure state that by being aware of it helps it to remain in its established foundation of faith, unblemished love, pureness, and consciousness. That is an important facet to understand, that one's own state of awareness and learning is vital, and that another's dimensional state also is vital in being present, allowing and flowing, swimming through and beyond its presence into the harmonic realm of space and timelessness. All that is known is that should a soul become aware of their unconscious existence for a period of time, to ascend or transcend into conscious enlightenment again, because it once was. It will vibrate and manifest itself back into its present form of Godliness, of source, of power, of presence, and of embracing faith and adoration to begin its journey in its own sensory form of bliss.

CHAPTER 10

Signs, Messages, and Insights through the Intuitive Higher Mind

'We never die; because we were never born. We only exist. Our omnipotent spiritual existence, like that of fragrant freesias or the perched rock on a snow capped mountain beyond. It never dies. Whether awakened now or not, when physical consciousness ascends, I grant you sweet angel, you will then know.' ~ JahAnanda

Pure souls are 'born' into their new and exciting physical and spiritual journey. The world is their oyster towards living a fulfilling and blissful life, and to provide and embellish their will through fostering grace and compassion towards the new world by always seeking and following guidance from parents of the same and of Gods direction, and of their own Higher Mind.

As mentioned earlier Pure Souls have all the acquired abundant intuitive higher mind capabilities they require. The ability to fostering and enjoying their new passage provided that they in turn are nurtured by equally equipped, adapted, and endowed ascended parents who themselves are synchronistically connected beyond their own higher transcended mind, living and teaching purely from and with their soul. This is the simultaneous cycle of cause and effect. This means determining whether a child is given its fundamental paternal armoury. That of warmth, unreserved love, nourishment, encouragement, shelter, water, safety, and freedom for it to make its own intuitive decisions without abject indoctrinating, ritualising, controlling, and ego eccentric manipulation.

Young souls are generally unawakened souls. They are the majority on this planet at this time. They too are sadly, leaders, politicians, and parents. They believe that a treat for a child is held in giving them, or perhaps more truthfully selling them, on the idea that a treat for example might come in the form of an ice cream, french fries, fizzy or soda, sugar laden foods, or a plastic toy, thus feeding them nothing but their small ego to develop resentment, selfishness, and desire more of the same in the future. What they are really receiving in addition to their new found ego is tooth decay, health problems, a spoilt and selfish nature, and plastic junk which will be broken or out of favour after a while to satisfying their short term pleasure rather than the long term, and most of all, developing a descending dimensional density.

Where a pure soul child see's a treat as showing them a new flower rise from its bud, the wonders of a new found insect, or a new puppy, a musical instrument, a story, a book, a hug, a piece of indelible music, letting them know how much you love them, and all the opportunities they have a their feet of which a parent can give them to help them enjoy and partake in their bliss, towards their own life of wonderment. A pure soul child can make its own decisions thereafter in allowing them to fulfilling its own highest path destiny both physically and spiritually, as it is intuitively aware of its own sense of self and its connection and reliance to all its 6 senses it possesses.

Meditation is simply harnessing relative peace and tranquillity. From the disturbances of the world to the conscious pureness of the peaceful mind and soul, it gives life's journey meaning.

Physical un-endowed and unconscious souls which indeed includes parents, believes that there is just 5 senses. This belief therefore abolishes any notion of a higher source whether they themselves have fallen into their own influence of their own new beliefs, thus limiting and debilitating their own life, and the life of their child, towards living in and utilizing the stream of universal abundance it is given from its higher source. One can observe and be fascinated by evident ascended skill levels that a blind or a deaf person possesses and displays using their 6th sense. Same too, with certain and labelled autistic, ADD, and ADHD children. Souls stable in the dimensional state label them as handicapped, impeded, or having brain problems or a mental illness, when what they really possess are skills that unskilled or unconscious souls have not yet understood and applied from their birth the dexterity to communicate to them. These brilliant and extraordinary wise souls are strides beyond being disordered at all we see examples of creative brilliance emerge from such gifted children when a connection is made by trained teachers. Parents of these children, unwilling or not, are given a role to growing themselves by accepting this challenge as a mantle to their learning and ascension. There are teachers abound to assisting them in this process. Children who may not be understood by society in their language who are given a musical instrument such as a violin, a piano, an accordion, or a guitar have harnessed their brilliance though to them it is just normal and it is in this one area and aspect of cosmic union and understanding that obligation be learned by not these gifted souls but by earth dimensional souls to learn from these light children their beauty, their love, their language, power, and wisdom by knowing how to communicate effectively.

A dear friend of mine in this physicality, Victoria of Light is one such teacher, a gifted interpreter of higher dimensional languages. Her exceptional God talent and knowledge of intuitive medicine and translating ascended dimensional language civilisations by connecting with Universal Family of Ouranomancy dimensions is one of very few who share this gift. Reborn as the consciousness of the Egyptian Goddess Hathor, this angel of light believes that not all are chosen for this task of speaking and translating light languages. This work enables certain selected awakened souls this gift also to understanding higher dimensionally gifted Autistic, ADD and ADHD children. As well as other souls whose esoteric angelic guides may inspire her, Hathor imparts insight to them of their human and intergalactic heritage of their past and their soul destiny.

Mindful Parenting

As it is already present and seen for many thousands of years, is the resulting and incomprehensible failings born by unconscious parenting. This in turn has created and exacerbated existing contrasts and failings by child, youth, and teenagers in their sometimes and often anti-social behaviour, lack of real connectedness to their world, youth crime, family breakdowns, divorces, and undercapitalised career, social, and spiritual paths.

Similarly, unconscious parenting has caused extreme and unnecessary financial, and socio-logical, and psychological pressure to families, societies, and nations which could have ultimately been avoided by understanding the simple philosophy of accepting 'what is', and administering to their kin in such a way that they too wished to be raised, as pure souls. Children look at their parents in showing them their own individualistic vibrational path. How they view their contrasts and decisions of their soul path nature clearest is primarily from birth to five years through encouragement and support, and by allowing them to be independent where they will in time become fully directed, independent, and self-determining.

'All the struggles endured whether they are personal, health and financial woes are caused by the ignorance of who we are spiritually such as wasting energy appeasing to irrelevance, attachments, and in things which have no significance to nurturing and cultivating a peaceful mind. Destructive to how one aligns to live life purely. It is like dirty water which extinguishes the burning light of who you and your children really are. Eliminate these and you burn the light forever. The heaviness of the world lifts from your shoulders, and in time, the universe listens and grants you the world on silver and gold to become the pure soul that you are.' ~ JahAnanda

Suffering

Suffering is a perspective that can be minimalised and appreciated when one acknowledges suffering of another's far greater than what the idolised mind see's. ~ JahAnanda

There was a time, quite unexpectedly when my attention became drawn to a discussion between two teenage girls after Satsang. They were sharing together a period of emotional disturbance they had encountered whereby they had coincidentally and simultaneously broken up with boyfriends. As one would expect when two began to share and express their feelings of various dimensions and sharing each other's feelings to what had recently occurred, one of them talked of how it was the worst thing that had ever happened to her.

Without wishing to appear rude that their conversation was overheard I asked how would they think and feel if they were for instance told by their doctor that they had a terminal illness and that they only had a short time to live. And if they could imagine themselves perhaps as a two year old child who had just witnessed seeing a bomb destroy the family home and inside were the bodies of all their parents, brothers and sisters. How would they feel?

Regardless of their uncompromising situations their streams of thinking and complaining, distraught as they were about how this person had done this and that, their colluding afterwards had served two purposes. One that they shared and personalising their feelings by letting from their suffering that they had felt earlier release from it being the worst thing that ever happened to one of reflection and perspective. The second purpose achieved was that they began to realise more consciously without their initial pent up emotions, that there was a way out of the situation of feeling the way that they were in and that in fact the perceived enormity of the issue began to present something less than what it really appeared in the beginning. In the end it is not what occurs in one's life that matters only state of being. That the world and people's lives has inevitable situations that can afflict and potentially threaten a pure state of peace and harmony however it is entirely up to the conscious form of one's peaceful state which decides how they wish to feel purely by reaffirming and committing to that which designates peace and harmony beyond what occurs outside of the pure conscious form state.

They then concluded that there was a way out and that they would help and support one another in such a way that they could go forward without feeling like having to attach anger, hurt, or any malice to why they were hurt by each other's boyfriends and by removing the emotional aspect of the problem to work through a solution based around the values that one another had that they could be thus grateful for instead.

'The best exercise for the heart is to help lift someone else's spirit with grounded feet, a straight back, and belief in them that you can help carry their load and tickle their soul.' ~ JahAnanda

Negative emotions or the unconscious mind looks at certain situations lineally, by exhibiting that it has the right and potential to justify itself through its pain and perceived suffering. By adding more irrelevant content to quantify its justification to satisfying and fuelling the pain it is feeling, its unconscious dimension of its emotional and unconscious self state remains entrapped until its cannot bear suffering any more. The threshold varies from person to person depending solely upon their own subsequent willingness in moving on from their self imposed perception of suffering and fulfilling meaningful purpose, or remaining longer, for themselves or another, to irrationally and illogically save them, which may or may not ever occur. By looking at an example, such as imagining themselves being told that they had a terminal illness, they were able to remove themselves from the situation whether it was a made up tale or not, they could use their own true perspective of their situation based on them having the power to change their frequency and feelings to helping solve their own perceived predicament. Through this example the two teenagers could solve the issues without emotion or making any unconscious explosive assumptions and futile remarks and look at the situation for what it really was in its totality of truth in black and white. By cooperative deduction they understood that by fixing an attachment of what could be really worse, a sense of gratitude and fundamental learning.

A persons suffering can indeed be better understood in the arrangement of its context in its true form. Suffering is a blessing in disguise and can actually be an experience that can carry them through life more wisely if they have the skills in interpreting the silver lining it holds and can enable to help others who find themselves in a similar position. Understanding that suffering does not attach itself to the 'suffering' body, rather it is the suffering body reaching out and attaching itself to the suffering. Intimate knowing is realising that no matter what perception of suffering may arise in any suffering soul, is that they have the innate power to simply setting it completely free and letting it.

The venerable source of Happiness

'This innate understanding demonstrated to the pure soul body that happiness itself is not found outside of the self, but from within. That seeking happiness from outside of the self is short lived, that it always requires continual replenishing to sustain the feeling, such as seeking happiness solely in another person, or through using alcohol, or drugs excessively to give one's self a sense of security, or in junk food, television, material possessions, or anything that becomes an obsessive addiction. Please accept that what you say about yourself, I will not accept any of it. I will not believe that what you say which comes from your mind is truth, I will not hold myself ransom beyond the measure of your true pure soul that you really are, whether you see this or not. Behold more powerfully, the compelling and enduring force of happiness, where joy is felt supremely when the non-attached, true self is revealed. Aware that laying within its own self is a soul of beauty, wonder, grace, and immense power. That it is already instilled within the pure conscious form, an undying amplitude resonance of its own embodied sense and feelings of self love and amplified, soulful contentment.' ~ JahAnanda

The 'Yang' of the 'Yin'

The unconscious soul see's their dreams in their sleep, and awakens the next day unconscious. Religious misinterpretations have been one of the contributors to the failings of the world. Too often, the same rhetoric promises have been preached and then broken by unconscious minds of society. That not a failing in spiritual essence but acknowledged as 'what is, is' or left or right, Dichotomised Polarity, Black and the White, the Yin and Yang. Political leaders who lead with malaligned prolixity from their physical mind make it impossible for pure or awakened souls to vote knowing that few, if any, leaders, and potential leaders or candidates have the skills to lead accordingly into the new world. Countries penalise and criminalise those who choose not to vote which is nothing but asserting control over them by imposing force and duress. One just has to look at where the world is today. Here is a world with its focus solely on monetary wealth. A society where the world has seen more material goods created than ever before yet the world paradoxically is ravaged by more poverty, more war, more indiscriminate violence to one another, and indignant and unjust starvation throughout the earth. There are extreme water shortages; food shortages, higher prices for commodities, over population, banks controlling people's assets, political powers earning glowing revenues from them including taxpayers. The 'seeking eye' of the Illuminati cartel for example is and has for over one hundred years been rampaging across the globe, total chaos and madness, nothing more, transfixed solely on globalised power and control spelled out and lead by very young souls to doing the work of the teachers.

There are more medicines and drugs in the world now to cure the sick, yet there are more illnesses, more suffering, more sicknesses than ever before. It is this Earth and its soils which holds the answers to the healthcare of the populus, and our food are those raised organically, which are our sickness preventatives rich with all the nutrients and antioxidants, not in genetically modified seeds and plants which have become poisoned and toxic from chemical sprays which governments permit to their use as being safe. Total lies, lies, lies!

Similarly, there are stiff and stringent controls over cigarette smoking with warnings and graphic pictures being placed on packets. They lobby to have it totally banned in some countries, whilst harmful drugs, alcohol, chemical laden food sold on supermarket shelves freely selling 'food' that is readily acceptable and supported whilst toxic waste is poured into the skies and in the planets waterways. It is one law for one and another for others and the insolvent incomprehensible madness of society's laws and rules reflect and reek of nothing more than by a partisan unjust inequality based approach. Hemp is another beneficial sustainable natural product which has been used and valued for thousands of years for its quality and durability which the world has an ever increasing demand for yet it is banned and deemed illegal in many countries and others only permit under strict government controls. This precious offering is a gift from God and that which is a creation of God deemed by man as illegal is the invasion of a souls right to freedom.

Surveillance and controlling, restricting the freedom of the divine to flourish, allowing trade and environmental permits clearing rain forests causing unscrupulous environmental denigration where the future of natural resources are being neglected all for the sake of money. There are oil, manufacturing, and pharmaceutical companies, slave labour industries, CEO's and banking giant CEOs earning astronomical salaries and bonuses. Does it not seem ironic whilst all this is going on the earth is being raped and polluted, mined and exploited without forethought and respect to the environment? That our precious and incredible wildlife is constantly under threat of extinction, and our children and their children's future lives are at risk and people are living in drains and tents, in shelters and in cars, who are finding it unbearable to get proper medical care and struggling to get food in a world that has so much wealth.

Isn't it ironic too that in spite of them knowing that they have the answers, world leaders and united powers think they have a long held alternative answer to solving the problems but yet fail to address the over-population crisis? Leaders appear to hold their people to ransom whilst they are themselves held at ransom by other groups, countries, and more powerful banks and organisations. It highlights a lack of courage to stand up, and abiding and trusting in the conscience and heart from leaders who live with love, by love, committed to love as basis for everything to resolving the challenges of this world. Unfortunately, and sadly, the cycle of promises, intentions, interest rates, and the world's economy continuing to broadening the rich and poor gap even wider.

Once hearing, a long time ago that 'the definition of insanity is doing the same thing over and over again and expecting a different result'. Of all insane defined injustices impeding the creation of the new world are these issues right here, still apparent, still confronting and perpetuated by ego, unjust selfishness, arrogance, and ignorance in a world where the self-proclaimed righteous are themselves acting unrighteously.

On a collective path to universal, sustainable, and spiritual global abundance is by having leaders and teachers who are old souls. These few are chosen for the tenure that possesses the tenable skills and integrity to work in accordance to living by and through their pure soul dimension which means the realm to be deemed justly fit and accountable to lead any nation. A proud moment it would be to witness earth's abundant destiny achieved for this most worthy, beautiful, and precious planet. There is only one earth and one shot at saving it, without haste.

'We hasten to allow flow, the child is scolded instead. 'You must think, you must do, you must act, you must achieve, strive to be something decent for it is why you are here!'

Amongst the tears and ruined heart, beneath the charade, placed within the pages of fiction, the child exclaims, 'I am all that I am, this is me and I am at that place now, I never left and it is here I will always stay – let me be, I am that more fully blessed than you know, I am free and father I want the same for thee!' – JahAnanda

Know heaven then be it

If there is an underlying and perhaps subtle message made as an offering, as a silver lining. By broadening and awakening the vision and wisdom of mankind and his destined path, is realising that rather than waiting for Jesus' impending return, that *'you be the change'*. Whilst they await the return of 'their' Messiah, unconscious souls are besieged to live their lives ravaged with worry, fear, greed and their ego. Controlling one another or being controlled themselves, and suffering. In the meantime, they rely on religious prophesies to duly save themselves.

The suffering of the planet has gone on unrelentingly for thousands of years, so why wait for the return of the Messiah? If He or She did arrive wouldn't they be pleased to see the good work already done? Know this; 'they' have already been arriving. Religious theologians, self confessed Christians, and many unfulfilled and unconvinced unconscious souls are awaiting a saviour, a Messiah, or a God to save their souls when in fact the Godly power to *'be the change'* is already and indelibly lying within each and every being within one's own self, in their own hands, your own hands, to beginning right now.

Once religious scriptures are interpreted and understood purely as contextual, metaphoric, and symbolic interpretations, then the establishment of the new earth, as is transcribed by Apostle John in Revelations, and trusting also the beliefs of intuitive pure souls, it can then rightfully begin.

Rather than allow the consciousness to believe, be fooled, delve, enter into, and listen to the chastising and opinionated views, and in many cases, the hatred towards other religions. And persecution of rhetoric politicians and their opinions rather prefer to seek now to find the Buddha Consciousness, the Jesus Consciousness, the Muhammad Consciousness, the Godliness within you. When you awaken to the discovery of your own prophecy that you too possess the pureness of the soul, life will have meaning and become pleased that you had a part to play in bringing the new heaven on earth.

'The divinity of the pure soul, the un-abiding spirit, is always present, never judging, never detracting itself in inconspicuous seclusion. Foremost when the mind is open and free of callous impulsion and egoism, the clarity of choices and its journey reveals the souls truth and purpose, provided to stay true to the fundamental direction and path of the higher quadrant of the mind' ~ JahAnanda

Money

~ Money is not a sin, tis how one uses it, wisely or not, which determines whether there is an understanding of karmic law and abundance.

Everyone at some point in their lives thinks about winning the jackpot. Whether it is the lottery or casino, sports or racing pools, people search for happiness through monetary means. When someone thinks about what they would do if they did win a large sum of money they will think perhaps of a new house, a new car, or even two cars, several trips away, shopping, or buying something special for a loved one, family or friends and giving to a charity. Many people splash out and even put some away into an investment account or trust fund. It may give a feeling of short-term happiness and often it refuses to become self perpetuating as is witnessed in the lives of people who have found conditional happiness and have felt also the pain of emptiness when they come to realise that happiness isn't found in monetary and material prosperity.

If someone is lucky enough to win any money they believe that what they will do with money will make them feel happy. However, what they are really wanting to experience is not the material homes, cars, new teeth, exotic trips, or investments. It is being in a position whereby they can simply experience the feeling of having the money. Money is just paper after all and what it offers is purely a feeling, a feeling of contentedness, a feeling that can be accessed by manifesting it already from the soul in spite of looking outside the consciousness. Any feeling one wants and desires can inevitably be achieved purely by changing to a preferred manifested vibration by having it already and being in the self perpetuating state of feeling gratitude, joy, compassion, unconditional love, peace, goodwill, and happiness becomes. Take a look at the faces of children and families, who live in impoverished homes, they emulate their joy and their happiness in their waking hours and in their sleep. They don't know what lies beyond their dimension of bliss wishing and desiring a new house, a new car, a plush fancy restaurant or a tropical holiday each year to instil their happiness. They already have it and as long as they have love for all their blessings, their loved ones and themselves, they simply are happiness.

Simply by being in synch and understanding the power of the mind and the laws of abundance that can be felt and experienced without the need for money and by ensuring and actively manifesting and living it as a self perpetuating vibration, the feeling remains fulfilling long term, the same feeling attained in the absence of things outside. The thing the soul awakened finds regarding happiness is that it is through their accumulation of things that they realise it wasn't in things after all.

'Misuse and greed, think of it like a sword, something to fall on if delinquency prevails.' ~ JahAnanda

It is not in material assets or investments, or trips to provide happiness but rather, the feeling felt for as we know it doesn't require money at all. Believing that it will arrive in the future will always bring the peaceful state back to the worrying, stressful, tiresome, fearful state.

Just 'be happy, be it' and 'remain being it' at this moment right now, take the thoughts away from everything, take a deep breath and relish this state of presence and reflect that state inside and outside. Comfort is a perspective and being comfortable is held by a state of appreciation rather than the desire to accumulate more things in order to feel more comfortable to feel happier. By following this simple manifestation I could relish presence constantly with this strategy and aligning to the karmic law and the laws of abundance reflect or mirror any vibration. Conversely, if money is abused say for buying drugs, power, stolen property, or wasting it on alcohol or extravagance in a wild tempestuous manner the karmic and abundance laws will immediately work accordingly mirroring thoughts, actions and manifestations and in no time at all it will feed those desires further, and as quickly, it will be gone.

Dreams

Dreams have for many centuries have held a mystical quality about them which mankind, cultures, and certain religions have attempted to understand and interpret their 'messages.

They belong to the form of the subconscious and the higher mind realm state.

The subtle and not so subtle meanings that come into the crevices of the deep consciousness in sleep have a guiding role to play in the life of the soul. They may appear as parabolic, playful, or sometimes frightening messages within subtle or completely abstract form, nevertheless a dream can enlighten and reveal to the consciousness a key descriptive to a particular 'story' that is being played out as a guide for ratification or quantifying. Each 'story' can be invariably, played out whether it is directly or indirectly connected to you, and what should be acknowledged is understanding to what aspect of the mind is playing in terms of being the 'interpreter' of the dream, whether it is the higher mind soul state or the irrationalising physical mind. They can both come together as interpreters, however the final analysis should always lay at the feet of the higher mind as the physical mind only has the ability to know 'what has happened', whereas the higher mind can illustrate more clearly 'what will or could happen' provided the interpretation is read, understood, and acted upon correctly.

Dreams in their abstract and sometimes perceivably confusing nature have indelibly planted an underlying message and direction from where the soul has been, how it has been affected or influenced, and can help shed light to the path going forward based on the natural state of being-ness in which the mind and hearts intentions it wishes to embody. It is at this critical phase of impartiality where the truth of the message is interpreted and used as a helpful guide to one's life for any dream to have a consequential benefit.

They may appear in a multitude of different forms from animals, birds, serpents, cosmic dimensions, friends, family, and past acquaintances including relationships and scenarios such as fear, or flying, falling, heavenly apparitions, disasters, water, the earth, the natural environment, bodily parts, and also conscious states of simple awareness.

Nightmares for example, will commonly expose an unconscious soul state of underlying fear reflecting an aspect of a person's life. Normally, it requires courage with a logical and simplistic approach to the nature of one's life without any fear or need to suffer however an answer to it will perpetuate and present itself with calmness and an open objective mind to equate the meaning that it is providing. They do not signify doom and despair as these apparitions remind the mind to remain connected to the soul whereby the soul asks the enquiring mind 'what does this thought doom and despair mean? The soul knows that these states are lost illusional conditions, that there is a deeper more innocent, productive and concise meaning that nightmares provide.

Dreams can in most cases, be lost from the memory very quickly after sleep is disturbed and it is suggested to have a pad and pencil beside you when you waken. In the busy world that one allows in this age there is a tendency to rush out of sleep and prepare for the day however the key to recalling dreams more clearly is to wake slowly, saviour what is being experienced and even during waking keep the dream close. Keep handy a pencil and note pad beside your bed and write down the key points as 'bullet points' from the dream. Once you have the main points written down, the dream will store and be retrievable in the mind more easily to analyse and interpret at that moment or later.

Offerings of Love

As these eyes cast the world from which I returned, the heavenly pureness beyond, and within them in Nirvana, the paradise of humility and bliss, a land of co-creators of love, souls who lived from their heart, as souls of revealed light. Exuding light and adoring. Justified in just simply Being, from this resonance of passion they drew themselves to remaining in peace, and relishing the light in their world they created, radiated the rapturous fulfilment for their love drew so much more of which love comprised.

In the street, in houses, their lives, their pains and fear, their relentless ego surging and obeying, feeding one another the gaps in their lives of which silence would have been the most adequate answer. Outside of silence the matted words and verbs of fear, the impudence of the maligned ego, the fight to reach out for love, to grasp as if it were concealed or out of reach, when it was lying already in them. As human nature subsists, it has learned and chosen realms of their lives unconsciously. By Yin and Yang, by light and dark, by pain and pleasure, to walk a narrow footbridge across a ravine or to wear a life jacket, or to put ones hand inside the cage of a panther, instinctively they know the outcome. If mankind on this earth permit themselves that something far greater exists and if they just knew that it wasn't 'out there' and out of reach, that it was already within to draw deep into their soul and reveal the glistening gem of their true joy they too can apply Yin and Yang to revealing more and wash away their pain.

The world might sell out; you don't have to ~ JahAnanda

Your embellishing mantle of joy can take great pleasure beyond the sacrosanct temperament of your love, like helping someone across the road, or inviting them to eat with you, or by just telling someone that you love them. The joy of sharing the gift of simply 'Being' with them, to sit together in presence together, in silence, and realising that you can communicate beyond thoughts with pure existence and peace. Relishing in your awareness and acquainting from the body to the soul, that this place really is ok. A difficult task made effortless by just living and being love within, from each breath, every heart beat; for that is where the earth provides itself to you, the seed, to grow a forest, the same forest you make by planting the same seed into the soil of the galvanising acquainted soul of those who see your light. ~ JahAnanda

For it is the soul where all precious gems are found, a heavenly land from where love resides, where romance and passion astound and lift the heart, and others, with the gifts you bring. The music you play and the portraits you paint, the brilliance and creations your soul desires, you will serve beyond not just you but for the world and wherever your dreams take you, for your devoted love will fill that place and afar. For this catalyst to sing, the song must in you already be sung, for the world needs to hear your voice, feel your rhythm and draw toward your elation. And when they bend an ear to hear the sound, you know that sooner or sooner still, your heart will be heard.

The new earth will be this above apocalyptic revelation or apocalypse itself. Whence they hear the sound of your heart beating the drum of love and what it holds by observing your peace. As they search for vestiges of ego or puffed up devotion, sooner they will trust that purist love is void of such self-worth and want to learn of the wisdom that love brings. Curse of the unconscious sufferings, the riddled and foiled, fighting to live and too who live to fight. Where fear strangles the minds, the same minds who fear losing more, and that holding and battling with their greed whilst setting free the answer they hold close, waiting to lend a hand, to help them let go of the noose they thought was valid to live a happy life. To feel blessed that you brought them to this place where the fight out of fear exists not, for within these walls lay solace and appreciation; to learn of the acquaintance and the relationship to peace, to learn the gifts love brings from the relinquished free soul.

For the greatest revelation you can convey is to reveal the revelation in your heart no less, and like a wild fire you will envelope this land all because of the joy and peace you bring. They will choke on your love until they cough up their fears and empty their life's abominable toil until they take a deep breath and open their awakened heart and taste the freedom of bliss brought by you. And by your sincerity and warmth that you laid at their feet, their eyes find the path that wasn't before there, they will touch the life of another and the wild fire you gave will set the whole world alight.

What they thought under the thousands of rocks they saw in their lives was the key to their happiness, the material ones and the uncanny disguises for the vacant mind to see. The Jones's can have their corporate stress and they can kick their cat too, and whilst his team work on a dead end road of dreams and hope, believing that toil was the key to being free. Yet we must keep up with the people, those whom we want them to admire us too as the noose round the neck pulls much tighter and the fear of being dead lies subtley ahead.

The mind tis like a new puppy or an inquisitive two year old child full of wonder and escapade, as innocent as the spring of which the mind pleads itself to be. It will seek out more joy and disregard any suffering it may bring where love of the soul possesses wisdom the same wisdom which consciousness allows the heart to lead always and for the mind to stay silent and remain. ~ JahAnanda

'This is your year. Don't relent, bend, falter, or adjust your soul plan to fit the ideals of young soul myriads on this Earth for they will weigh you down . . . they have many lifetimes to ascend yet, and you cannot wait for them or anyone. You at this time are already there. Be a miserably domiciled delinquent of penchant authenticity, radical freedom and voluptuous expression, and let the rain fall mercilessly down until you say stop. The weak souls will cast their eye waiting to hear you call out and pass over waiting to see you falter, and you would have played your role for them and for you. No-one makes it happen in this life for you, only you. Life is so very, very short, so make each breath count and don't count on them for your next breath. Live with truth and know that you will never die in the garden of bliss' ~ JahAnanda

Blessed awakened souls are free to choose their own highest joy ever more preferable if it is found in their work, as long as it is true, a source of giving that hurts no-one. It is the greatest freedom of all. Enjoy. Peace. Love, Be.' ~ JahAnanda

Know this. You are more a being than the flesh, bone, feet, hands and blood that you see. You are an energy field, a radiance of immeasurable power and inconceivable wisdom and knowledge through which the very nature of your Life's Journey, Your Path is laid out infinitely more than what you are actually seeing and believing in your constrained belief of limited reality. It is time to let go, with courage, of the 'old you' and step from the confines of the disturbed and untrue' ~ JahAnanda

'Here lies within us, fears to heal of which we must face; and a sleeping giant of love that yearns inside to be awakened and nourished with every breath, understood to ascertain for it to be love, must be given to be true.' ~ JahAnanda

'You are given just this one life at this moment, why live being someone else when God gave you all that you require, He designed to make YOU already great. Trust.' ~ JahAnanda

'Pure souls are lovers of art. If you believe that you are not then ask yourself 'what is art?' Should you still not agree then your time here has expired. 'Life IS art and life is beautiful and art is the expression of its beauty' ~ JahAnanda

'When the beauty of a flower reveals to the consciousness, or the wonder of a painting from a child, or the blessed-ness of a dew drop in the morning sun glistening, an awakening will reveal money has no meaning in life's journey whatsoever, and freedom refuses to permit that it was ever so.' ~ JahAnanda

'Belief changes any experience. And being masters of destiny is manifested by the mind, physical, or higher, from the soul, from this position one can mould, change, radiate, or project more or less of the reality created by the stable and soulful belief state that the pure conscious mind desires to following the path along ones higher joy and excitement. If doubt precedes which belief is preferred or not then it is best to remove all beliefs and remain as pure thoughtlessness and then you will know which path then to take.' ~ JahAnanda

'A master of one's destiny is the one who thinks, breathes, listens, feels, smells and visualises. The author of materialising ones destiny is he who believes thoughts to be owned rather than purely observed in awareness, whether it being at peace, in love, appreciative, humble, or compassionate, or whether it is misery of being controlled, self loathing, humiliation, illness, distrust, or hatred. Be conscious of what is believed as the power of intention will surmise your requests on a silver platter graced between gold or what you choose not.' ~ JahAnanda

'Freedom does not seek the existence of another person to set them free. It lies always embodied as one with the consciousness. Constrict in the belief that belies any attempt to prove otherwise is merely ones belief that a boulder has blocked ones path. The boulder is nothing but ego, the chain which anchors it is nothing but the mind. Hold close to your heart awareness, for that is the unmistakable truth. Let peace flow from the revelation that freedom never left, only the door of one's mind allowed the perception of something that was never there but freedom itself. Now fly and stay free!' ~ JahAnanda

The miracle of alchemy or that of walking on water, or turning water into wine is not what this world wants to manifest change. The miracle is mastering the art of impermanence; touching our feet upon the earth, embracing the beauty of a flower, the pureness in a new born baby's eyes, the invisible force through the bending trees in a breeze, the song in your heart. There is no judgement here, only that of grace and happiness. Stay here forever. Never leave. The world will follow soon. The miracle created by you.' ~ JahAnanda

Have the courage to let go of those whom you are not resonating to, and the things in life that do not matter or cultivate true happiness as the liturgy to Gods wisdom. Be it materialism, hatred, money, self indulgence and war. Lay down your symbolic olive branch and seek the knowledge and wisdom as depicted in apostle Pauls letter in Romans 11:23,24 He explains: 'They (natural Jews) also, if they do not remain in their lack of faith, will be grafted in; for God is able to graft them in again. For if you were cut out of the olive tree that is wild by nature and were grafted contrary to nature into the garden olive tree, how much rather will these who are natural be grafted into their own olive tree!'

'At times of any earnest struggle, cometh crucial challenges when there are mountains to scale that must be conquered. The greater the pain of our struggles is determined by the perception of it being relative to our will, of the fighting spirit. For the will and of the knowing; of true and undying faith gives anyone, absolutely anyone has the strength to attain that in which knowledge and self realisation brings us at the gates of Bodhisattva and onwards towards this, our enlightened journey.' ~ JahAnanda

'There's no validity or truth to dying a thousand deaths over something in the future. Ultimately, it will fade like the blink of an eye compared to the timelessly greater torture of enlisting worry as your friend. For a man who masters worry fails to master himself, but a man who masters trust masters his undying faith in his destiny.' ~ JahAnanda

Visualisation essentially is that which stimulates all the senses. Never insular or alone, it stands equally and unabated through sound, touch, smell, in prayer and manifested meditation. Recognise that not all stimulation is the same for other soul brothers and sisters. Imagination is the seed, and visualisation is exercising the seeds of imagination through manifestation. Visualisation is changing the vibration, the feeling, the state of having the goals manifested already in your life in this present moment, and by being happy and having them felt in the emotive form. Perception, will, and the universal realm of the intelligence, keep playing with it, mould it, and allow it to materialise naturally, effortlessly using the Law of the Universal Mind and the Law of Attraction. A way upon the realisation to revealing Heaven on the Earth, it starts from within and like a ripple from a pebble tossed into a pool, it radiates out. Be the pebble of love first in You. ~ JahAnanda

'Feelings of the heart lets the love body know of its connection to the soul, the pure soul.' ~ JahAnanda

'When a challenge, a sticking point, or a mind or mental block occurs, let it go, let it flow . . . in its own time the power of what you seek will return and fill you up naturally, effortlessly, radiantly. Know who God really is. Much frustration, perhaps hesitancy, worse still giving up even, causes only more dis-ease within the mind because we allow the mind to take control by forcing it.

The analogy is like trying to force a square peg into a round hole. It is about releasing and laying more manifested seeds to desires and accepting 'what is' to receiving more which is a paradox truth to coercing the physical mind to do a function it is unadapted to perform. The higher the unabated disembodied consciousness views the platform to receive more clearly than the physical minds entity is able to cope or deal with. To catch fish, you must first throw out your net, just let it go. Let your heart fill the truth of your desires for there are many paths your soul seeks. ~ JahAnanda.

'When we are faced with any kind of challenge in life there is a human desire to search for an answer outside of ourselves. Look deep inside your heart first. Place peace and appreciation at your door in all that surrounds you. Give to yourself, and the world unblemished kindness and reverent love. Practise solemn undying faith, for the answer reveals in giving eternally. That is the paradox of life' ~ JahAnanda

"Suis ton coeur, pour que ton visage brille durant le temps de ta vie." "I am your heart, so that your face shines during the time of your life." ~ JahAnanda

When we allow our true light to shine, it is the difference between accomplishment and that of laying your legacy of light amongst the stars that will shine on earth and mankind forever' ~ JahAnanda

If it speaks to you solemnly, expressively to your heart, it can only be the
    guidance from that of God.
If truth sits at your feet, then never let your feet stop walking the path of
    truth,
And should you stop, let it be to close your eyes quietly to give praise,
and humble expression of the thanks to your existence and appreciation
    to God.
For God lives in every one of us,
And let God's love fill your heart ~ JahAnanda

Happiness foremost is an inside job' ~ JahAnanda

'When we are threatened . . . In solidarity and meditation, our collusion together as peaceful spirits focuses our intentions on remaining calm, still, holding close the essence of self love and projecting love unconditionally to all beings regardless of their actions and intentions.' ~ JahAnanda

'Self becomes relevant when thoughts are understood to be irrelevant. Thoughts, even inspiring or powerful thoughts exempt of truth fade in time . . . . they are only beliefs, but they are not that of the evolving self of BEing-ness that is YOU' ~ JahAnanda

'Impulses and guidance are quantified when it comes from a place of unconditional love. The more truth one becomes inside the heart, the authenticity of the vibration radiates and reflects multiplicity to mirror those who seek and align to the change taking place on the planet. The power of change comes from heartfelt love for one another.' ~ JahAnanda

Recognition of what is 'Amazing' . . . this benediction, this discovery of truth in its nakedness comes in meditation, the presence of Being. When nothing gets in the way, when the mind is empty of intention, identification, notion, and expectation, intelligence flows into pureness of total peace' ~ JahAnanda

The body is mortal, the consciousness however is immortal. What matters more in maintaining peace, inner peaceful quality of entrenched vibration harmony. Is seeing and feeling our consciousness for what it IS. Not what we or anyone else wants it to be. It is pure, it is alive. It is YOU' ~ JahAnanda

'Your dreams come to fruition in a powerful and distinct way when eternal gratitude is the foundation sitting upon the rock of unconditional love and compassion for others in every breath you take, enveloped in the light of undying faith' ~ JahAnanda

'Self love is the seed in which true compassion and love for all others can be planted. Even those who may hate you or show anger, jealousy, or contempt towards you, what we feel inside in remaining at peace, and loving at all times, is fundamental truth. We can only give love and show compassion to others until we first truly love our self. Selfishness is allied to traits such as materialism, anger, greed, and hatred. This is the opposite of self love. The love of one's-self, above anything else, is critical within the state of understanding and practise until ones journey of self discovery can truly begin.' ~ JahAnanda

'If anything can be considered the most treasured value in life, it is that of making mistakes. The greatest achievers relied on persistence in the knowledge that each mistake they encountered meant they were that much closer to finding the answer, the goal, their dream. For nothing was ever gained by being perfect. Imperfection is humanities and Gods 'perfection' that. It is the prerequisite to being the greatest achiever you know that is the essence of who you are and always will be.' ~ JahAnanda

'When external stress and suffering afflicts the mind, it is not external situations that reinstates presence of inner peace rather, making a conscious choice to feel inner peace within.' ~ JahAnanda

'The past is unchangeable. There is no reason to feel remorse, regret nor is there substance in trying to repair what's done. It happened for a reason beneficial to your journey's unfolding. The door of joy, happiness, excitement, enlightenment and discovery now awaits you. Behold my child, to be blessed with the courage to just walk through it. The nature to heal lies to what you do right now' ~ JahAnanda

'There is a place from which, when the heart takes over and moves mountains and the brain and its ego hangs itself out to dry, in amazement from its dictatorship puzzled how it occurred. That love created the heart and God created, not love, for God IS love' ~ JahAnanda

'When we realise life's journey is absent of material possessions, money, power, animosity towards others, hatred, judgement, greed, patriotism, worry, insecurity of what is lacking in our self, and life. True meaning comes from knowing unconditional love, self love, preservation and protection of our earth, and the conscious state of being through the pureness of gratitude, faith, prayer, meditation, and compassion for others. We will then embark on the first step in knowing who we truly are and the true fundamental purpose of life begins.' ~ JahAnanda

'Like a rose petal, touched by the morning suns dew, gently cascading, it falls, two and fro til it touches the outstretched arms of our Earth Mother below, whence born, we are blessed.

Dear Mother, other than warmth, love and nurture I ask. I seek only to be loved, like any other new soul to this Earth we are born with all the skills we need to follow our chosen and blessed path, entrusted by God through the eternal light from which we have always shone. Peace is the stillness of our offering, enshrined eternally' ~ JahAnanda

'Imagination is more important than what is learnt, intellect has contributed and amassed very little for this Earth, hard work is a proverb, soul direction is pronouncement' ~ Namaste. ~ JahAnanda

'La conscience ne consiste pas à chercher constamment des réponses sous les rochers mais la reconnaissance et permettre à son cœur d'agir comme une porte ouverte, un conduit, prêt à recevoir tout ce qui est. C'est le lancer du regard, le souffle embellisseur, l'assemblement de la pensée, l'esprit satisfaisant, les sens évocateurs. Ses compagnons sont la foi et l'acceptation, . . . Sa luminosité, qu'elle provienne du Bouddha, de Dieu, ou de l'Univers, étale devant vous, le voile interrogateur des dimensions parallèles et variées de la vérité, à votre porte.' ~ JahAnanda

'The song of the ocean never sleeps. Sultry, ever alluring, it seeks to soothe, speaks in reminiscent whispers of peace, of solitude, of reverence, of love. It touches your soul as it knocks at your door . . . all it asks is truth and in return it will light your way.' ~ JahAnanda

'Your heart is your deepest sanctuary; your inner peace of love. Guard it with your life from seething tongues and reckless souls. Sing songs of joy, and poems of love; ascend to the light of the enlightened, lay in the arms of the uplifted, and melt in the glory that is you.' ~ JahAnanda

'Man has become emptier, poverty stricken, more accountable to the system of things, out of temptation and Evading Gods Order. Zacchaeus found peace and happiness once he found true happiness was absent of things' ~ JahAnanda

'Whatever disturbs your vibrational harmony; don't walk away from it, don't hold negativity towards it. Make peace with it. Realign your discourse so that you re-tap back into source that the universe wants for you, as long as you clear out that which you choose not and begin receiving what you truly desire and enjoy in your life that you do want. That is aligning to your truth, your inner being; it is reacquainting you back to who you truly are. Make peace and feel the energy flow once again.' ~ JahAnanda

'In the stillness of early dawn, meditate and give praise. Place your soul in peaceful silence amongst the birdsongs at play. God lays before you serenity detached far from the madding crowd; for nothing is more blessed than the peace within you.' ~ JahAnanda

'What is paranormal is not what's contained in the 'what's out there' universe; but what isn't. There is no 'out there' until the blessed soul in you is discovered first. Contained within mans very own meek existence of his work, worry, survival, ego, fight or die complex. The dexterity of mans evolution has created who we are today as we sit proud of our achievements nevertheless . . . yet quietly ashamed to admit, we still don't know what we don't know and look desparingly at what the world has become.' ~ JahAnanda

'Live your life with reverence and utmost respect. Only then can you know the thankfulness and love in the reverence and respect you give to others' ~ JahAnanda

'In physical reality, time is everywhere where the rat-race runs, where conditioning and deadlines strain the soul. The New Age will again seek to use the sun and the stars, and that of the moon for they are our clocks. For time in reality is infinite and present, not seconds and minutes but accepting, allowing, and knowing timelessness.' ~ JahAnanda

'If being happy is about fighting with an ego, a car, a luxurious home, travel, money, or the way to appear on the outside to impress others, then why are there more problems, more war, more insecurity, more unsettling of the mind, more destruction of the planet, more worry, more fear, more hatred, more anguish, more injustice, more divorces, more suffering and more un-happiness? . . . Are they just illusions or is it that the key to happiness isn't really found in material things and fighting one another in order to be and feel happy? Has the planet arrived full circle that in spite of searching it has eluded man still? After all the science, after all the scepticism of what was always known of what happiness was, yet succumbed to allow what was thought of as truth; to trust in those whom was thought to know the answer and believed in them and trusted them more and at the end of the day, it wasn't really there and apparent in 'things'?

In spite of the illuminated few who control the agony of the world, happiness remains to this day a state of mind. No matter how one is affected outside one's own conscious state of inner peace, happiness nevertheless remains as a timeless state of appreciation. Never let it leave your side. Grant yourself peace as YOU are the centre of the universe, your universe, your truth. The dimension all enveloped in a deeper love you thought not so. It does exist. Love listens, love is pure. It begins with you loving you. Reflect the states you dream, the state of your dreams reside at the seat of your heart, your guides, your desires, and the pureness of your soul. Let your happiness be fuelled by your journey to know a greater love and your deepest desire to remain always at peace. To allow gratitude to BE you, like a river always finds the sea. Let love keep you safe for nothing but excitement and joy of you being the greatest You. Celebrate always, be blessed and Rejoice' ~ JahAnanda . . .

'Being indebted eliminates anger, dissolves worry, accepts and realigns one's self to the purpose of truth. It opens the doors of abundance to flow, filling the heart, deserving of humility. It is the seed to meditation to finding peace and discovering inner sanctity of one's true self. Being loving unreservedly is not the path to which thankfulness comes but rather being thankful is the door to knowing love beyond no other. Live always a life of appreciation and trust what is yours.' ~ JahAnanda

Miracles Abound

On the 13th of October 2010, the world has been waiting and praying for this momentous occasion as 33 Chilean miners undertake their 'final journey' one by one in a vehicle called the Phoenix from almost a kilometre beneath the earth.

Let this incredible story of love and faith resonate to all of us who take for granted the unsurmountable blessings that we all have in our hands. To have the right each and every day to give thanks and living with unconditional love and to be humbly grateful to the knowledge that we too can be reborn. In times like this, one's life comes to a crossroad. Life has not changed, but the true perspective of one's own life no matter what has occurred. If you were given six months to live, oh how the knoweth of one's purpose to life and love reveals. These men's lives will never be the same again. Be this story shared with mankind that life is truly a gift and not to take one day for granted. Live each day like it is your last, life means so much more.' ~ JahAnanda.

'Life's journey isn't meant to be always how we want it to be. Flagrance trussed with turmoil and digression reveals its light in time. The serenity of downstream peace we find when we hold our sanctity and conviction that only our belief in faith and trusting to what the universe will reveal to the awakened one. In the meantime be patient and indebted, as they are your lights.' ~ JahAnanda

'The earth may see our ancestors as primitive. In centuries to come 20th and 21st century man will be considered primitive as those who endured self sacrificial manifestations endured through this time, this Age, The Age of Limitation.' ~ JahAnanda

'Awareness is not about constantly searching under rocks for answers but the acknowledgement and allowing the heart to be an open door, a conduit to receive all that is. It is the eye casting, the breath adorning, the thought gathering, the spirit fulfilling, the senses feeling. Its companions are faith and acceptance. Its light, whether it be Buddha, God or the Universe lays before you the wondrous veil of parallel and assorted dimensions of truth at your door.' ~ JahAnanda

'The mysticism of the eternal tugs always to the seekers of truth in that the path of now lies immortally entrenched beside the river of love that flows to the requiem songs of the ancient ones' ~ JahAnanda

'There is nothing that is more important to our existence than imagination. Imagination is who we are, what we are, what we feel, what we become. If we can understand the real power of faith and belief, through disciplined purpose of following joy and excitement in our hearts . . . . we will never question the road we travel ever again.' ~ JahAnanda

'You are so much more than what you think and believe you are. God and the Universe want you to know this. The story you read is written by others, believed by you, a novel of untruths through solitude lost. Write your own in a hardcover of faith and gold. Appreciation and humility and unconditional love are your kings, your queens, your masters. Believe in the ecstatic essence you are in this moment, without judgment or fear . . . celebrate your uniqueness, there is no-one quite like you! Allow now, your pages to unfold.' ~ JahAnanda

Life's contrasts is like the pristine ocean, a panacea of glistening beauty, vastness to wonder, solemn in its pleasures, courage tried, tossed in torrential turmoil, peaceful in its depths of silence, resplendent with nourished souls, soothing when nature seeks its stillness forced upon its aching limb. ~ JahAnanda

If it is said, 'The sky's the limit', then tell me, why are there footprints on the moon? Be careful what you read or listen to, you just might believe it. If it is said, 'To think outside the square, know this to be true. There is no square' ~ JahAnanda

'It is not the length of time that brings an understanding of someone you care to fruition, but the time spent absent of hurt, judgement, fear, anger, despair and egoistic delvement of. It is the time spent with hearts open, forever devoted, unlimited of timeless ritual, expressed sharing entwined with love for everlasting, like the meeting of your twin flame, you've known them forever yet you've only just met in this moment.

You may have friends who say they have known you for 10, 20, 30 years or more and they say they know you; the fact of the matter is THEY DO NOT. Time is only physical world illusion, timeless connections flow eternally.' ~ JahAnanda

'Knowing who we really are begins through the process of divine meditation, prayer, faith, patience, structured and disciplined elements of daily ritual, committed for a day, a month, a year, a lifetime. Absent of the past, of who you think you are in the eyes of others. Absent of your perception of what the future may unfold. Be still, be silent, be nothing but free. In time the truth will reveal. In the empty darkness of space and time, practise this, even if you feel nothing, be at peace, comfortable with it, and when the universe is ready for you to receive your gift, you will then know. The virtual offering of one's own patience towards inner peace will arrive. The light to which will transform not what you want to be, but what you always were. Beneath the layers of conditioned futility evading Gods order. You will know when you have arrived. The knowing, the knoweth. Deliverance abiding.' ~ JahAnanda

'If you don't love yourself, you cannot truly love others with the heart of the loved. When one hates another, they hate only themself. When one complains, it reflects their own pain, the vibration created unjust, when others are creating in making the world a better place. When one shows anger or exposes their struggles up stream, against the flow, what does it serve? Peace, unreserved love, humility, respect for all beings, brings abundance, joy and happiness in this world of co-creators. Downstream is effortless harmony, it is peace to the heart, peace to the soul, where beauty within and outward is born. It radiates out into the cosmos, and the universe, and God smiles back at his creation made in His image. That is always His plan for the future, I see.
And it will be.' ~ JahAnanda

'By loving who you are and in creating the things or the alignment you want whether it is appreciation, joy, abundance, peace, love, or excitement in your life; then practice being kinder to yourself. Let go of the 'baggage' of what people think you are. Laugh more, play more. And not only will you enjoy the process along the way, you will accomplish the offering made to the one. The kill two birds with one stone theory as co-creators, exponentially the convergence will cause the explosion of critical mass you were a part of. And through your vibrational alignment in trusting your higher mind, your divine faith and your love, the new earth will be born, before it is too late.' ~ JahAnanda

'Revelation of truth lies deep within the soul. In the illusion, the calamity, the ego, and senseless chatter of the mind; of fear, despair, anger, matted and entwined so tight. When it is time, the time will be it, to cast all aside, trembling and naked. We never die, yet we die a thousand 'deaths', but all is merely illusion, til we awaken to the truth, as it comes home to rest.' ~ JahAnanda

'The day of your birth, the coming of you, a celebration, a wondrous occasion to rejoice, and celebrate. Celebrate it as equally as any of your days. Worthy is life, as giving as the sun, and as blessed as the moon. The divine and solemn reason to celebrate life, a blessed purpose to revel in your being; recreating, reliving. Re-born each day, welcome, welcome, welcome!' ~ JahAnanda

'Give credit and appreciation to you, to the blessedness of your love, your thoughts, your work, and your consequences.' ~ JahAnanda

Life is so very short, and before you realise how fast the years have gone rushing by, consider this. Living your life to make others happy is a dead-end road unless you first love you yourself above anything. Avoid listening to the chatter of others criticisms attempting in succumbing your inner desires and dreams. Follow your heart, live with passion, laugh so hard you pee, be truthful to yourself, never take things personally and practise every day with appreciation to the absolute, with love in your heart. The rest in life is just drama and baggage, just drop it and be free. ~ JahAnanda

'Allow the unequivocal, peaceful mind to observe the one who is larger than life, for in their quiet moments, themselves to be less sure of themself.' ~ JahAnanda

Strength in this time of world events and Mother Nature's vengeance, we want more of everything; money, happiness, compassion, and love. However the paradox is actually the reverse. It is simply having the strength to let go. Let go of envy, let go of ego, let go of materialism, let go of greed and let go of what your neighbour, your world, and what the mind is believing. Listen closely to the feelings and the beating desires of the heart. Letting go of the lies and idiocy requires no strength at all, simply the courage to do it. ~ JahAnanda

CHAPTER 11

Where to from Here? ~ *Its Hellish!*

One of the most common questions asked to me was 'did you see hell for if you didn't repent surely you must have?'

'The place, I explained, was heavenly. It was like no other beautifully serene, peaceful, and colourful world I had ever seen, and yet, I was a sinner. It was familiar, like I'd been there before, but not was it on this earth. There were beautiful faces glowing with light, in light, full of light. There were trees, and flowers, mountains and fields more colourful than this earth. But more than that, there was this ever present, totalling embellished and overwhelming presence of love.

To say it is like the love that is felt when we fall in love, or when we hold our new born child in our arms for the very first time. Or when we see the light in a little baby's eyes, or when a little cub or baby whale snuggles to suckle to its mother. Or the heartfelt pride in seeing your child's eyes light up when they receive an award, for they are all striking and breathtaking expressions of love. Love more powerful, even words cannot express, but this love was more and even much more than that. It is found only in this place yet, I did eventually arrive to this place they call Hell.

It was true what I'd heard, and more horridly that could prepare a soul,
Who was looking to find.
There was hate and distrust, and fire like no other.
People dying and crying,
Their faces told of their tale.
There wasn't a man with horns growing out of his head,
Nor a pitched fork in his hands,
Nor was he red.

There were many,
Upon thousands of evil men and women hurting one another,
From mothers and fathers, children, sisters, and brothers,
There was stench in the air and muck on the ground,
The dying and the dead, their bodies lay all around.
Some were just hungry,
Holding their hands out to be fed,
Whilst others picked through their pockets wearing suits and smiling instead,
Their laughter was so scary,
Their greed was too ugly to dwell, and yet this place, it was a disgrace,
You could tell by the smell.

The stench was overwhelming,
Made me sick right down to my teeth,
I deserved to be here I thought,
For not repenting with fervent belief,
I hated to be there, I just wanted to be home,
I felt scared and oh so lonely,
I couldn't face anymore of this alone.

But I chose to be here, over heavens heaven above,
For the sake of those little children,
And mothers and fathers whom we love,
I accepted the agreement to forfeit heaven to enter hell,
But I would have thought of more than twice,
If I'd known how the torment I would dwell.

For the evil and deception, the ego and crime,
The selfish and angry, dictators, politicians all standing in line.
For this is the place,
The place they fear degrading worse of its worth,
For no other planet, heaven, or star, lives like this stench,
For this place that is known, as Earth,

For hell lies right here,
Hidden behind suits with pens of power and greed,
Whose eyes look left and right,
Forming powers with alliances to bleed,
The earth is just a place,
A place to squaller their harvested reaps of reward,
And suck off the helpless and poor,
To line their pockets, their boats, and their holiday homes,
Leaving the starving children lying dead at their door

So yes, I did go to hell, and after all was said and done,
To the hell that couldn't be worse than anywhere,
A place that makes laws by a gun

So I'm sorry I never repented,
I should have thought but never had a chance,
And now that I'm here my works to make a difference,
To bring heaven on this earth and while in this rain,
I shall dance.

'Hating is such an effort. It is like carrying around a heavy load of heartache, frowns, and wrinkles compared to love which is like floating on a cloud and raining flowers, rainbows and kisses.' ~ JahAnanda

'The nature of man kinds current situation by inflicting harm, control, hurt and war, upon others including mother earth determines the state, ridicule and primitiveness of mans thinking separate from his peaceful, harmonic, compassionate and loving state of its true soul.'. ~ JahAnanda

'When someone attacks, hurts, annoys, displeases, or disgusts you. In your heart, thank them for helping you gain a better understanding of yourself . . . for it is these souls who create the contrasts in your life to making you the unique person you are to see the beauty in everything regardless of any vibration they choose to emit.' ~ JahAnanda

The real truth, please reveal

Over the past few years since the reports have come out about the capture and death of Osama Bin Laden there appears deep resentment and hundreds of questions unanswered about the 9/11 attacks among the suffering of victims and their families. The seemingly supposed unusual constructed design of the collapses falling to the ground when other aircraft that have hit buildings remained standing, explosions heard on the lower floors and basements. The Pentagon suffering very minimal damage with no wreckage found whatsoever with claims that it had vaporised. That Israelis were found nearby the attacks in NYC at the time dressed as Arabs with documents pertaining to the attacks and certain government departments moved out from ground zero just weeks before the attacks. The list of questions will continue to continue but no matter who are the real perpetrators, they for now, will be kept safe.

What then was the real reason this man was made to look like the causal agent of 9/11, to defer attention from the real perpetrators? To close a number of deals perhaps oil related and alliance forming of the reaffirmed World Bank conglomerates? Whatever this compelling story shares, we think of Vietnam, Nazism, Fascism, Illuminati, Nuclear Energy and pollution of the planet, the displacement and murder of indigenous peoples. Here is a world which has generated more wealth in mankind's history yet paradoxically, there are more people living in poverty, hunger, and even in homes worldwide, people are struggling to survive.

The world knows it can survive without oil and nuclear energy so why the lure towards these dangerous commodities? Is it all about money and commodities or more specifically, the idea to creating a scarcity of a commodity to ensure its value is upheld to a market? Where the choice of a commodity is deep in the ground so it is out of reach of the market so if it is needed, it then has a price? And, by having a price to a commodity in demand, then wouldn't owners, refining companies, and countries generate enormous revenues from it in profit, taxes, and subsequent sales from it in spite of the pollution it creates to the world's environment?

Whatever happened to the renditions of old fashion values of simple honesty and accountability? If 911 was a big mistake, then shouldn't someone just own up? Nevertheless the past is the past, what has happened has happened and to help heal everything is through love and forgiveness for it conquers all. Jesus, Martin Luther King, Muhammad, Mahatma Gandhi, Mother Theresa, John Lennon all preached the same message. Imagine.

Energy

Serving human existence and life for thousands of years, energy has come a vast distance since fire and fur. Although Ra, our sun, has been in our galaxy for millions of years has driven and fed all life on this Earth by its light and energy, both spiritually and physically.

Its force is considered infinite by the energy it provides to humanity and to earth. It is also responsible for our weather and seasons including that of wind.

In spite of Ra's unlimited and sustainably puritan supply of solar, wind and light energy, the need to venture into the earth itself and to its limited gas and oil resources has largely been noticed purely as a means of profiteering. Laws are in place to control its development, not long after, using scarcity as a potential profiteering tool since the advent of the monetary system a great many years earlier.

The irony now is the unjustifiable need for finite energy resources to serving governments and rulers more so than people themselves when there are more sustainable energy systems which have been evident for over one hundred years. The way many countries view the costs of it as valid and the enormous returns they reap in passing on these costs to hard working families who just want to travel from point A to point B, or to warm or cool their homes, to heat water, and providing electricity to hospitals, factories, and other businesses is primarily because the world is lead to believe it is the only means available.

Has it not that the technology been prevalent for decades for hydrogen cars for example? Hasn't wind technology been available for decades where a hard working family can use another sustainable, renewable, non-polluting God given resource without the need for nuclear generation for electricity? Governments justify their stance that owning a home wind turbine causes noise pollution? Raucous or not, the noise the millions upon millions of cars, trucks, trains and planes emit would not compare. Just imagine the ease and amount of money a family would save each year on both these so called, scarce commodities and yet we are not talking about wind, sunlight, or water for they are free and non-polluting and sustainable. We are talking about oil, gas, and nuclear energy. There is a real possibility where a one world government will cease power over countries, nations and people, to control food, oil, water, and money in an attempt to crush the universal source of God given free energy thus widening the gap even further between the rich and poor.

Transportation

In the early 1900's Dr Ferdinand Porshe designed and developed one of the first prototype of its first electric hybrid motor. Not long after he designed and made one of the first hydrogen cars. It was also a revolutionary change to the new emerging and rapidly growing transport industry market.

With hydrogen being simply water, countries could also see that with hydrogen transportation technology, this would almost eliminate their ability to tax a commodity that is readily and easily available virtually at no cost whatsoever to the consumer after all, water as an energy source is practically everywhere, and it is free. This meant that governments and oil companies capacity to raking in trillions of dollars was being threatened so licensing laws were introduced to block hydrogen technology transportation to allow the mass production and rolling out of oil fuel cars instead for the average hard working household family. Governments, States, and countries could also see that by the fact of its scarcity, that they could control what price they put on it, as to a commodity that was generally free and easy to obtain is what the world is lead to believe. It does seem ironic that revolutionised hydrogen technology inventors suspiciously 'disappear' or are paid off handsomely to 'go away.'

"I am poor and naked, but I am the chief of the nation. We do not want riches but we do want to train our children right. Riches would do us no good. We could not take them with us to the other world. We do not want riches. We want peace and love."
-Chief Red Cloud (Sioux)

The World doesn't know what it doesn't know, and the world likes it like that.

If world powers choose to spend $100 million every hour on arms, just think what if that kind of money would do to solve poverty and suffering?

There is a resolve separate from what media hungry capitalists are 'fed' by government press releases to so-call mind sabotage its readers and consumers.

Are pharmaceuticals meant to be the new age medicine? Perhaps we can think again. Let us ask ourselves. Why are there barriers imposed on holistic, natural, indigenous medicines? Similarly, why are these barriers being enforced and made more difficult for growers to preventing their organic fruit and vegetables being sold on a corner street, in a market, or outside a grower's farm gate? And why is the paranoia prevalent to governments and powers that see medicinal, social, and medicinal hemp marijuana production as a threat? In the US it was advocated and compulsory for farmers to produce this delicately beneficial natural product and now it is hindered and difficult to gain a permit on their own land. Is it to brainwash society to believing that it is harmful? If it is, then can we ask them why? When they make comparisons to alcohol as being far fetchingly detrimental on society yet they feel compelled to gain extraordinary tax revenue on a commodity which used excessively socially and anti-socially yet as a result, causes more deaths on the road and in the home and in society. Who really funds pharmaceuticals and who supplies them to the people?

Who visits doctors, the everyday, the elderly, the young and hardworking people who are unconscious to the fact that they are being fed a short term solution to remain on a medication for the remainder of their lives which costs consumers directly and indirectly to purchase? More and more I began to look at life differently, openly, objectively and free of the sheep mentality that I and many other people had once possessed when it came down to our food, health, laws, and transportation. Continuously, there seemed an apparent belief that the world in general had this belief that freedom was abundant and that belief was less evident by the fact that the world was less free, that the congestive crisis of over population, the increase in chemical and industrial poisoning of what was once a harmonious and already complete God arranged medicinally organic planet. This demonstrates that mankind's leaders appear to divert this obviously acknowledgeable stance solely for the purpose of making money at the detriment of mankind and the future life and sustainability of the planet.

As a people, regardless of what purpose others have outside of this reality choose to commit, there is a resolve and reinstated importance of knowing the truth, and aligning to manifest with other likeminded souls, to seeing a 'heaven' on this earth. Living with undying kindness and consideration for all people including adversaries, serving to protecting the planets resources, and dissolving ego and greed and looking to helping and loving our fellow man. Overall it is freedom which is being jeopardised primarily to serve and underlined as a means to reaping taxation money for what?

Like a long chain of defensive rationale, at the end of the day the question 'what does that mean?' In opposition, by questioning where does the money go? And 'what does that mean?' who pays for it and 'what does that mean?' and 'what about the planet, what does it really mean to the future of the planet?' And who wins and who loses?' 'Why is there so much red tape and beauocracy? Why do planes spray chemical toxic aluminium in the skies, the poisons that the world thinks are harmless vapour trails?' 'Why does the most important news never make the news and what does that mean?' Is the world really being lead to believe that the occupants of this great land lives in a free world, with so many rules and regulatory obligations, charges, blockades and laws how can this be called a free world?' And, the world really hide a secret they don't want the people to know about the choking and rapidly rising world population crisis, hitting 9 billion people on the planet and soon growing well beyond that figure, guess how long it will take to double and reach 18 billion people and view how over populated the planet is right now?' 'So what will that mean?' Who makes the extra revenue in taxes as a result of the rising population and who gets the money, and what do they spend it on that you don't really know about? Where does the money come from that countries spend each year on warfare and rather than helping to feed the sick and the hungry and giving them an education and hope, then why are they ignored so they can buy guns, bombs and missiles instead? By not standing up to hapless governments, banks, dictators, rulers, Kings and Queens, where could the world be in 2025? How many more people will be killed by war, and how many men, women and children will die of starvation and malnutrition? By spending enormous amounts of money on space exploration when the world has done so much damage to this planet, do they really believe that they have the right to infiltrate and pollute space and other planets as well? How much of our natural forests will there be left and what animals will be extinct by 2025 because of sanctimonious greed and ignorance, where eventually the reality the world will not be able to feed itself? 'What would that mean?'

If heavenly love was a university degree that the world completed before they leave high school to be a parent, environmentalist, scientist, philosopher, ruler, a teacher, or a leader, what would that ultimately do to their path and this great planet? If all the world leaders met to meditate and pray to listen to Gods Plan, to learn of alignment and love, and they hugged their new brothers and sisters, what would that mean? And if the world's population was 4 Billion and everyone had grass and trees and gardens at their door and miles and miles of native forests and rainforests all around, and guns and bombs would no more be, where Nuclear Energy plants became merely monuments of an unforgotten period of ludicrously torrid times gone by? To look back upon the earth in years to come and say 'what were they ever thinking' all those years ago? To envision the new world where meditation and prayer was as important as breathing, in a world where the aligned for ever will instil that love is the foundation to everything; a new Earth where prisons were no more because they were taught love and became lovers and teachers themselves, the same love gifted from Heaven. Love which is the soil for all seeds of love for our children to grow; the seeds to create the new Heaven on this Earth.' What would that mean?' I think I already know and believe it possible. It is the role of each and every awakened soul on this Earth to converge.

'Build your castle in the sky, resplendent with all that you wish and desire. Make peace with your soul and live within the radiant beauty of the light that you shine. For the castle built on sand succumbs to the tide of doubt, anger and ego. Build your castle on the foundation of unreserved love, faith, and humility. Receive all from the seeds and grace you sow' ~ JahAnanda

CHAPTER 12

Invisibleness of the Scriptural Annunciate

'The mysticism of the eternal tugs always to the seekers of truth in that the path of now lies immortally entrenched beside the river of love that flows from the requiem songs of the ancient ones' - JahAnanda

JahAnanda

I am that I am.
That, of peace,
One who has not pious heart, despair or despondency?
Nor rage from thine heart,
Only love and remorse,
Who speaks from which a place of peace and knoweth change dwells,
Wanting for the souls of the broken hearted,
The troubled and the worrisome,
The thwart, the hateful and the unjust,
The misguided and the cheated,
The angered and revenged,

From a place where jealousy dwells not,
And never will,
And the words of the fledging are unbound for
they are dissolved by the eyes of the just,
And the ruined,
The healed heart of a suffered soul speaks words that
the awakened soul desires, suffered or not.
For to awaken demands only courage to let go unjust
thoughts to live a life not of the world, but of truth,
Commence the journey of life, the journey
that speak of richness and joy,
And of abundance unfolding,
Revealing forever in your heart
~ JahAnanda

'Sit. In stillness,
In quiet peaceful bliss,
Now listen. Wait, patiently, quietly.
Listen to your breath, though that is not the sound.
This sound streams of knowledge, wisdom, peace, connection, abundance.
Swim amongst the noise, bath in letting the world pass
sullenly, effortlessly, unenquiringly, absolute.
Radiance is forthwith, filling the veins with peace.
It has arrived. Ananda.
Pleasure in its song,
The song of the absolute,
The song of Silence'
~ JahAnanda

It Exists in Creation

Does a spider think when it's tucked up in its web?
Does the moon smile when it gazes upon the earth?
Does the new plant from its seed stretch its arms out in appreciation?
Does the ocean, on a still moon lit night sleep?
Does the Owl dream through the day?
Does the Tree wish it had legs to walk?
Does the river feel alive that it is free to follow its own path?
Does the mind believe that this could be so?
Does was already done, in the imaginative heart and soul who already
   caused it to be

For all are creators, an 'I magical nation of magicians' of the collective
consciousness, co-creators of whatever you dare to dream, it will be.
~ JahAnanda

Peace

What are our thoughts if we sit surrounded by noise or
In the quietest midst of our breath,
Embraced in secluded silence and solitude,
From dawn to dusk,
Nourished by the stream,
What will we delight outside of our human-ness,
In the voluptuous depths of our heart
~ JahAnanda

You are

You are born with all the skills and wisdom to fulfil this journey.
If there is anything to learn, it is this.
Remove the false acquaintances; false friends you thought were true.
The illusions, the labels, beliefs,
And any ritualised indoctrinations placed in
the mind you thought of as legitimacy.
Negative perceptions of which you thought you were
are just lies and untruths. And, perceptions of whom
you are, it is all fabrication and falsehoods.
Set free the ego, the evasion of Gods order.
You are none of them.
Emptiness of all judgement, worry, and fear,
To this place of pureness and unassuming,
selfless, awakened consciousness,
For this is the commencement of.
You are blessed in pureness of total peace and to your
devotion towards faith and the absolute of your love.
You are conviction by letting your truth flow from Gods love.
That of your own life force, your awakened Bodhisattva.
Free to fear not, but to follow only your heart.
If I am to teach you one thing further from this day on,
It is this,
Nothing,
For you are already here, and here you shall remain,
Now go and be free
Namaskar and Eternal Love
~ JahAnanda.

I found it in You

Inside a cave lay the most precious gem.
Nestled in beauty and warmth, known only by its grace, it light
shines in radiance like the ray of sunshine through a prism.
Glistening colours, a myriad of beams and sparkles
deep as the Caribbean turquoise blue its beauty, its
love, shines for the one who is searching to find.

It's not her hair, her eyes, her legs, her skin.
I fell in love with what I saw within.
The gem was her heart, her eyes her soul,
Like a mountain of memories that flood the depths and valleys below.

So precious and soft, in the glow she sits.
My eyes were captured, fixed at this sight,
Of this heavenly entity, in hearts she reaches out,
Her gaze casts over the horizon as the wind combs her hair.

She exists, this creature of encapsulating love,
Her mind free to follow the stars,
Those who see her smile as they pass by,
But not for the boy who's transfixed by her soul,
And the depth of love from those blue eyes.

His world has stood still, for a moment it seems,
For the house is on fire and the wind through the trees.
Let it burn, let it burn, let the big wind blow,
I need just to pause and consume it all,
To be captivated by her spell.

They kiss and it's sealed, the magic was true,
Who would have dream he been bungling through.
Their eyes fixed together over oceans and stars,
The pain of their past released by their love,

The tenderness of her kiss,
Again and again,
Like roses in springtime with flowers in her hair.
They talk hand in hand as they walk along the shore,
He offers his love beyond death, to love her forever more.

Her strength, his rosebud, their hearts come to be one,
He whispers, 'I love you always, until the heat fades from the sun,'
Until the stars fall from the sky,
Til the moon promises gold,
I'll love you forever,
In sweet bliss we will die.
For I found it in you
~ JahAnanda

Twin-Flames Vows Reprise

If perfection comes only once in a lifetime,
I saw it in the beauty of the one whom I fell in love.
Rivers and oceans, mountains and vast open plains,
Gaping forests and hauntingly beautiful swathed deserts,
And the peachiness of the sun, the romance of the moon above,

The spring flowers that awaken, expelling from
its midst of its bud, its fragrant beauty
Graced and gifted from heaven and the stars.

As clear deep, spring waters flow, to the song of the waves of the
oceans rushing swiftly across the clusters of sand grains below.

The straining roar of a stag on the brow,
beckoning its lullaby to its frond,
Its mist heralds its presence mellowing,
echoing through the valley below.
And the insects and birds play cat and mouse, cleaning
and preening themselves in their pristine land.

The wide space of darkness and stars, galaxies
stretch beyond the eyes grasp,
Lies the immenseness wane of infinite realm of space, and time

As sleeping whales breach and schools of amphibian forms grace
in their Neptunian land in search of sustenance and recluse.
A mother gives birth and embraces its newborn vowed by
generous applause and love from observers glistening.

This is the radiance of our land, the sounds, the music,
from our Earth Mother, we are blessed.
There was never a beginning; it is evolvement
in its present, nothing more.
There will never be an end, its song forever more.

That is the gift we are offered in this life,
Of physical and of realms we receive and appreciate.
This heavenly embodiment of life as we desire to include,
Fills our unbroken heart for an awakened spirits life is always true.

As is the gift of love, more precious than we know,
The life force of consciousness we allow into our heart.
For one cannot live in fullness without its search revealed,

Until it meets its Twin and through their kiss,
their devotion forever it is sealed.

Their love breathes with love, from their hearts deep within,
Guarding with their lives, the treasure no–one else shall ever know.
Jealously protecting and loving all that they are and seek,
He cradles his love in his arms, from the angels' mouth she speaks.

No touch, no words can ever match what they possess.
Their love locked forever, the key thrown away.
Their universe is complete.
~ JahAnanda

If Only

There is a stream,
A stream, by a tree passing,
Under the willows it flows,
Effortlessly, graceful, free, like it knows no–one's there,
Attachments release of the world rushing by,
Just me and the stream, like friends I met when I sat next to you.

If only,
You could see yourself through my eyes,
You will know how much
You mean to me.

~ JahAnanda

It is Now

There comes a time, when it comes down to you,
Weighing up options, points of view,
The mind invites itself in.
This is the time, to know this is true,
That the heart is the light and trusting comes down to you.
Cast out the mind and follow your heart,
Above all challenges,
Let this be the only one.
~ JahAnanda

When Spirit comes to Call

I now know when spirit comes to call,
It is then I am reminded that the dimension of our senses
operates above what we were led to believe that there were five.
As innocent as a baby puppy,
as inquisitive as a lamb.
Blocking out the world around,
To take a deep breath,
Eyes closed,
Focussed on the pitch black screen in the centre of the mind,
It comes as no sweet surprise to who knocks on our door,
Or rather silently waves a waft of scent.
A feeling embraces the body,
Just to let me know that they're there,
And the screen begins to play.
~ JahAnanda

End it Now

This world lives in a
Hypoxic dead zone,
The raucous killing of a mother whale,
Her screams heard as her brain is exploded as her calf beckons to her,
Helpless as she cries out for mercy.
Animals in torture chambers,
Stuffed in cages for their lives,
Scratching and clawing at their skin, their feathers,
Their minds strewed their place on the earth.
Cutting off their heads,
Humane slaughter there is not,
In a world where we teach children to care for animals,
Whilst they witness governments who permit the barbaric
exploitation of lives and land, all in the name of progress
and profit over and beyond the beautiful creation of nature
and God's will, in a world where love is merely a myth.
And gleaned from the tables of epicurean and culinary masters,
To put an end to this madness right now.
~ JahAnanda

Grace ~

Perfection embracing upon these things He has created,
'Tis Grace.
The light in a child's eyes, to the dawn sun's rays reaching,
'Tis Grace.
Never fearing with faith always on your side,
'Tis Grace,
The mist of warmth rising from a monsoon sun glistening,
'Tis Grace.

Migrating birds in flight, aligned and sharing the load,
T'is elegant Grace.
Symbolic appraisal to the One, who gives life,
T'is Grace.
Falling leaves and waterfalls in slow motion,
Its movement formed in eloquent Grace.
Acknowledging praise and goodwill at the table giving thanks,
T'is Grace.
Falling in Love, two hearts now become one,
Bonded in fortified Grace,
Seeking and finding, all is well and not lost,
Trust comes knowing Grace.
Never fearing always trusting,
Evolutionary Grace,
As the sun rises the moon sets, and like
effortless refrain, forms each day,
Timed perfectly by Grace,
Hidden by the hand, a cheeky smile escapes
but not that of smiling eyes,
Expressed precisely with Grace,
Thus Grace exhibits itself, through the passing of time,
As a teacher of love, an expression held in thine.
Take note of the subtle creations and wonders we let by,
For the answers lie in the divinity of Grace,
Grace born from Love'
~ JahAnanda

Heavenly Deliverance, Divine

'Like leavened bread,
You are a mould in the likeness of His son Jesus Christ.
Imperfect perhaps but always seeking to know your truth,

To be set free.
It pains me to see such suffering in this evil system of things,
But with faith and knowing that this will bring change,
But first, let you be the change.

Like a the crimson sky,
And the fragrance in spring,
God wants you to know that is the new earth, He shall bring,
And it too comes from you,
Let His love mould your true light,
To shed His righteousness,
Upon this system of things'
~ JahAnanda

Heal

They say heal the heart,
From junk food they feed our poor children.
They say heal the lungs,
From pollution they fill the skies.
They say heal the eyes,
And offer television to spread lies and doom in their news.
They say heal the skin,
With their radiation skies,
They say heal the poor,
And grant them credit to bind them to pay.
They say heal the liver,
When their pills and toxins lethally disturb,
But never do they say heal the mind,
For it belongs to them.
Look beyond the hype and the reason,
It paints a path to you,

Lead thus not into temptation,
Tis the only place to healing the world,
Lies in feeding the mind with love,
And filling the heart with compassion,
It starts by the change,
The change deep within you
~ JahAnanda

Let it be You . . .

Let it be you to be the change.
To turn anger into understanding,
To seek peace over war,
To give love when there is hatred,
To show forgiveness in times of hurt,
To bring light where there is darkness,
To hold out your hand to the lonely,
To help build a bridge in times of conflict,
To show compassion in times of pain,
To offer food and water to the weak and the weary,
To bring laughter to the worried and fearful,
There are always two sides to every coin.
And it is through you that reveals an answer
Is always at hand,
To shed fortune to the misfortunate,
To give shelter to the exposed,
To know what is right and what is wrong,
And help our brothers and sisters know Gods plan for us all.
~ JahAnanda

Suffer No More

Spells and collusion,
Intent with deed and void of knowing thy true self,
Promises made to climb a ladder that was never there,
A step into the unknown,
A step further, into the bosom of hell,
Exclaiming they bring peace, wearing a facade full of light,
That their way is their truth whilst the knowing witness their plight.
And those governments spill dollars, to feather their oily nest,
For there's none to be found in hydrogen cars,
So they keep its secret at rest.
And the world knows of their plan,
To dumb down the masses belief,
Tax to drive their polluting money making devices,
To bring poverty, control and grief,
For the word they love are taxes,
And bound by the necessities of life,
They seek to have power having a garden, and nature's medicine,
Fill their pockets from pharmaceutical coffers,
In exchange for heartache and strife,
Electricity you must have,
More importantly it must come from us.
It's we, who will look after you,
It's our wind you must buy,
Imploding a soul's vision thought rightful and just.

So they speak from this place of entrusting,
Expelling sovereignty, legacy, and myth,
For the new world lies with us all,
In their minds the worlds demise into an abyss.

Yet their mouths speak undying compassion,

Whilst their eyes look left and the right,
Espousing that their hearts lie with God,
Grasping the spoils of their riches,
From the poverty stricken sight,

And they preach their intentions,
From parliamentary pulpits deemed from heaven above.
And the world can see they're from Uranus,
Nothing more without knowing their own love,

For the awakened envision a heaven,
A blessed sanctuary,
A blessed heaven on earth,
To give back the rights of true freedom,
And seek to be free from ones birth.

Fighting fire with fire for the dollar,
Back pocket gestures kept well from view,
For greed, self, and material gains,
Whilst the world remains suffering except for the few.

And the weak want notoriety,
With the badge of honour, to their lapel,
With a sword and a gun at their side,
Upon it, like a fool they fell.

If its gain for oneself, it begins giving to others,
The path is compassion,
To our sisters, brothers, fathers, and mothers,
And to the children of tomorrow,
Who will take hold this land?
Want to be free to touch a tree,
To hold out our hand,

To play with the whales,
To grace upon beautiful soils,
And lie in a Garden of Eden,
Treating our earth as our mother,
who gives eternal life for our toil.
~ JahAnanda

Faith

'Faith is like breathing.
The consciousness aware to the blessedness of life by
each breath it takes to physical life. The awakened
conscious self embodies faith because without it,
Like love, it does not exist.
Faith does not rest once adversity has passed
or until any storm has subsided.
Faith continues on to accepting and revealing all things it bears
through patience. Attracting abundance, giving, sharing, loving
Live and breathe faith in all things especially within you,
And forbid anyone who seeks to question faith for they know not it,
Nor their own true power,
Through which faith will lie patiently dormant
until it is placed upon the throne of love.'
~ JahAnanda

Life is to be lived in joy and bliss.

Suffering does not allow these to become a reality in one hand when
suffering is in the other. But remember this. It is not holding you.
YOU are holding it. Once you believe this truth you can release the
traps of contempt and despair disclosing no one was responsible for

your suffering but you. Your pure soul lives by truth, and through
awakening you will live as you deserve to be joyful and blissful forever.
~ JahAnanda

I've learned

I've learned that if someone says something unkind about me, I must live so that no one will believe it.

'I've learned that if a person plans on being happy, it never comes, until he or she decides to be happy right now. The idea that it lies in the future is the illusion of confusion, conceived and believed by the attitude conscience, the ego, the ransomed mind, the fool. '

I've learned that no matter how bad at times, life it seems, how we truly want to feel regardless remains always.

I've learned that no matter what happened, or how bad it seems today, life goes on, and it will be better when you chose to be right now.

I've learned to be blamed is announcing the self reflection of he who blames.

I've learned that the greater a person's sense of guilt, the greater is his or her need to cast blame on others.

I've learned that there is revelation in celebrating the variances of family even through clouds of perception.

I've learned that life sometimes gives you no second chance, only you.

I've learned that awakening occurred before and after this life and the opportunity reveals the same in this life when you realise it never had a dollar value on it.

I've learned that working to make a living is not the same as making a life by living in bliss.

I've learned that living to survive is not the same as living in gratitude.

I've learned that we have two hands, one to receive and the other to give.

I've learned that if you pursue happiness, it will elude you. But if you focus on your family your friends, the needs of others, your work and doing the very best you can, happiness will find you.

I've learned that whenever I decide something with an open heart, I usually make the right decision.

I've learned that when I have pains, I don't have to be one.

I've learned that every day you should reach out and touch someone. People love the human touch—holding hands, a warm hug, or just a kiss on the cheek.

I've learned that there is still a lot to learn, but appreciative for what I have.
~ JahAnanda

'A soul is damned and labelled as crazy, disturbed, even demented: whereas as a collective group of souls are labelled as a religion, a group, or sect. The one thing they possess in common, is having a label, in the view of the observer, and its ego' ~ JahAnanda.

CHAPTER 13

With or Without You, It Exists

Arrangement of Density elements, or Dimensions of Facetal Intelligence

The cosmos is vast. Many on earth think that the solar system resides within one universe and the totality of the universe is all in which all things where the 'seen' and unseen exists. For tens of thousands of years the evidence of astounding sophistication of ancient civilisations has been known and continues to become an intrinsic and fundamentally emphasised understanding of the inter-galactic relationship early man had with their extraterrestrial cousins. That connection has been exchanged now by spiritual atonement and relinquishment by spending billions of dollars on scientific research which could have helped the homeless and hungry with the sullen conclusion that our ancestors knew extraordinarily more than man does now.

The solar system along with the multitude of stars, planets, their moons, and gases are domiciled within the universe and beyond it there are many more universes, many more stars, planets, even suns, which have not been discovered, or if they ever will, nevertheless they do exist. There is a sense of dichotomised despise when I hear that an organisation such as NASA has discovered new planets. All that money spent on something that is already known, that could have instead been spent on feeding the hungry and medications for the sick in this world however our universe is like a grain of sand on a beach which lies among millions upon millions of other ever expanding 'grains of sands' how does that knowledge feed the hungry, shelter the impoverished, empower the victimised?,

The physical mind of mankind has an insatiable appetite for wanting to know what lies 'beyond' and what other forms of life there may be in far reaching galaxies, and whether there could be other planets in which humans could occupy and live. They have a wonder about whether other civilisations exist outside of their own. And if there are, whether they could communicate, learn from, and perhaps even cohabitate with in years to come. Physical minds too commonly think of our family civilisations as aliens or Martians, and that they may possibly be the link between them and the sightings of what is referred to on this planet as Unidentified Flying Objects or UFO's. They are and have been in existence for millions of years in earth time physicality. This being the case, the physical mind of mankind is attempting to go further in establishing whether there is intelligence in these civilisations, and if so, to what degree or how far advanced are they or not, to their own.

To use 'their own' rather than 'our own' them been suggested of being not of this world but of the divine, or star-seed, if you call it that, or nothing at all, presently justifiably in their minds as not of this world.

It should be stated that there certainly are multi-dimensional, universally connected and divinely intelligent civilisations existing in a multitude of vastly complexes, non-physical timeless dimensional realms and realities. They are advanced beyond comprehension to this human reality. To think of them in any definition of alien must not be confused or interpreted at all to any thought, assumption, definition, or belief that they are themselves primitive. Rather the paradox could be said instinctively about the human physical mind of the demeaning unconsciousness of this planet remembering that the universal dimensions in which these civilisations live in is timeless. They are our cosmos family and beyond this time of physicality, and indeed are their own occupiers existing amongst a broad stream of highly evolved universal levels of density dimensional intelligence of which ancient earth civilisations including Maori are innately aware of their power, direction, and wisdom.

To add thus then is the belief that they are determining a possible attack or invasion of this planet. That again could be more a direct reflection of the confused human physical mind instinct and its evasive complexity of distancing themselves from Gods order of light to one of egoistic defensive insecurity similar to how man has lived for thousands of years, and in particular the past one hundred years. One has merely to look at the world which has been created by the hands of man. Beyond vast developments in technology and science, wealth has created more poverty, greed has become epidemic upon numerous political and corporate levels with little thought to serving mans highest good and treating the earth with the respect as he would with his own child. Wars have ravaged mankind for thousands of years and still the real threat of Judgement Day looms as realised by prophets again and again. If mankind believes it hasn't done enough damage to the planet, rather than feeding the hungry and impoverished nations of the world and saving it from pollution and decimation. What of the dire extinction of animals and mammals such as polar and panda bear species, shrimp and kelp species declining as a result of global ice retreating in which whales rely on these species for survival and compounded with these beautiful animals being hunted and decimated by certain countries indiscriminately, the real threat to their existence remains significantly important. Rainforests as too the diminishing Arctic and Antarctica

287

hinterlands, and rapidly growing deserts, mankind now wants to conquer other planets and have a disillusional paranoic mindset that makes our inter-galactic friends nothing more than potentially destructive enemies?

It must be thus known that it is only arrangement of low density elements, or Descended Dimensions of Facetal Intelligence which arrives to the physicality of mankind's conclusions to showcasing their shameful extremities as an abominable compelling species which has derived from pure soul distinction at birth en route to a descended humanistic level as they physically mature.

Extra-terrestrial civilisations learn from earth not by the known fact that they can physically visit this planet but in the way that they have the ability to move multi-dimensionally through time and space, that is to say, they can move through time beyond this time scope here on earth. It must be known that they are more highly evolved as they can create their realities with ease collectively amongst themselves and other civilisations and they can create and relate to states of mankind as well as most mammals, plants, and birds through telepathic and electro-magnetic transcription and translation. They learn from connecting with various forms of telepathy emitted through human consciousness as well as mammals, plants, and birds, and trees included by their electro-magnetic and telepathic dexterity which they have developed over millions of years in human time analysis. This means that by having this skill and ability to tap into heart and conscious states they already know of mans past, present and destiny by collating together the strongest vibratory signals they receive from earth. They are completely aware of mans destiny at this point and by using the same advanced intelligence our ancestors used tens of thousands of years ago, our extra-terrestrial brothers even in their non-physical form, wish to assist to not improving the outcome of this planets destiny but to elevating the conscious state of humanity to creating an eternal manifestation that changing anything on the planet is achieved simply by altering the state of conscious towards a pure state of relative form. This will ensure a more permanent embedded structure in which to set a foundation that will assist mankind's ability to ascend into love, heart, and higher dimensionally states and frequencies including the non-physical. This is what has been talked about on earth in the 1960-70's as moving from third dimension states to fourth and onwards into the fifth dimensions.

As an evolving civilisation also, mankind must always look inwards to finding the answers because that is where the answers lie. The ultimate goal for ascension is to realising a substantially greater dimension of love, bliss, happiness, and sustainability to the planet. The possibility of paradigm shift ascension exists already and all it requires is the collective culmination of conscious states to become teachers and guides to those existing in their unconscious paradigm to help them ascend also. The time it takes to achieving the prosperity of abundance as defined by the true definition of what abundance means, laws of attraction will in due course tip the collective conscious state once critical point mass occurs. The family of the Uranomancy are simply guides, teachers, and part of our conscious power if mankind chooses to use their help in the correct way and that is by treating them as family, no more in the way that a parent loves and protects their child. It is widely known and accepted that babies are born pure and that they also possess, consciously or unconsciously recognisable by its parent, abilities that they seem to not be able to put their finger on what it is exactly however that they do possess that something that makes them so special.

Ascended Facetal Intelligence, Indigo, and Pure Soul Children

To put this into simpler terms, a child is born as an Ascended Dimension of Facetal Intelligence, or Indigo, or Pure Soul dimensions.

They originate from spirit dimension cleansed and fluidly embellished in love from the divine realm of heavenly embodiment. They have all the skills they require to take care of their journey in their physical life other than the important requirement of their parents to provide for them absolute love in their nurturing, encouragement, freedom to be, food, water, warmth and shelter in a safe environment of teaching and growth. That is all. From there, an ADFI, Indigo or Pure Soul child have all the necessary skills to embark and embrace their new path provided they themselves are raised with and among other ADFI, Indigo, Pure Soul children cohabitate alongside equally skilled and equipped parents to ensure their rightful path forward. They are connected dimensionally, spiritually, and are physically pure towards being not only being enabled to fledge forward, but to become leaders of truth as God had intended without symbolism, idolatry, conditioning, ritualising, racial distrust, greed empowered, attachment, controlling dictatorship, religious binding and dissent towards themselves and others.

These children generally behave in quite a contrasting way to other children and at times can be chastised, labelled, and misinterpreted in the way that they are related and how they should be treated. You yourself may find that you too may hold the same or very similar characteristics already or that your awakening will reveal more and more about you having the soul density traits of the ascended consciousness and should that be the case then you could almost certainly have been in other past lives as well. What matters more appreciatively, is this moment, and any wisdom that doth bring forth comes with experience of non-attachment in a completely giving and loving way. To these souls, knowing comes not from what they choose to make right, only to be, and remain always in touch with self and the breath, and trusting. That their will surrounding unblemished faithful love holds the key to downstream peace which others too will follow the same path, not necessary with words at all. Think of a pair of devoted parrots. They have been Soul-mates or Twin-flames for years and years. And perhaps, in that time, they have collected food, bred, played and possibly even teased another bird or two in their happy lives, and maybe watched the setting sun go down on dozens of occasions, and, the same number watching the sunrise in early morn dusk.

Indeed, when one observes their connection, they don't need to talk, they just watch from a branch, in a tree, together. Then without a sound and in a flash they're gone, together, like bullets, in the same direction, flying almost the same distance apart, at exactly the same speed, the same tract and direction, until they land together at their destination together, and without a word. Ascended souls who understand that being is the most universal language of connection, and truth is the most decipherable form of peace, then flow occurs too through trusting, where others will naturally align according to what vibration you prefer is your most least resistant source of resonance, happiness, and tranquillity and that vibrates to a concordance being drawn to the same collective stream. This facet of connection is universal to all that possesses energy and matter and ascended souls already know of this inherently, and instinctively.

They only require being free and accepted and allowed to express them exactly how these children choose. Parents and care-givers determine how well they are able to teach others by allowing their own freedom and expression of who they are to be relevant whilst parents and care-givers to nurture them through encouragement, safety, affection, spiritual guidance, and unreserved love.

The definition on this planet of insanity is doing the same thing over and over again and expecting a different result. Those who know this as truth must invariably be congratulated as it is known for the reason that it is through this recognition that change must commence. The aspect of recognising the need for change is a great step forward to becoming a society of love, sustainability, and potentially, a heavenly place on earth by breaking down the barriers of what was the usual or the norm. The next stage ultimately is one in which formalising a plan of such measures to establishing a doctrine that reflects the philosophies and ideals based on Ascended Dimensional protocols of the Higher Mind. This means, fulfilling the order to raising the consciousness globally of physical mind theories into a broader, achieving, and sustainable compassionate civilisation centred in preservation, conservation, and sustainability with love as its primary foundation. One which embraces unreserved love and teachings in such a way that the need to incorporate the ego will be viewed upon by future generations as a period of primitive, unconscious, demonstrative, and morally destructive. To be recognised purely as a soul destroying period in man-kinds bleak, greedy, and disparagingly caustic history. The right to exist goes beyond any notion or belief that right passes to manipulating the existence of another.

There have been numerous philosophies, beliefs, codes of conducts, portrayals, insights, and justifications in history over many thousands of years based from teachings and religious scriptures. Some various leaders may have charged scribes to rewrite prophetic insights and in turn rewrote translations by other scribes who themselves have become tired or reworded scriptures to reflect either their own beliefs or that of their egoistic ruler. Original scriptures have been copied many times and in subsequent occasions, hundreds of times from original translations until the so called 'truth' of a final religious document have become no more than that of the common mans writings. The true intentions of supplicating mans spiritual path may well be fostered and administered with honest and righteous intent, however it must also be acknowledged and agreed that a divisive, accurate, and articulate moderation process must be of the highest non-evasive and sound standard.

The arts of healing and learning divine inspiration are God specified gifts in which the chosen ones hold in absolute homage to their art form based on the foundations of unreserved love and their talent born to then through God to impart. It is through this understanding that they themselves live each day supremely grateful to the Highest for their skill and blessing for the reason that anyone who dares to claim their talent as their own potentially allows the egoic state to manifest thus relinquishing their foundation of love and humility, and realising their humanistic physical mind dimension to reveal as earthly.

Electro-magnetic radiation is the food for cancer, so is the food from mans science, and the invisible force of stress. The paradox is that he can live happily in peace without any of them'. ~ JahAnanda

UFO

~ Universal Family of Ouranomancy ~ Divination of the Ethereal realm.

Whether the idea is understood, believed, agreed with or not, the human physical state on the earth plane is multi-dimensional. Babies are born into the earthly physical dimension, and an extraordinarily rare number of adults are 10th dimensional pure souls with some almost equally rare beings vibrating in 7th, 8th, and 9th Dimensions. Nevertheless, they come with the inherent DNA and wisdom from their past lives and their ancestors.

Babies although deriving their DNA from each of their parents, contain a 'capsule' of DNA which too is the link to their cosmos and Nirvanic heavenly family. They are aware of their divine power of light and pureness of their soul although more so they use their intuitive ability to assisting themselves and those who align to them towards ascension.

Babies, as mentioned earlier in this book are enlightened beings equipped with all the knowledge of 'what is'. Their distinct understanding of and their interconnectedness with the myriads of other realms of multi-dimensional realities embodied externally and within their consciousness and the cosmos is well understood. Some of these babies have lived many past lives and come as what is referred as 'old souls.' This includes their innate understanding of UFO's or what is referred to in Dimension of the 3rd existence as unidentified flying objects, but is understood more affectionately to higher realms as the Universal Family of Ouranomancy. JahAnanda for example resides in the 12 dimensional realm of Lyra and is an ascended teacher of the chosen twelve.

The paradox is that mankind can use babies as teachers simply through observation as a means to justly learn from, for they are ascended dimensional souls. Similarly, there are adults too who are pure in their soul state although as mentioned the instances are much rare, less than one quarter of a percent. In the physical earth dimension of human existence however, operating in these ascended realms does come with some agreements.

'There is nothing paranormal about the after-life, psychic, extraterrestrial inhabitants, and ghosts from opinions, watching Sci-fi movies, the practices of witches, Halloween, indoctrinated religions, and gothic emo-fashionistas parading like they'd 'seen the light.' Or from creative expressionless explosions just waiting to cause a wave of their own explosional adage of 'I'm not afraid'. It is this earth at this time that is abnormally ex-paranormal to the paranormal. Let them be free to love and be free as well to you my child.' ~ JahAnanda

The first key law in creation understood by the Dimensional 5th realm and higher, is the knowledge that they exist. The second law is the fundamental premise of knowing that they exist within a greater structure of things being one amongst 'the all' of not just their existence on the planet but also being an integral member of the greater intergalactic association. It is at this point that the pure soul feels complete and connected to that within and outside of themselves and that their soul alliance has different points of rule depending on the dimension it resides in at that particular point in time. This including cohabitating, advancing their learning, and connecting with their divine Universal Family of Ouranomancy.

This may seem strange perhaps ridiculous, even feeling threatening to 3rd dimensional physical beings and this has been noticed by higher dimensional civilisations who believe that anyone in the physical earth plane should not at all feel afraid, concerned, threatened, or paranoid to the idea of what is labelled as an alien invasion. Once physical beings can develop themselves in such a way through courage to first trust, and letting go and surrendering all attachments and everything that has nothing to do with themselves, they will then realise that their life will be more tranquil, more peaceful, more trusting, more accepting, more forgiving, more tolerant, more compassionate, and dare we say it, more loving.

It bears a question, what has this got to do with UFOs and how will I know when I am ready to ascend into the next dimension, and the next? And why choose to ascend anyway?

The word ascension does not signify or attempt to demonstrate that is above or more superior to any other dimensional phase of consciousness existence. Ascension merely points to the point where a threshold of a particular conscious state has occurred in a particular direction toward living entirely with unconditional love. As mentioned, babies are of elevated or ascended dimensional realms. This simply means that they have certain strengths and weaknesses much like any other dimensional realm however they come from pureness state characterised by both their 'free spirit' trait and their empathetic and compassionate facet of living and loving unconditionally. The only difference is where these types of strengths and weaknesses can be similar to their identically dimensional compatriots whom dwell at that specific vibratory frequency, the strengths and weaknesses of other dimensionally classed compatriots will

295

be quite different. This will be explained in a little more detail below however the contrasting and perhaps 'quantum negative effect' that babies are exposed to in their new physical humanistic life journey is that which is primarily determined by 'in which and how' they are raised, and by whom. This is one of the most critical challenges for mankind to realise, comprehend, and fulfil.

For example, if a 5th Dimensionally born baby is raised however not necessarily born to 3rd Dimensional parents they can and most likely are affected by QNE, or the Quantum Negative Effect through their parental influence or nurturing. In other words, they will most likely be susceptible to their dimensional structure of being affected and influenced by QNE until the child becomes aligned to his or her parent's dimensional vibration or somewhere in between, unless the baby or child is a highly evolved strong love embraced soul.

The alarming and interesting feature of a baby (including adults) being affected by QNE is they can descend towards the levels of 3rd or 4th Density, 3rd or 4th Dimension as quickly as by age four. This may seem startling to think or imagine, however this has been an epidemic on this planet for thousands of years due to egoistic, ritualistic, conditioned, and in some cases, singular religious binding beyond literalised interpretation. However, this does not need to happen and through awakening releases all that brings truth and realisation.

Below is a broad yet easy to track outline where the contained order the characteristics each Dimensional or Density phases of unconscious/conscious states determines at the level of Dimension or Density they reside in or close to, depending on their soul characteristic nature.

Dimensional Density Level Characteristic Traits (Nature)

3rd Dimensional Density - Physically Centred, Submissive, Territorial, Insecure, Self-Sacrificing, Fearful, Egoistic, Irrational, Easily Angered, Volatile, Wasteful, Vicious, Controlling, Violent, Materialistic, Attachment Orientated, Greedy, Selfish, Limiting, Loving, Extravagant, Self Indulgent, Arrogant, Ruthless, Self-Centred. God Fearing, Unconscious

4th Dimensional Density - Compassionate, Creative, Independant, Hardworking, Instinctive, Dynamic, Instigator, Harrowing, Forceful, Productive, Humble, Loving, Reverent, Accepting, Energetic, God Embracing

5th Dimensional Density - Non-Physical, Ethereal, Creative, Imaginative, Delinquent, Compassionate, Intuitive, Respectful, Direct, Irrevocably Loving, Purifying, Peaceful, Immaterialistic.

6th Dimensional Density - Evolving, Prophetic, Trusting, Intelligent, Instinctive, Proponent of Universal Mind Consciousness

7th Dimensional Density - Philosophical, Impartial, Faithful, Connected, Indigo/Light Child, Star Seed, Teacher.

8th Dimensional Density - Collectively Linked to the Cosmos, Interpreter.

Synergistic Co-binding

When a soul is ascending or descending, they can take with them remnants and possess what is referred to as OIF or 'Ounce In Favour.' This means that almost all souls which transcend or descend an order of

Dimensional Density, they can take with them, for a given time, several remnants of their Dimensional past, or Ounce in Favour or (OIF).

OIF is an element of the stream called Synergistic Co-binding, or (SCb). Souls will continue to carry these distinctive and unique traits with them until such time as their entrance into their new Dimensional Density is become fully residing within its new placement within the order.

Portal Opening of Ascension

On the 11.11.11 at 11 minutes and 11 seconds past 11pm was one example of a portal opening of Divine Ascension of Collective Awakening. The next and final portal is 12.12-21.12. This divine period for those who understand the connection of universal power within the cosmos occurs when the vibration of 'all that is' is accepted as divine power in unifying Love once again, where God or Source is constantly tuning in to our own vibration and likewise and more importantly when one chooses to realign to another realm or stream of conscious and awakened ascending.

Anyone who seeks with courage and faith has this innate power to synchronise their love and acceptance to 'all that is' and live in a vibration of blessedness, whatever is desired. Meditating, giving prayer and thanks to whatever is desired in this present moment, be they troubles, or challenges, struggles and strife, knowing that through one door, another door of awakening opens ready in which a purpose or reason for that experience was necessary much like Yin and Yang or The Law of Attraction, or What one thinks, they become. It is merely a portal of grace. There are messages God presents in times of silence understanding always that this Godly power resides within and only until one acknowledges its vital strength and power. It may at times involve releasing all that has nothing to do with our lives but of the higher realms of the consciousness. This connection reminds those who align toward this vortex to remove anything that has no connection or relevance to the purity of one's life for they are nothing but illusions, distractions, to the fundamental power of the pure soul disciple, of conscious power awakened.

The phase of dimensional change and transcending allows one to seeing the strength in the invisible, reflecting the mirror of the unobliterated true heart to flow naturally, effortlessly, peacefully. It aligns to seek by reaffirming once more towards bringing forth compassion, happiness, joy, bliss, wisdom, and love. By opening their newly inspired heart to source and faithfully walking in its grace to serving its soulful purpose with freewill, truth and endearing love. Laying first the most critical aspect of ascension, the love we have for ourselves, as this opens the greatest door to being aware of existence and abundance remembering that 3rd dimension civilisations, which is the majority of the people in this world at this time, who believe abundance means for them money for example. It does not necessarily though it *can* include money however when 3rd dimensional beings focus on just money the universe close's all other potential doors from where abundance can bring forth and thus the cycle of poverty perpetuates and reflects its nature and form.

When one chooses in laying forth a commitment by manifesting gratitude and humbly accepting and allowing love to flow for all things, even the simplest of things beautiful, tragic and traumatic periods as they also hold what is called on this earth as a silver lining. Thus then, like seeing the beauty in a simple flower, its fragrance, the face of peace in a baby's eyes, a sunset, the stars, even a thunderstorm, a good book, a sumptuous meal, spices, the sun on our skin, even the cold wind. By simply doing this in the complete and unobstructed manifested awareness and in the total presence of the moment to nothing but accepting and opening ones awareness to space and presence. Attachment to nothing at all in thought: no past, no future, just simply being present in this moment. That all things are given in grace from God, through God, by God inside you and yet it was you who first opened your heart to discover. Allowing the irreverent light of God's love flow and when one can see 'all that is' is in its radiant beauty including ones own self in the true form of pure unabated peace and spiritual connection to 'all that is', one will begin to see and feel more and more of 'all that is' and to this the universe recognises this open portal of love connect with 'the all', thus it will receive and respond to opening many more doors through the law of simply trusting and allowing, whatever they desire. This is abundance.

Give praise and prayer, meditating and giving thanks for all things in your present, in the present moment, even should they be troubles, or challenges, whatever. Knowing that one has the power to release suffering and through one door of awakening, another door is ready to open and reveal another portal of abundant stream. There are messages God, and the universe presents itself and ones preeminent path is in moments of silence, in prayer and meditation, And releasing all that has nothing to do with our lives, much like cleaning out a messy home of debris, remove everything and anything that has no connection or relevance to one's own existence. Placing that which is pure, non-physical and powerful that we want to enjoy peace, goodwill, compassion for others, happiness, and unreserved love. ~ JahAnanda

'Sit in stillness, in quiet peaceful bliss. Now listen, wait patiently, quietly. Listen to your breath though that is not the sound but the doorway to awareness of existence and peace. This sound streams of knowledge, wisdom, peace, connection, abundance. Bathe in its purity, letting the world pass sullenly, effortlessly, unenquiring, absolute. Radiance forthwith, filling your veins and soul with peace, it has arrived. Ananda. Pleasure in its song laced intricately, beautifully, and solemnly in silence'.
~ JahAnanda

What are our thoughts if we sit surrounded by noise, or in quietest midst of our breath? Embraced in secluded silence and solitude, from dawn to dusk, being nourished by the stream. What will we delight outside of our human-ness, in the depth of our heart? ~ JahAnanda

There is a stream,
A stream in passing,
Under the willows it flows,
Effortlessly graceful like it knows no-one's there.
Attachments release of the world rushing by,
Just me and the stream, and friends I met when I sat next to you.

If only,
You could see yourself through my eyes,
You will know how much
You mean to me.

There comes a time, when it comes down to you.
Weighing up options, points of view, and the mind invites itself in.
This is the time, to know this is true,
That the heart is light and trusting comes down to you.
Cast out the mind and follow your soul,
Above all challenges,
Let this be the only one.

I now know when spirit comes to call, it is then I am
reminded that the dimension of our senses operates above
what the world was lead to believe that there were five.
As innocent as a baby puppy,
as inquisitive as a lamb.
I stop, blocking out the entire world around me,
And take a deep breath, eyes closed, focussed on the
pitch black screen in the centre of the mind's eye.

It comes as sweet surprise that knocks, or
rather silently waves a waft of scent.
A feeling wraps this body just to let me know that they're there,
And the screen begins to play.
~ JahAnanda

'Like leavened bread,
You are a mould in the likeness of His son Jesus Christ.
Imperfect perhaps but always seeking to know your truth,
To be set free.
It pains me to see such suffering in this evil system of things,
But with faith and knowing that this will bring change.
Like a the crimson sky,
And the fragrance in spring,
God wants you to know that is the new earth, He shall bring.
And let His love mould your true light,
To shed His righteousness,
Upon this system of things'
   ~ JahAnanda

Let You to be the change.

To turn anger into understanding,
To seek peace over war;
To give love when there is hatred,
To show forgiveness in times of hurt,
To bring light where there is darkness,
To hold out your hand to the lonely,
To help build a bridge in times of conflict,
To show compassion in times of pain,
To offer food to the weak and the weary,
To bring laughter to the sad and fearful,

To shed fortune to the misfortunate,
To give shelter to the exposed,
To know what is right and what is not,
And help our brothers and sisters know Gods plan for us all.
For there are always two sides to every coin,
And it is through You that reveals an answer
Is always at hand
  ~ JahAnanda

CHAPTER 14

Purification to Heal

There comes a time when reflection on what has become and where the road has brought us to unravels itself without abject emotion and self sacrificial suffering. The bearing of any burdens reaches a point of healing through understanding that the power always lies within the sufferer to letting it go as holding on to any pain and suffering holds us back from living life to the full.

'To create Heaven on Earth starts from looking within' ~ JahAnanda

'Truth is freedom, and freedom is bliss, to which the road unravels like a ribbon of peace and rivers of dreams. Where once there was a road of fallen rocks and broken hearts lays now a path of silver and gold.' ~ JahAnanda

'If anything can be considered the most treasured value in life, it is that of making mistakes. The greatest achievers relied on persistence in the knowledge that each mistake they encountered meant they were that much closer to finding the answer, the goal, their dream. For nothing was ever gained by being perfect. Imperfection is humanities perfection to adorn and embrace. It is the prerequisite to being the greatest achiever you know being that which is the hallowed uniqueness of you.' ~ JahAnanda

Insomnia ~ is a human name for restlessness. Release any belief, subtle or otherwise, which permits the lured mind to thinking that 8 hours sleep is what you 'should' have. Humans can be like that. Your soul is your purist light; let it simply demonstrate for you that you have much more important tasks of bliss at this time, following your love and highest deepest desires and remaining too that peace in this moment is at your door. Just open it and let your harmonic state, once again resume, and flow like the constancy of a waterfall and in time your soul will tell you it is time to sleep, and you will, peacefully. In the meantime, simply play, fulfil your journey, embellish, and love.

Sample the Smorgasbord of Life

We have now arrived at this point of acceptance, through the discovery of personal power, freedom, and the irrefutable state of awareness and accepting 'what is.' There is an understanding of acceptance, the acceptance to the knowing, acceptance to the allowing, whilst the thrill is its acquainting sojourn with the discovered purity of the pure soul in training. As the new journey forward unfolds the foundations of existence, one comprising of simply being love and accepting; and by fostering the deep essence of living in harmony, humility, blessedness, and appreciation. Aware that Godliness lies within the one who acknowledges their intimate divine sanctuary of love, power, insight, and wisdom, the step is remaining in this place of giving, sharing, offering, and growing together and holding close to ones heart, the preciousness of existence.

There is by now, an understanding that we are all dissimilar in the innate construct of which we are, that we all on this earth have diverse passions, that we have diverse wants, that we have diverse courses in each of one's own delicate and exuberant life. We also know and accept now that the distinct pureness of our lives once it is revealed and discovered is completely and eloquently revered and sanctified. And that outside of the consciousness is afforded to further its illuminate path, in tune with maintaining bliss, passion, and excitement, for if life isn't blissful, passionate, and exciting, then what else should life be if we choose to live without a loving heart? Therefore, as complete and separate souls living as Oneness with the all, as it is the second law of creation, the pure soul albeit disciple lends towards soul pureness, it can venture forth far and beyond the realms of the unconscious soul, to play, enjoy, revel in peace and harmony, and love explicitly to the dimensional nature of who they are.

This can be viewed as a somewhat precise overview. One of having a smorgasbord of choices by fostering and nurturing the soul in its own unique and fundamentally vortexual sense, in which the soul can allow anything it chooses along its fulfilling path of learning and discovery.

A pure soul disciple may have an attraction and desire to peering into the nature of Buddhism, or the nature of Jesus' life, or Nichiren Buddhism, or that of Muhammad or that of one's own sense of Spiritual Self Discovery, it does not matter. The danger lies in attachment thereof. What matters is accepting all faiths for what they are in their own unique contexts and knowing also that these elements lie outside of the dimension of one's own sense of truth. Being-ness, peace, harmony, and the acquainted pure love form, and knowing that one can filter what resonates and what does not, much like choosing particular items of food from a smorgasbord. What is important from what is learnt is not as important to what you arrive to finding as your truth, your own truth without attachment, ritualising, or allowing the mind and ego to take lead as none of these paths has any relevance to knowing truth.

Life is discovering and revealing more and more about who we truly are. It is nothing but having the freedom to following bliss. Free of judgement, free of fear, free of guilt, free of evading Gods order, or allowing the ego to permeate; free of pain, free of suffering, and free of exemplifying permanence in any such way which can disturb the harmony of the soul. This is what we can say, is the path of enlightenment, truth, your own truth in allowing.

'The idea of who you are based on your past history, actions, thoughts, conquests, failures and beliefs do not equate to who you are right at this moment. It is all in the past, it cannot be changed and it doesn't need to change. Don't let it hold you back or use it to inflate the ego. The infinince of who you are, lies in trusting, and vibrating with the knowledge that you have the power to expand, grow, and develop into the most extraordinary powerful you YOU can be and that it starts right here in this moment of now to redesign the true soulful, beautiful, loving, creative, powerful, free, and expressive You.' ~ JahAnanda

'Conscious awakening does not bring the aligned to this place, nor does suffering. Forbearance to this ambient light of bliss; freedom and truth comes with that which unravels like silk and cuts through the ego like a blade through the stubborn door of opiaty. It is courage, it is persistence, it is courage' ~ JahAnanda

Much like musical tastes, one may choose to follow classical music, another country music, another spiritual music, another drum and bass, another reggae, and others may enjoy them all. Likewise some souls have a passion to knit, some to fly aeroplanes, paint, design and teach, some seek adrenaline rush sports, and some choose to simply play chess. The more the soul follows and allows its instinct and drive towards its wondrous excitement it can repel them fluidly from that vibration onto another. Over time, an ascending soul will choose more discerningly as to what works and what it is negated. That too, is the learning aspect of life as is any life dimension one enters, provided it remains bound at the ascended levels of its universal dimension state, always seeking and always thriving to ascend to the next level. It is that beautifully unique aspect of the individual soul characteristic nature that makes the world such a beautiful, varied, and fundamentally stimulating paradise if we allow and accept all others to enjoying their bliss and happiness whilst you in turn, revel in your own.

Study and practice are both very important, but they must go hand in hand. Faith without knowledge is not sufficient. Faith needs to be supported by reason. However intellectual understanding that is not applied in practice is also of little use. Whatever we learn from study we need to apply sincerely in our daily lives. ~ Dalai Lama

Satsang

During the 12 months period of rehabilitation after leaving hospital, after the media attention subsided, there were literally thousands of emails and messages from people around the world. Among them were a handful which seemed to appear almost within a similar time frame apart which aroused my attention and questioning exactly what they meant.

They people did not know me personally, but felt perhaps they did spiritually. There was a bound sense of understanding, compassion, and a direction which they spoke of regarding an unknown philosophy to me back then called Satsang. Because of the simultaneous arrival of this name I had not heard of curiously I trusted yet their wisdom and believed that they knew something that I did not. These messages came far away, from Germany, Canada, US, and India. They outlined that they had a belief that my survival was for a reason which I was already aware of, and further, that it was to reiterate this purpose to teach, to become a teacher of the ancient art and philosophy of Satsang with a directive to being a Satsang master. Knowing this as to what the agreement had arranged.

Encompassing was the time spent with my eternal soul brother in Bethany. He too talked of his travels when he was merely a teenager across the vast deserts across Assyria and on to the holy lands of Asia.

He himself had heard of the great teachings of Buddha and upon his awareness of anger and hostility by marginal factionist Jewish Pharisees, Herod the one, Egyptians, and Babylonian adherents opposed and composed with jealousy and riled puffed chests and scorn to the One, my brother Jesus, of his teachings and his mantle, knowing in his heart, that his life was to be short. For those short years he had spent and shared unduly his wisdom to Hindu and Buddhists, and met with guru and renouncing together Gods love, and that it lies within the deep crevasses of the truly wakened soul. He taught himself the teachings of Buddha in the offering that peace and silence is sacred which filled his heart with much joy and appreciation. He talked of God's love and that God lives purely in ones heart amongst the ravings and mistrust of the earth; that solemness and peace lies deep within the soul.

Over many long nights we would spend talking until dawns light over wine, and with anointments, Spike Nard and Frankincense, Patuoli, and Rose. The tranquil space of solitude and silence was blessed, yet feeling the resonant comfort and peace together of simply being, together offering the sentient blessing of love for one another and for those who chose also to follow His path. Thus this offering was brought peacefully and amicably to the One amidst the sufferings upon the Earth at that time was viewed as timely and accepted to those who too saw the need for restitution, peace, and the formulate restoration of harmony among the people, men, women and children.

The blessing we all have in our lives,
Is the ability to right wrongs in ones heart?
That no matter what has occurred in this life,
There is always a place of healing and atonement,
No matter how devastating or contrasting our influences have
Affected the pained,
Or how much their actions have affected others,

There is,
Always a path to heal'
~ JahAnanda

Compassion

Inauguration of courage is not in recognising the exploitation mankind has done to Earth Mother, humanity, and mankind himself. These acts were and still are the results of nothing more than greed, control, power, and his destructible hunger to accumulate massive amounts of monetary wealth, worthless notoriety, with little regard for his consequential and inevitable outcomes.

Courage heralded is that in which love runs deeper than ignorance, ego, greed, and apathy, towards a universal place of caring and kindness to all souls on this earth, this approach being the first indicating step to awakening. Let this be the revolutionary change in spite of the perpetuation of political and corporate greed, money, and power that this world permits, such that mankind has created to its demise and suffering. By having the courage to confront one's own fears to say 'enough is enough'. It is only through courage and conviction to serve with unrestricted love that heaven on earth will come to be.' ~ JahAnanda

Eph 6 v10. For our struggle is not against flesh and blood, but against the rulers, against the powers, against the world forces of this darkness, against the spiritual forces of wickedness in the heavenly places.

When we are threatened . . . In solidarity and meditation, our collusion together as peaceful spirits focuses our intentions on remaining calm, still, holding close the essence of self love and projecting kindness and love unconditionally to all beings regardless of any actions and intentions. This may confuse them rather than incite further conflict and in doing this they too may see an approach of love cannot be attacked thus placing the state into one of understanding and giving. Fellowship between spiritual souls, reminding ourselves that unconditional love is everlasting and eternal in spite of turmoil that may reign in the lives of the unjust . . . . always be of light and love to them.

'There is no romance in searching for happiness in money other than romance itself. For to seek true romance with the one you love is found in the happiness you feel within, therefore inconsequential of money itself. The wealthy will agree this is so.' - JahAnanda

Through suffering among the Maori populous, some of the greatest expressive talents have evolved to combat the burgeoning suffering to women, children and families of physical violence and abuse. This problem exists worldwide. 'Once Were Warriors' now a historic yet true portrayal and graphically horrific Aotearoa New Zealand movie of our times which highlights the social and cultural issues that surround elements of Maori life but not entirely endemic solely within this sector of Aotearoa but throughout the world. Exacerbated with issues of alcohol, drugs and generational replication of parenting it has come a time where a stringent answer now lies in accordance to stemming the harm brought upon families to stop the cycle through education, edification, and moderated practises by fundamental teachers.

The result split's victims into two mainstream directions. One group, unconscious, who continues the cycle on to the next generation of children to affect their off-spring with the other mainstream group, conscious, choosing to break the cycle and understanding that there is a more productive means to serving self and showing their children that peer pressure, violence, alcohol and drug addictions are inconclusively caused by ego centred behaviours. They are behaviours collected by the minds state of unconscious attachment to something which appears as a fabric of reality where by the wounded soul or the perpetrator is at a loss to find a more approved or identifiable recourse to solve the problem which forces the unconscious mind to lapse towards anger, frustration, and despondency.

A great deal of these talented sports, creative and literary icons are choosing to pursue their own interests, their inner talents and desires by seeing that the world has opportunities beyond measure.

The way out from this demise to all sectors of societies begins by indentifying the values that each person has in contributing to themselves first outside of antisocial behaviours. By helping to lay down their own truth and legacy infinitely as their God given contribution towards strengthening mankind as a whole and by directing perpetrators to role models and teachers who have the skills and talents to assist and enabling them onto a path of sanctified change.

Governments could look to invest entirely in prisons towards an outcome. Rather than locking them up but by becoming teaching and educational organisations. Above anything else, if they are to prevent reoffending and preventing more public funding being wasted and compounding year after year. By just locking offenders up and throwing away the key as is the case in many western and even many eastern countries, is like putting a sticking plaster over a festering boil. Not only does it perpetuate an already growing and burdening population, socially and economically on again to society's tax payers, but the growing problem will continue festering until it bursts, and the cycle of reoffending and being admitted back into the prison system as it is exemplified now in this current situation. The outcomes still of repatriation back into society are simply not being met at this time and threatens to only worsening this trend.

Every human being must be given love, respect, compassion, and hope for their crimes no matter what they have done. This may be indeed a difficult stand point in this age for such reprehensible crimes however no war was one with more war, no outburst of anger was won by yelling, and no darkness can bring light into someone's world with more darkness. And locking them up and throwing away the key creates more anger and disassociation. All individuals have enormous power and value to participate and contribute to society, mankind, their families, spiritually, psychologically, emotionally, compassionately, and financially. The world has an enormous untapped resource to helping one another. No-one is lacking of talent, courage, or persistent drive when clearness of the egoistic and destructive mind is unseated, forgiveness ultimately heals.

Denouncing all behaviours which in the past stymied healing by nondescript intervention to a position of 'clearing the slate' to starting again through healing is challenging for all concerned however it is up to governments and society to see the benefits over the common prospect of reoffending by perpetrators

The Laws of the Land

We are temporary occupants on this god given earth and how we live and learn on this great journey is inevitable once we find the blessedness of the awakened heart. Each living being has a contract to participate in the world for we are the guardians of the land, and of this great earth, a chosen participant and disciple in the world where respect, tolerance, treasuring of, and acceptance of its many gifts and of one another is apparent.

What was quite odd about life growing up was no matter how intriguing, or how exciting, and even how tedious at times life appeared; each one of those periods were an invitation to develop and configure our path by using the synergy of such experiences created and allowed to create the next more preferable steps in life. No machine or computer will have the will to make a decision. Our perception about what are important in our lives are what grows us therefore we must allow ourselves to grow and reveal more and more of who we are based on new experiences, expressions and learning's in our lives. Courage is very important. When you can examine thoroughly anything in life you have a duty to sell your view and opinion of living from the soul. There may be significant difference in matters relating to points of view but having the freedom and nous to provide a point of view of robust examination and abiding to the law of Godliness, there is honour to uphold by residing on the facts based upon the foundational premise of love. Pure souls have a right to sit in any case or situation as proposed with a will and rightful means to settle. Wild horse's would extract anyone who in their mind who has the obvious intentions of reinstating their authority wielding a sword and absent of a peaceful heart and an irreverent mind. Jurisdictional errors are an unfortunate fact of life and when the minds of the resolved and the unresolved meet can only be rectified and settled by the authority of one who has the wisdom of God's insight.

A somewhat surprising feature is that life develops by the great gifts and democratic right of humanity whereby mankind has a right to disagree. It is important that all matters of an individual's case are presented fully, to be heard and an accurate opinion can then be formed. Making any decision when any challenging scenario is met is the idea of asking the question 'what does that mean?' allows the concept or case of a person's view to be heard. In all matters of resolving anything involves being courteous and showing dignity and respect even when another person has a differing point of view. God's Law is not corrupt, they are honest and meet with integrity and independent to humanity's physical mind view and it is important that advocates maintaining of integrity. Everyone has values and beliefs and others may have differing values and beliefs but there is no corruption in God's Law and this is something the earth should embrace, trust, and be proud of.

Constitution comes from God's Law and is founded outside of earth and biblical laws by knowing how to soulfully analyse a problem with purist love in ones heart and absent of ego.

CHAPTER 15

Gods Message

God

If it speaks to you solemnly,
Expressively to your heart,
It can only be the guidance from that of God.
If truth sits at your feet,
Then never let your feet stop walking the path of truth.
And should you stop,
Let it be to close your eyes quietly to give praise,
And humble expression of the thanks to your
existence and appreciation to God.
For God lives in every one upon this earth,
Let God fill your heart.

He is always by your side,
Believe,
Breathe,
And bathe in Gods glory.
The truth is your hearts light,

JOHN EDMONDS

Expression in His love,
Faith forever be,
Blessedness that is You.
Graciousness in
His solemn divine wisdom,
To reach out,
Is all God asks of You.

Source from Highest

This message unto him was given in love,
To do for Him,
His work,

The sacrament of Ones journey he speaks, that of knowing remains indelibly quiescent, sleeping, fortuitous, and dormant. It waits to be unlocked until the awakening of the soul, the beginning of truth. Then will the heart lift up, its impermanence known to make haste to sit still for offerings subsidence will cease, to rouse and draw near. That is more simply than the complications of the world, to let go of materialistic gain for identity and power, to relinquish control of awakened souls knowing of truth and those disciples of learning. The greed of the unjust will forebode their own demise in time to stipulate themselves upon the corpses upon that they feed. The ravishing governments, dictators, and tyrants, who plead rule from upon high, who force them to ballot and should they not they rain down judgement for not becoming their slavered flock. They will further bring ruin the same of the hundred year reign to hinder ascended souls who seek heaven to the new earth.

Those who seek and announce heaven's land on this Earth, and to prepare themselves for their place in the heavenly kingdom and for now in the intervening time to do good, that indelible sign is to uphold the truth of one's remaining presence to the love and ensure the wrath of evading Gods order is kept far removed from thee.

Gods plan was succinct in His desire to seek a land of truth, love, and justice, to reign as in heaven and too unto earth.

The scribes of God who envisage truth in His will,
Who deem to write with goodwill and good intentions in their heart,
Who pervade the truth to be told from tired eyes and blemished minds
who nevertheless sought right notwithstanding their literal and moral
intent upon themselves to do His work.

Daniel 2:30 ~ 'And as for me, it is not through any wisdom that exists in me more than in any others alive that this secret is revealed to me, except to the intent that the interpretation may be known to the king himself and that the thoughts of your heart you may know.'

In the Prophet Daniel's wisdom, is shown and revealed in many of his testimonies. The explanation in this scripture is that his vision for mans destiny is his interpretation of the new kingdom. His belief and vision was his insight of things to come. His interpretation of a new kingdom, and a new earth, as was expressed also by Apostle John in Revelations in his longing for the same new earth to be created after judgement is passed. The planet based on their own observations of the wickedness occurring.

Those who in themselves, set forth a path to seeing the creation, the establishment of the new kingdom, a new earth born from pain and suffering from the old. One dealt out at the hands of the wicked and egoistic kings, dictators, politicians, and rulers. They will reign no more. There will be more pain and suffering to come, from the bombs and invisible cloak, but hold faith close to thine heart and trusting that God has a plan. Those who raise their hand to do the good work will become part of the new creation, the new kingdom. God is within the hearts of all righteous men to be part of the change. The power lies within all to seek peace, respect of the Earth and its water, wildlife, plants, creatures and mammals, refusing materialistic endeavours, monetary competition, endeavours and controls, burdensome over population to two billion, the dismantling of all non-organic production, to cease all expenditure on space, oil and coal exploration until all these policies are met first. Foremost, the courage to see these changes through for the children of the future and to healing the destructive damage seen over the past 100 years to this planet before there is none to save. It starts first with you.

This land is now seeing virtuous reckoning summarised as revelations many centuries ago foretelling signs that people on this planet are experiencing now today. To feel more pain, more heartache, more undeserved suffering or learn now to be kind. That is the choice. Avoid the senselessness and lay down all arms, dismantle all nuclear power plants and war-heads, and materialistic endeavours. End the destruction and pollution our Earth Mother, and Gods creation, but to create heaven on earth as it should have been those thousands of years ago. End ego struggles for the struggle is with nothing but the self. Devote tirelessly to instilling and practising the truth of being humbly grateful and compassionate in our nature, and in our giving. Truth to embracing unreservedness in loving all people; now is the time to shine your light, haste leaving it another day longer, for we are all one of the blessed Oneness. ~ JahAnanda

Trust

Trust, if you feel scared and unsure about where your life takes you.
Trust, if someone you love turns their back on you.
Trust, when you believe in something that no-one else see's.
Trust, even when the world chooses to incite violence
and harm upon another soul or nation.
Trust, when you feel that your prayers are not being answered.

Trust, when you're all alone.
Trust that miracles do happen at the least opportunistic moments.
Trust, that someone see's the beauty in you even when you don't.
Trust, your feelings and your heart, more than science and your head,
Trust, that your determination and courage
will always amount to something good.
Trust, when you feel God is closer than you think.
Trust, that the world would be lost without
your contribution to this planet.
Trust when you are tired, shattered and lost
that tomorrow will bring a better day.
Trust, that the centre of the universe is You.
Trust, with all your heart,
Because God never gives up on you, because Gods trust in you is
eternal and never failing if you need only reach out to Him.
~ JahAnanda

God warns of ego, that of Evading Gods Order, more brutal when two ego's collude in alliance with one another to serve a purpose for themselves, neglecting the wellbeing of other earthly souls. Reaffirm the sustainable and determinable force involving unreserved love and empathy for one another; this means is the only ideological truth. ~ JahAnanda

Gratitude

'Being-ness reaches its peak of maturity in knowing truest, purist love, peace within the soul, an abiding humility state, and a compassionate heart, when it understands the infinity and cruciality of living with tranquillity' ~ JahAnanda

Depression

A fashion of the past, no more will it be, in the new world.

'Be reminded, that should family disturbance, conflict, judgments of you by someone else, hostile implications aimed at you, or notions of insecure comparisons by anyone towards you, are squarely not any of your business . . . just keep thanking, giving, forgiving, and loving, and demand always of yourself the peace, joy, harmony, compassion, and wisdom that rightfully is yours, unconditionally.' ~ JahAnanda

'Freedom does not seek ones existence to set them free. It lies always embodied as one with the consciousness. Constrict in the belief that belies any attempt to prove otherwise is merely ones belief that a boulder has blocked ones path. The boulder is nothing but ego, the chain which anchors it is nothing but the mind. Hold close to your heart awareness, for that is the unmistakable truth. Let peace flow from the revelation that freedom never left, only the door of one's mind allowed the perception of something that was never there but freedom itself. Now fly and stay free!' ~ JahAnanda

Death

'We have 'died' many times. You grieve not for the person but yourself. The pure consciousness is aware simply that it has entered an unlimited realm of universal multi-dimensional streams of reality since its existence. You grieve more that it is nothing but the mind controlled by the self which sabotages the self to believing that they must remain in this limited dimension of ritualistic physical reality entwinement of which the mind has no part to play at all' ~ JahAnanda

Death envy is sometimes a perceived ostentatiously as a temporary callous trait of the few who understand what occurs when someone crosses the threshold into the light. Its cause is subsequent to knowing where the departing soul ventures onto its next journey beyond their once previous life. The awakened soul understands intimately the course of transcendental realisation into the next exciting phase of a souls' journey for it has done once or many dozens of times before. It is acceptance of the knowing, a time of celebration and a time for loved ones to draw to the Oneness of continual connection to their own soul power to know love beyond realisation that the love of a loved one is lost for it is not. The mind holds grief as a belief as true and ever-lasting however it is your planets subconscious grieving in them self for thinking that they are powerless. This is not the case outside the human (mind) dimension as any soul has the gift and potential to recapture resonant peace of mind by entrusting the soul to shining the light of healing and heavens hand to heal as higher dimensions remain aware and connected through source, for this is where the power of knowing and allowing lies.

Any suffering surrounding grief is understandably accepted as human and through having faith that in time it will soon pass and understanding allows any suffering of grief to be solely in the hands of the suffered to realise its own truth.

'Death' is conscious reawakening, a celebration, and another new road of light. The sadness of grief lies on this physical plane and the acknowledgement of loss lies within the self and the physical minds forced perilous detachment from their spiritual connected loss within themself more so than the loss of a loved one once it is realised as truth. The only death is the body 'earth to earth, ashes to ashes and dust to dust.' The body is nothing but the vehicle for the soul and the spirit in which it lives on eternally' - JahAnanda

Knowing this and knowing too that death is not death at all, being the fastidiously unintelligent way that the world looks and labels ascension, crossing over, or passing, as death. Whether it is talked about or written in the newspapers and television we hear that someone died or that there was a death. Sadly, real death, if any, is how people live in their physical life before they ascend. By not realising their own truth and living according to how other unconscious souls live and being self entrapped in thinking that the world is holding them ransom rather than it is quite the contrary. To ascend peacefully is always the preferred route and attaining this state is to live abidingly in peace, in each breath and each heartbeat.

Healing

'When life seems dark and despairing, when life appears all doom, when life feels gloomy and destitute, a pain, stressful, worrisome, or just feeling down, ask yourself, is it the world out there, or someone else's negativity, or perhaps is it the voice in the mind? Life can feel like sitting in a pile of shit. You can stay in it, or stand up. Clean yourself off, walk away from it, and bask in your power, in your will, your ability, your freedom, your highest desires, to seek excitement, to be happy, to be free. To be the blessed you who recognised that nothing can affect state of being unless we give it permission. If a permission slip to be depressed arrives at your door, refuse it. Follow your heart, your love, your joy, and like a frog on a lily pad, you simply choose to jump onto another and another until you find one that suits you, one with an inspiration to share.' ~ JahAnanda

'Winning any war is more ideologically simplistic than the trillions spent on it than on our earths starving children and poverty stricken nations. The paradox to conquering any enemy rather than 'fighting fire with fire' is defeat through undying love, sincerest compassion, rekindled solemn and eternal kindness' ~ JahAnanda

'The nature of man kinds current situation by inflicting harm, control, hurt and war, upon others including mother earth determines the state, ridicule and primitiveness of mans thinking separate from his peaceful, harmonic, compassionate and loving state of its true soul form. God warns of ego and more so where two egos collude in alliance with one another to serve a purpose for themselves and neglecting the wellbeing of other earthly souls is a source to be rejected and refused. Reaffirm the sustainable and determinable force involving unconditional love and compassion for one another if collusion is deemed necessary, this path being the only ideological truth to realising acceptance and true meaning to understanding the fabric of a pure soul identity which encompasses love'. ~ JahAnanda

Of all accomplishments, nothing affects mankind's destiny more honourably than conquering the vast abyss from that of one's ego to the heart' ~ JahAnanda

Forgiving

'Only a courageous soul, a brave soul, a surrendering soul, a pure soul who acknowledges the strength within themselves that regardless of perceived turmoil and unjustness that exists, understands that the paved path, the planted seed, the fruition of irreverence to absolute everlasting peace and unconditional love first is borne through knowing that of undying forgiveness.' ~ JahAnanda

'There is a dance created by you, the free soul, and the soaring light. Fortunate we are to behold that within ourselves. Refute imitating to dance in someone's shoes, to dance someone else's dance, to live your life through another. If you wish for knowledge in this place then seek it elsewhere. All discoverers of the enlightened heart come not for this but for the surety and reality that it lies embedded within. Remove all that is believed as being truth, even assumptions, for truth does not lie there, except that of your own. Forgiveness is the restorative road to freedom and understanding life and truth means forgiving all that you held against you for doing this was just holding you back from your freedom. Forgive everything and forgive yourself. Feel your freedom lift your wings from this day forward and remain to be the soaring light of love, forever blessed and true.' ~ JahAnanda

Truth ~

I am not religion, nor saint, nor your beliefs, nor your findings of truth. I am that which I Am, that of love which I am not like, or what I give, or what I seek. I Am Love. I Am the Creator and whoever goes forth in your new journey to seek me, will find me when they seek to finding their own pure heart. Know that god lives in you and He is always there waiting to serve you. He speaks with love and wisdom solely for you. You too will say, I am not like love for I Am love. I Am God, I Am Yaweh, Allah, Atua, Jah, whatever you use, make my name holy and sacred. Be hallowed in remembering thy Name. I am here for you as you are my son and daughter, your guiding light, centre of your universe, your creation. You are created, my creation, existing because you are compellingly more, and nothing less. You are the One of the many, the many of the One, of creation. Hold Your Love close to thine heart. Never judge, never fear, never forsake your brothers and sisters, never seek to make right, for it rests already in you. Never bow down to make wrong from your restorative and righteous mind. Seek only me, have faith in me. I am your light and Love. Seek me and you will find wisdom through my truth. Blessed are those who do.' ~ JahAnanda

Spend not a whole life living unconsciously and measuring to the standards of others. When we arrive to this place, that of knowing who we truly are soulfully, spiritually, and in awareness to the innateness and purity of our own divine essence of Love and Being-ness, the path we assumed as true becomes obsolete and irrelevant. It does not take an NDE, or trauma, accident, or even someone to 'switch' a light on to reach this place, just a decision, a choice to live through truth to be the change.

The many souls who live unconsciously, whether in a third dimensional or descended realm may not be aware that they are unconscious at all. Life, God, the Universe, makes known signs to all souls, conscious or not. They will continue to flow into the consciousness over and over again, disclosing signs to new paths, new journeys, new opportunities, and new connections, to the Oneness of source as guidance and direction. The quality of truth paths, signs, and messages are distinctive. Quality in the sense that based on the identity which is known by the soul in its purity, reflects the direct line of vibration that the conscious or unconscious soul emits from its frequency it focuses mostly onto. This unfolds a path, truth or not, which draws it towards that which holds an avenue or doorway of least resistance to unveil and present itself to the soul. If any sign or message that is not read, seen, felt, heard, experienced, understood, or agreed at that given point in time, the unconscious soul will revert to its status quo or current contained vibration that is least resistant to its own perpetual state of its awareness. ~ JahAnanda

An unconscious soul may live many lifetimes. Unconscious souls generally are those who have lived single digit lifetimes, to those souls who have lived 17-35 lifetimes who hold the wisdom of the ascended masters. Any sign that gives rise to itself in the consciousness that become unobligatory, they will resume their present state of learning unconsciously. There are beautiful aspects and features by what can be perceived as perplexing, confounding, or baffling, in which signs or distinct messages are present. Yet if they are not amassed and composed in such a way that would utilize to thrust them forward, above and beyond their present state of existence to knowing both their truth, and themselves from a pure soul level, the Universal Law of 'What is, Is', applies. ~ JahAnanda

Pure Soul Disciple ~ Bodhisattva

Pure souls who witness unconscious souls in their awareness purely observe, they do not judge, try to change, or administer to them in any way. They are accepting of the Universal Law of 'What is, Is.' They do not invite themselves into any frequency or vibration that does not align to that of other dimensions or densities other than from a point of sincere observation and humility. Pure souls are compassionate, loving, offering of their truth, and obliging. But like two cars going in different directions on a freeway, they can only offer guidance and direction only when they are summoned. Until then, they let pass, achieving and moving toward each their own perceived vortex of highest excitement, anticipation, enthused device. Pure souls do not take any aspect of another unconscious soul's path emotionally or personally. They are aware of the Universal Law as they say on this planet, as being either 'black or white'. They are instinctively and compassionately aware that each other's path is for a purpose whether it is to feel more or less pain or suffering, or more or less joy, peace, love, wisdom, and harmony. ~ JahAnanda

Righting the Imbalance

Forget everything, forget troubles, and forget fear, worry or any notion of despair. Forget any interpreting, forget it all . . . even the worlds troubles. Embrace faith. The world is not destructive, nor degraded, it is merely correcting, realigning. So is your body mind. Be still, be quiet. Fill your entirety with all of which resonate pureness of love and offer as your mantra your blessedness in giving thanks to all that lays at your feet.' ~ JahAnanda

This is the corrective path for change. Power can be ill fated like dictatorship has seen before. However power too can reveal compassion when the absence of an unforgiving heart and reckless thought of abusive man is refuted, removed, and forever cast out. For now is the time to grace the hearts of the healed; to share in thy offerings, to seek justice with love for all the hearts of the new and awakened.

'There is only one true God. Who lives within You. God was always present, though you didn't know. Like the olive branch, His hand was always there reaching out for you. Praise Jah! Glorify Him, the creator of all things, 'The maker of Heaven and Earth, the suns and all the stars, including you. Denounce false worship and idolatry! Dispel money as sole path of abundance: and stand steadfast and strong to receiving the grace of His might and glory that was always waiting for you to accepting Him into your life and rejoice in praising Hallelujah!' ~ JahAnanda

The Earth's Suffering

The fruits of my work are for you, and all animals, your livestock, and all creatures, my creations. Drink the water from the lakes and the rivers, pay homage to life and its spirit and seek that you and your people repay my work that the earth and its riches is kept sacred in your hands. Put back the trees, the land and speak my name when you approach, when you drive the first metal into her skin, and when you put back the trees. For if you do not, the land will be holes, like craters of the moon, dead children, and their children, and theirs forever, the shame will be eternal and lie with you. The black gold has served you, but look beyond, far beyond, before the thick smokes chokes your skies and kills your land, and your women and children and their children more. All for the sake of losing sight, eyes covered with money, blinding you by your greed. It shall not be so should you think of your children above money, silver, copper, and gold, and coins and of paper, they can take from the earth but not nourish their bellies nor yours. Look beyond, look up to the sun, for its power is there and beyond to the universes flares. That is my creation and my creation to you, to seek out beyond the blackness of smoke which will blind your view and your plants and your trees.

Use your heart not your head the blackness seeps and kills the oceans dead, I warn you, I beg you, my will I give to you, think of your children and their children, before your greed kills you too. Heed my words. And the same, the same, of that I give to you. Pay attention and look beyond what you need is shining down on you. It gives to my work, my animals and creations, its light and its power, its warmth. You will know beyond three decades and six winters after the millennium of two that life amongst the stars will reveal a contact to meet you. By 14 more winters and summers you will know them as one, as part of your family, they will become your intergalactic friends. Make peace with them make peace for they only know love, they are not puffed up nor full of self pride, they know not hate but reveal purest love. They will teach and take you to the ends of the universe to a place where time goes so fast, beyond ten thousand full moons and beyond and bring you back to this earth. You will sail past your machines as primitive as they are, and wonder why you starved your children to build ornaments for the stars. The dimensions, as preparing, to lay Gods heaven on earth, while this day man on the earth strains to make four, from three, two, and one. There is ice and there is water, there's rays, and there's hope, there's air that you can breathe, make for you from your hidden inventions the things that you need. A sword is a waste, like a gun is on Mars, there's just one weapon you need not bring, that which evades Gods order stays at home. You will not see heaven, but yes you will find love, with Intergalactic ancestors and yours a home, in the stars above.

My creation brings forth a new world, many worlds, so much more than this earth brings, but you will return here your home for the new earth is heavens mighty new birth blessed by the Angel named Michael returns as the King. The new earth will have teachers numbering two fours preceding one, they lived here and died here and ascended and again back to this earth they have come. There will be plenty to eat, to share, to enjoy, but never forget me and as hallowed be thy name. God I am, the one and only true God YHWH praise Jah. Seek me, like I seek you, teach your children, teach them well.

And, the ruler of this earth will forever be cast out. ~ JahAnanda

'You are given just this one life at this moment, why live being someone else when God gave you all He designed to make YOU already great. Trust.' ~ JahAnanda

To Him, living the impossible is not a consideration, for when the succinct pureness of the heart is found. Trust in Him, everything is possible.' ~ JahAnanda

Daniel 2:44-45 ~ 'And in the days of those kings the God of heaven will set up a kingdom that will never be brought to ruin.

'Evading Gods order is thwart with indulgence. It is unconsciously comparing of itself and that of others absent of kindness, detached from its own peace of mind. Feelings of inferiority and superiority subjects state of being to illusionary judgment detrimental to understand its own self worth.' ~ JahAnanda

'Accept that you all are separate bodies, separate beings, separate souls, in awareness of the Oneness formed by that which is not separate, but connected, aligned, through love, the purest love, unconditional love.' ~ JahAnanda

Commanding, Oh thee Blessed Soul

We come unto this earth blessed, to be nurtured, to be loved, to be fed.

Verifying how it, to nurturing ourselves and our brothers and sisters.

How being loved validates how to love another as we would love our self.

How being fed confirms how we choose to feed this body, mind and soul.

The contradiction is that we came upon this soil, already born as nurturers, for we we're born from the blessed nursery of love and harmonious light to bring upon this land.

And we came upon this cradle of joy to being the most affectionate and wisest of lovers, far from the sacred place of heaven's love is where the esteemed seed to which the garden of love was planted upon.

And we came upon this table to be feeders of food and of light, blessed with soul so pure to immerse our hearts in soulful rejoice beside our brothers and sisters.

Yet, erroneous is the one who schools to become leaders, for we were born to lead, to go blessedly beyond the path of being mere followers, like sheep, we paved the way for our insight, and Gods love shone like a light unto the path that we walk.

And erroneous is the one who schools to become doctors, for we were already born as doctors and healers and that the earth and the stars were our pharmacy given by God and we need nothing more.

And erroneous is the one who schools to become teachers, for we we're born teachers, schooled from the school of love and from the wise souls of heavens light, once more prearranged by God.

And erroneous is the one who schools destined to become artists, and writers, and painters, musicians and dancers, for we were born to express from the moment we were born and upon the canvas of life we danced and spun lyrical bliss and colourful glee until they reflected the expressions of this fairy tale land here, and all the way back to our home.

And erroneous is the one who schools to learn and embrace peace, for peaceful is how we were all born as peaceful as earths filtering sunlight through trees and the autumn leaf is it gently flows down the peaceful stream, free in a world that knows no borders where we can hug our brothers and sisters from faraway lands.

Erroneous is the version that mans mind seeks them to abide in accord to their earthly bounds of their own nurture and their love. Who paints a picture of just and of cause to those born unto this world. They may crush the jewel that they hold in their hands and feed the child's blemished fate and fear until the jewels body of purity suffers into the tempest whirlwind of plight and despair. Feeding their minds and feeding their struggle with notions of victimised bearing until the pure light shines no more.

For one day, the ancient bells will toll and soon will call you back to this land, to the seed of your existence and the guidance of Gods hand. To the one who truly believeth that miracles can come true, will spell out your life's true meaning and its power will again, be graced upon you.
~ JahAnanda

Offering of Thankfulness

Penance was due,
Expiation of suffering, reconcile to the One,
Lambasted with love, defiant with joy,
The solemn prayer, it seeks to the known,
The One highest of high, more precious than gold,
More beautiful than the mysticism of the full moon blazoned,
Or the radiant touches of morning light in silent sombre dawning
shines bright,
For without this existence, this awareness of offering bequest to thee
Blessed God, thy guide, thy breath, graced to thou,
For Ananda is delight, to rise from the spoil,
To receive,
I Love You Jah,
I LOVE YOU MY LORD,
I LOVE YOU,
I LOVE YOU,

You are

You are the person in charge of you,
The wings you wear are yours,
The freedom you have belongs to no-one but you,
Be free, for you are a creator,
A child of the divine,
In this universe placed in this time,
This moment, this place to be,
The You that you are and who you want to be right now, be it!
Holding Your truth always close to your being,
Close to your heart and soul.
With the knowledge that everything that fills your being,

Your senses reaping of the vibrations and dreams you want to for you
on your journey right now, in this moment.
Celebrate You!
Go in love and harmony, and in peace.
~ JahAnanda

I say, Just Have Faith!

'If in our hearts we feel tormented by angst, pain, suffering, guilt, worry, or fear . . . God is reminding you that faith is your saviour and through His love and the blessedness you lost in the turmoil of knowing your own love. Know Gods beauty and his strength; for suffering relinquishes its hold, to know intimately that faith is real if you live with it embraced always in your heart. That which escapes rationalisation or kindness deed, the invisible entity more acquainted to man than he knows. The world might know violence for they've been doing it for thousands of years, they have the money, they do it for money, that's what they know and they're very good at doing it. Living the life of a martyr whether they do it by bombs or poison or bullets or inciting enough fear to force people to turn on people. They return looking like the peace makers and you will vote and you have a choice to support violence or support someone who lives peace, someone who doesn't have a litany of bloodshed on their hands, someone lured through love not money. At this time those of the knoweth sanctity of truth can stand together and stand tall for sooner or later peace will prevail. Whether you pray for peace, go to school for peace, make an effort for anything in this world, through even the smallest effort you make right now and forever, always live your truth, your own power, and by your own grace and the grace of God, just do it for peace. Blessed is its force, embrace it with truth for faith knows no other way. ~ JahAnanda

When one holds faith as sacred as breathing, you are never afraid'
~ JahAnanda

'There is only one true God and the God living within you is always
present. Like the olive branch, His hand was always there reaching out
for you. Praise Jah! Glorify Him, the creator of all things, 'The maker
of Heaven and Earth' (Ps 124:8). You are the maker of your heaven and
your earth and if you must choose this also, your hell. It is your choice.
Dispel money as sole path of abundance: and stand steadfast and strong
to receive the grace of His might and glory that was always waiting for
you to accept Him into your life and rejoice in the praise of Hallelujah!'
~ JahAnanda

The 10 Commandments
Guilt and Shame

Tis is evil, tis is dread.
Tis the dark cloak they wrap,
Around body and head,
It plays on their conscience, weighing heavy on their mind,
Precise in their aim,
To them, it's not a crime.
They may listen and believe them,
Or take to heart, their venging feud,
Succeed in creating, this disgust thou exude.
To turn and walk away,
And pity their life,
Or be a slave to persecution,
When what was believed was right.
There's no point in holding it,
There's certainly no claim,
Whence the notion of this demeaning pointed finger,

That comes from a place of jealousy and blame.
For if you have done wrong,
It may rightfully be so,
Let karma be the service to your crime,
For it's the universe who knows,
For it is karma which balances, and corrects right from wrong,
And seeks out its justice,
Where forgotten remorse is left too long,
For, if injustice is done,
And forgiveness is sought,
Leave it in the hands of karma to serve,
The balancing out it brought.
Alas, shame is not worthy,
Tis' merely a dead end if you choose it so.
If guilty and unrepentant,
To the accuser then shame, it does not know.

So let go of the sneering, and damnation,
Tis not worth opinions at all,
To the accused, to the remorseless soul,
Onto it, the hammer will fall.

Let karma seek out its own justice,
Have faith in its power to it.
Whether guilty, unproven, or innocent,
Sooner or later,
Its sentence to the accused will be met.
Still love them all the same.
~ JahAnanda

Sacred message of God

'The feeble existence of mans recent attempts during the past century. Thwart with inciting harm, control, and extraordinary suffering to one another and to this Earth is now standing at the edge of critical and insightful reckoning far beyond the greatest inventions ever mastered and achieved in this world. That reckoning is by abolishing the ego once and for all. For in it is this miniscule manifestation that has created the most compelling and cataclysmic harm and devastation seen in this period than any millennia prior. By having the will and undying courage to disassociating the ego in exchange for redeemable and forgiving love; to each and every living being on this planet, beginning now at this present moment. No other challenge means more to mans existence, the simplest and easiest means to resolve any conflict whether financial, political, social, personal, environmental, and spiritual. Guilt and judgement replaced by irrevocable unconditional love. It is at this point and time when the nature of the truthful soul, the revealing soul, the purest state of the soul river of peace and sustainability for many years to come, and prosperity and peace never felt or seen before will give rise to the 'new heaven on the new earth (Rev 21:1)' ~ God wants you to know this ~ JahAnanda.

'God is not a homophobe. If he was I would not be part of His creation and would not wish to be. However, I am, like you are, and He created all with the intention of Love in his heart, no different to the love a woman or man has for that of another. He desired free expression. There is no judgement or impartiality or indigence to what Moses believed he inspired from God in Leviticus 18:22. Only misconstrued error at the time those many millennia it was written. Such blunders have only created division, war, suffering, the loss of millions of lives, and believe that if Moses would have retracted that scripture if he knew it would cause such separation and hatred towards mankind. Acceptance in this instance prevails. One Love, unconditional Love. Namaste Hallelujah. ~

'Before one commits to even considering inhabiting another civilisations planets it is best warned now to serve first to heal your own planets damage and destruction and taking care of them before wasting money and your existence' ~ JahAnanda

I met a Man

I met a man one day; he was dressed all in white,
He had a great beard, frail and wise,
And failing was his sight.

We sat down on a tree stump together, beside the river below,
As I threw, into it, a pebble I found,
And watched as the ripples did grow,

I asked him, what was life like as a boy,
And did he have family close to him.
He smiled and recalled that yes he did once have,
As his eyes lit up, revealing a grin.

He told me of his family, he created upon this land,
And that he came from a place oh so far,
And planted all the trees, and all the butterflies we see,
The animals, the fish, and the stars,

I looked at him perplexed and confused and
Asked him how could that be,
You're too old and you're so frail,
You carry a walking stick,
And you barely can see.

I created what you see, with the heavens high above,
To build a land with promise and pride,

To grace upon the people a life to be joyous,
With happy children to build for them a new life,

But a mistake I did create,
A fleetingly innocent one at that,
A tree bearing fruit, but disguised,
And made a temptation by suggesting its danger,
To unsuspecting partners, to whom they tried,

It wasn't their fault for it was me, the tree I did create,
To test of their strength and their devotion to me,
Not to eat it, but sadly they ate.

So for millions years, I've sat at this spot,
Rueing and cursing myself,
For what I had done by tempting that fate,
To two people whom sin reigns forever,
How can I make right for this sin for I have cried,
You're only a child, you can't help.

I thought for a while as I picked up a pebble,
And another I handed to him,
He held it in his hand and I asked him to stand,
And see how far into the river, he could throw it in.

He looked at me strange though he lifted his arm,
And threw it with all of his might,
It didn't go far but into the river it did land,
As the ripples glimmered out beyond sight,

He smiled with his eyes,
And he took a deep breath,
As his face suddenly beamed like a child,

That felt so good, great here is another,
And like two crazy kids,
We spent the whole day,
Laughing and playing, going wild.

We laughed and we played and after a while we sat down,
As two angels came down next to us,
It was the angel of love,
And the angel of peace,
To sit and listen with us,

But don't you bring good news, of love and of light,
to bless this boys future and path?
You are both angels said the man,
I created you to be,
To you, whom they look to from afar,

To be guiding lights for this young boy,
But not worthy is me,
For the fruit I did make in unjust,
And pertinent to thee, it's quite easy to see,
That I command you to help him you must!

The angels sat quiet as they turned to look at me,
My heart filled with power and their grace,
I started to speak with words from my mouth,
But truly whose wisdom did I take?

'Tis mine said the man, I'm too old and I am weak,
It's time for you to go out and be known.
I give you my blessing and I will give my command,
In return, all I ask is my throne.

For you is the one who taught me to laugh,
To learn about life with a smile,
And the pebble you gave,
Brought a smile to my face,
I haven't done that for a while.

It is you, whom has the courage,
And it's you, who has faith,
And it's to you whom the wisdom I bestow.
With passion in your eyes,
And streaming love in your heart,
Go out and share what you know!

I said, Father I will do the task that you offer,
And your throne you will sit and remain,
But the blessing I have is my wisdom that you gave,
The same of your love,
For the people who suffer in vain.

And the people will look back all those years long ago,
When cars ran on polluting the skies,
Where man ruled with guns,
And fools ran the world,
With eyes that glisten dollar signs.

When they sold in their markets,
Food and drinks with chemicals,
And people with cancerous bodies,
And pharmaceutical drugs to poison their minds,
And televisions to brainwash their commodities,

That they read all the news that the world wanted them to say,
To make them all think like merciless robots,

Whilst the earth and trees were our medicines for disease,
Not the drugs and the pills that they sold us.

It was money go round but not for the man,
Who worked and toiled for his keep,
Who tried to raise his children,
And a roof overhead,
Not knowing that he was merely a sheep.

For it's the taxes they pay,
And the cars and fuel that they buy,
And the electricity must come from them,
You can't have a windmill and you can't have hydrogen,
What about our salaries and corporate,
We are your leaders and we can't live like them!

For it is the sheep we program, so to keep them alike,
We don't need a poverty story,
Long as you pay all your taxes,
And buy all our food,
And our drug to you is your glory!

Though the earth's populated there's plenty of room,
For more people to come into our den,
Just herd them all here,
In front of the television sets,
And let the brainwashing begin.

They'll look all those years of an earth once there was,
Where destiny was thought of as money and power,
And home mortgages were for you not for the banks,
To siphon the equity devoured,
Where freedom was thought of as living under rule,

To buy and consume what you wanted,
But organic fruit and vegetables,
Was against those old laws,
With your taxes and drug money they squandered.

So life way back then will be thought of as sad,
Emptiness worse than betrayal,
Where malnourished children with decaying teeth,
Sought to fight and ended up in jail.

In growing prisons they did find guinea pigs to lock away,
No teaching or love provided.
Just spit in their faces,
And slam shut the door,
Their role in justice has been decided.

So I sit here right now, my works nearly done,
Since the day I met that kind man.
I think he said God was his name,
And he gave me the reign,
And primitive man has set like the sun.

And now I am an old man and here is the choice,
We must learn to love one another.
To this boy approaching me,
He wants to see,
If I am his wise great grandfather;

If he asks me about who really 'Am I',
I'll not say that I am God or another,
But is just a happy man,
Doing the best that I can,

And hand him a pebble,
And by the river, we'll discover;

For that man I once did meet,
Who showed me the way,
By saying he gave me the power.
For God was in me,
And I found it that day,
When he asked me to help my sister and brother;

And I'll say to this boy,
Who is seeking his joy,
That God lives in him eternally.
Just peel back the layers,
Of gun slinging slayers,
And God will reveal to him,
Just like me.

Live with faith.
Be blessed.
Namaste.
~ JahAnanda

Don't you feel it? Now is the Time

There is a constant unravelling,
A constant unravelling, unfolding,
Awakening,
Like a new seed, the seed from which you have discovered.
The seed within you, the seed of discovery,
The seed of truth,
Of whom you truly are.

And what light this incredible, vibrational discovery holds,
Now that it is in your hands.

This is the time,
This is the moment.
We cannot believe that through the complications
and processes we thought were obviously and ruefully
convinced were important in this life, weren't.
We cannot believe that through the mind trapping beliefs of
the physical nature that held you captive all these years,
Was nothing but one's own sense of fear,
Hesitancy and trust,
And thinking,

Thinking that you needed to be connected to something 'out there'
In the world,
Thinking that your survival was dependant on being fed by the world,
By the system, by your husband, by your wife, by your children,
Beyond your own love,

Knowing now that survival is just an illusion,
You are already here now!
You are existence, you are excited, you are love and you are love,
You are joy.
You are pure and you are beautiful.
You are reborn. You are radiant. You are life,
And you are existence,
You are adoring just the way you have desired, and more.
And, you are eternal.

It is in believing,
Believing in this revelation,
That you are energy,

That you ARE the power,
That you are part of the multitude richness of collective source,
The vibrational source interconnected with others who,
Like you are coming into the alignment stream of vibrational energy,
Not just on this planet,
But in alignment with the collective
concordance of all within the cosmos,
Who, like you,
Are of the Oneness,
Believing that by the power of collective consciousness,
More and more souls will co-align to the
radiance that they feel in their lives.
That they too feel different,
That they feel drawn to,
That they feel themselves being drawn more
and more closer to the love,
And doing so,
Discovering more of who you truly are,
And who they truly are,

It is alive.
It is vibrant. It is felt not in your mind,
But in your heart,
It is the living, breathing essence of Mauri,
Life force, source, of God, and your soul,
For it is you who holds the key to being alive,
To being happy, living in truth,
Living in the total pureness of unconditional love in
all aspects of this blessed life and existence,
Even through the contrasts and dire times of your life,
It too holds the doorway in which new light permits itself to shine in.

Have faith,
Be faith, live in faith.
For no matter what holds you to ransom,
Know that you have the power to let it all go,
To be higher than that which attempts to permeate your wisdom of
knowing.

Knowing the wisdom,
And allowing whatever you choose to have in your life,
It shall be, for that is the law, the Law of
Abundance, the Law of Truth.
Knowing that you can allow peace in your life right now and you
certainly hold the power to share it, and show it, and be it.
And by coming on board to join the growing ascension to the Oneness,
The Oneness of love and alignment to being
that who you really are, then that
Oneness will bring more enlightened and
awakened souls into their own alignment.

And the discernment and mass ascension to
the Oneness provided by source,
By the Universe, and through God,
It will be all because of you choosing to align.

You are it,
You are part of the great expansion of what is going on in the world,
What you see for the world, want you want for the world.
Know this that you are eternal, and you are
beautiful in your own unique way.
That you can let go of burdens,
That struggles and ego is not a true reflection of who you really are.
That you can walk up to another person on this planet
and say that you don't know who they are, or what they

want in their life, or where they've come from, or how
they see life, or that they are different from you.
But just to let them know that you love them.
And love that for who they are.

And even though they may be in a completely
different alignment than you,
That you can stand by them and celebrate the incredible diversity that
this existence has brought together to making this life on this earth,
The beautiful world in which all souls, animals,
mammals, plants and creatures can enjoy,
And that it does not stop there.
It goes on and on and on and on and ON.

So why live it outside of the loving person that you are?
Why keep yourself from the joy and happiness
that you can have and enjoy right now?
Because you can,

Imagine

Just imagine what joy you would feel if you
touched the life of a dictator,
Or politician, a ruler, a loyalist to the suffering,
Just imagine seeing them change into knowing
their true self by the love that you shared,
Or by the hope in them that you gave,
Or by just showing them a better way,
Just imagine if you held out your hand to someone else,
Who themselves touched the life of a dictator, a
politician, a ruler, or a loyalist to the suffering.

351

Imagine the power of multiplicity, of working
together to achieving critical mass,
And knowing you had an integral part to play,
In this collective direction and alignment towards the love,

The love for others,
To our earth, and its creatures, the land, and oceans,
The love for the planet, the love for all things powerful and invisible,
Don't you feel it?
Ride the wave, hop on board.
Take this step, this leap into the frontier of alignment
and experiencing the joy and wonders of life.
To share in the wonder of the simple things in this life,
To say enough is enough and I choose to be happy and I
choose to be love, and I choose to be joyful, and I choose to
make a difference, and I choose it right this minute.
To live life complete,
Don't you feel it?
Be the change. Have courage, have faith.
Express, create, be blessed.
Be.
Good health,
Until we meet again
Ayubowan
Namaste ~ JahAnanda

The Coming of the New Age

What this Earth has seen in recent times has shown man more of himself, and appreciatively, the answer to his actions and suffering from his chronological knowing through historical accounts of recent times. From where civilisations outside of your planet experience timelessness of presence, there is no measure of time at all where on your earth it is measured by centuries, years, months, days, hours, minutes and seconds.

The basis in which time was invented on your earth was merely a need to improve ancient time measurement tools which were doing a function that really did not need improvement at all. Thus from that point the clock was invented and people on your planet based their lives concurrently around time as a 'means achievement' factor of shall we say to make efficient time as a measure to do more of whatever they chose. That the fact that time itself came into being more and more on your planet was not the result of centuries of turmoil, war, starvation, poisoning of your planet and relationship upheavals between one another but through the acceleration of certain manifestations of ego centred ideals in which time became a measurement of doing what was needed to be done outside the pure soul domain. From a time where love was previously held much greater before times invention, and love itself was simply timeless and the domain in which love was held was in accord to the Laws of Creation of which awareness of conscious existence was the beginning. As one understands more and more, the contrasts and sufferings which have created the imbalance of harmony between people and planet, as a consequence for so many centuries, the law thus mirrors the thoughts and actions of history to permeate more by the repetitive nature of moving ones conscious state outside and into the reflective manifested states. Those of repeating more and more ritualised disharmony, pain, war, suffering and living in a fear based existence rather than one based around simply allowing that which reflects a state of love for all things and trusting.

Remaining and living in light

Awakening is a virtuous celebratory time; one which signals the attainment of something precious and powerful. It may have taken a lifetime or many lifetimes, perhaps making the same unconscious errors over and over again until arrival to this place came. It does not matter how or when it occurred, only that it did. This is all that matters, and now that you are holding it in your hands. Nurture and treasure it always, for the light of awakening is the dawn of the path to your joy rising, your peace, your paradise and whom you are, and whom you choose to be.

You will know too whether you will become a teacher or not. That too does not matter, what matters is holding close what you have discovered and realising that there are many more important things about life and existence that cannot be learnt at school or by living in fear or with scorn. Those who see your light shining will follow. And by not holding back emotions; for to do so only subject's dissemination of your newly found connectedness to spiritual growth, of learning and following the heart. Go back only if you wish to reflect more suffering for in this place you are now is absolute resonant peace and love.

By viewing everything in life going forward, with appreciation, God will reflect so much more in this life worth appreciating just by employing solemn faith and living with gratitude, peace and humility. Such as the love and respect in holding nature close to your heart, that it too becomes a mirror of how one wish's for the planet and souls on this earth while the purpose of such a test sometimes necessitates going out and beyond, and at times, alone. That by simply following and being a slave to the crowd and the beasts of the code embroiled already in this world, life finds oneself still nestled always among the crowd, abandoning the universal language of love, and recognizing that courage through suffering is not the only singular path to love and awakening.

For the unblemished soul of purist love fears nothing nor situations, or people, for the light of their heart shines bright eternally and divine. A token of enumerable blessings to the awakened soul and from the very first step into this moving and liberating aspect of harmony and peace, opens the doorway to paradise like a new soul born unto the world.

As perfect as the setting sun, as definitive as the perfect balance of life and seasons. And, as spontaneous and precise as has always been the case on this Earth for millions upon millions of years, the pondering and the most supremely lingering of questions of one's life, sooner or later, and in time, do get answered. Many knew of the answers before they arrived here, and then they unknowingly relinquished them; and some, unfortunately or not, didn't know them at all. It is not just the chosen who behold this wisdom of knowledge and truth; this truth that makes known life and purpose, existence, the many lives trodden. Janna, Heaven, Hell, Angels, Spirit, Twin-flames, Soul-mates, Death, Ascended and dimensional realms, all this knowledge becomes an exciting, redeeming, blissful open door from your heart when the face you see looking back in the mirror is your truth appreciating and smiling back with love and acceptance at you. The birth of your new conscious and present self; no longer sabotaged again by fear, being lead, and living in the past, and if there is a weight on the shoulders of the newly discovered soul of the blessed, then let it be the soothing weight of love for you to share among the loved, and the lost.

I have not arrived at this place nor was I the solely chosen one. I, like you are always arriving, and your arriving and constant desire to continuing the new path you hold now in your hands, will in time, disclose and reveal more of who you are. If you have come to this place, I say to you, welcome.

And, as the Torus and existence has shown too, that imminent and significant wisdom is held within the soul, not within the unconscious domain of the physical mind. Where definitive power resides ready and patiently waiting for anyone willing to finding their truth, and one day soon, you too will find it. Discovering your truth; your truth 'Beyond

Your Horizon, onwards Into Your Exquisite Light.' Be blessed. Namaskar,
Amen, Ayubowan, Tihei Mauriora!

Ka nui te mihi aroha ki i a tatau katoa.
(Extending and expressing my deepest love to you all)

GLOSSARY

Ahua	Verb: to form, make. Noun: character, likeness, appearance, figure.
Ahuatanga	Way, Likeness, Circumstance, Aspect, Characteristic
Aoraki	Aotearoa's highest mountain (Mt Cook)
Aotearoa	New Zealand ~ Land of the Long White Cloud
Aroha	Love
Atua	God
Hangi	Earthen food cooking method
Hui	Meeting/ gathering
Io	Maori name for God
Kai	Food
Kaimoana	Seafood
Karakia	Prayer
Kawa	Beliefs
Kereru	Native wood pigeon
Kia ora	Hello/ Thank you
Kiore	Native rat (food source)
Kina	Sea Egg/ Urchin

Kohanga Reo	Maori Pre-school
Kumara	Sweet potato
Manuhiri	Visitors/ Guests
Marama	Moon
Marae	Traditional Central Maori Meeting House
Mauri	Life-force
Mere	Maori Clubbing weapon usually made from greenstone
Moana	Sea/Lake, Lakes
Moko	Maori tattoo worn by women on the chin/ Grandchild
Mokopuna	Grandchildren
Ngahere	Forest
Noke	Intestinal worm
Papatuanuku	God of the Earth (Earth Mother)
Puku	Stomach
Rata	Native tree
Rangatira	Chief
Rangi-nui	God of the Sky (Sky Father)
Rimu	Native tree
Taiaha	Maori Spear-like clubbing weapon
Tamariki	Children
Tane	God of the Forest
Tangata whenua	Sovereign people of the land
Tangi	Funeral/ To Cry

Te Reo	Maori language
Te Ika A Maui	North Island of Aotearoa
Te Wai Pounamu	South Island of Aotearoa
Te Ao	The World
Tipuna/Tupuna	Ancestors
Tikanga	Customs
Tohunga	Spiritual chief
Totara	Native tree
Tui	Native bird of Aotearoa
Urupa	Burial ground
Whanau	Family
Whanaungatanga	Family togetherness
Waiata	Maori song/s
Wairua	Spirit
Waka	Canoe
Whare	House
Wharenui	Large Family home
Whenua	The Land
Whangai	Traditionally adopted child